Weekly Assessments

Mc
Graw
Hill
Education

www.mheonline.com/readingwonders

Send all inquiries to:
McGraw-Hill Education
Two Penn Plaza
New York, New York 10121

ISBN: 978-0-07-680141-1
MHID: 0-07-680141-1

Printed in the United States of America.

1 2 3 4 5 6 7 8 9 RHR 20 19 18 17 16 15

A

Table of Contents

Table of Contents– Cont'd.

Teacher Introduction

Weekly Assessments

The *Weekly Assessments* component is an integral part of the complete assessment program aligned with *Reading Wonders* and state standards.

Purpose of *Weekly Assessments*

Weekly Assessments offers the opportunity to monitor student progress in a steady and structured manner while providing formative assessment data. As students complete each week of the reading program, they will be assessed on their understanding of key instructional content. The results of the assessments can be used to inform subsequent instruction.

The results of *Weekly Assessments* provide a status of current achievement in relation to student progress through the curriculum.

Focus of *Weekly Assessments*

The focus of *Weekly Assessments* is on two key areas of English Language Arts—Reading and Language. Students will read two selections each week and respond to items focusing on Comprehension Skills and Vocabulary Strategies. These items assess the ability to access meaning from the text and demonstrate understanding of unknown and multiple-meaning words and phrases.

Administering *Weekly Assessments*

Each weekly assessment should be administered once the instruction for the specific week is completed. Make copies of the weekly assessment for the class. You will need one copy of the Answer Key page for each student taking the assessment. The scoring table at the bottom of the Answer Key provides a place to list student scores. The accumulated data from each weekly assessment charts student progress and underscores strengths and weaknesses.

After each student has a copy of the assessment, provide a version of the following directions: **Say:** *Write your name and the date on the question pages for this assessment.* (When students are finished, continue with the directions.) *You will read two selections and answer questions about them. Read each selection and the questions that follow it carefully. For the multiple-choice items, completely fill in the circle next to the correct answer. For items that require a written response, write that response clearly in the space provided. For the constructed response item, write your response on the lines provided. When you have completed the assessment, put your pencil down and turn the pages over. You may begin now.*

Answer procedural questions during the assessment, but do not provide any assistance on the items or selections. After the class has completed the assessment, ask students to verify that their names and the date are written on the necessary pages.

Teacher Introduction

Overview of *Weekly Assessments*

Each weekly assessment is comprised of the following

- 2 "Cold Read" selections
- 10 items assessing Comprehension Skills and Vocabulary Strategies
- 1 constructed response item assessing Comprehension and the ability to write across texts

Reading Selections

Each weekly assessment features two selections on which the assessment items are based. (In instances where poetry is used, multiple poems may be set as a selection.) The selections reflect the unit theme and/or weekly Essential Question to support the focus of the classroom instruction. Because the weekly assessments have been composed to assess student application of the skills rather than genre or genre knowledge, selections are not always the same genre as the reading selections in the Literature Anthology or RWW.

Selections increase in complexity as the school year progresses to mirror the rigor of reading materials students encounter in the classroom. The Lexile goal by unit is as follows—Unit 1: 740L; Unit 2: 780L; Unit 3: 820L; Unit 4: 860L; Unit 5: 900L; and Unit 6: 940L.

Assessment Items

Weekly assessments feature the following item types—selected response (SR), multiple selected response (MSR), evidence-based selected response (EBSR), constructed response (CR), technology-enhanced constructed response (TECR), and extended constructed response (ECR). (Please note that the print versions of TECR items are available in this component; the full functionality of the items is available only through the online assessment.) This variety of item types provides multiple methods of assessing student understanding, allows for deeper investigation into skills and strategies, and provides students an opportunity to become familiar with the kinds of questions they will encounter in next generation assessments, both consortia-related and state-mandated.

Comprehension Items

Each selection is followed by items that assess student understanding of the text through the use of Comprehension Skills—both that week's Comprehension Skill focus and a review Comprehension Skill. The review skill is taken from a week as near as possible to the current week and aligns with the instruction.

Vocabulary Items

Each selection is followed by items that ask students to demonstrate the ability to uncover the meanings of unknown and multiple-meaning words and phrases using Vocabulary Strategies.

Comprehension—Extended Constructed Response

At the close of each weekly assessment is a constructed response item that provides students the opportunity to craft a written response that shows their critical thinking skills and allows them to support an opinion/position by using text evidence from one or both selections.

NOTE: Please consider this item as an optional assessment that allows students to show comprehension of a text in a more in-depth manner as they make connections between and within texts.

Teacher Introduction

Scoring *Weekly Assessments*

Items 1–10 are each worth two points, for a twenty-point assessment. Each part of a EBSR is worth 1 point; MSR and TECR items should be answered correctly in full, though you may choose to provide partial credit. If you decide to have students complete the constructed response, use the correct response parameters provided in the Answer Key along with the scoring rubric listed below to assign a score of 0 through 4.

Score: 4
- The student understands the question/prompt and responds suitably using the appropriate text evidence from the selection or selections.
- The response is an acceptably complete answer to the question/prompt.
- The organization of the response is meaningful.
- The response stays on-topic; ideas are linked to one another with effective transitions.
- The response has correct spelling, grammar, usage, and mechanics, and it is written neatly and legibly.

Score: 3
- The student understands the question/prompt and responds suitably using the appropriate text evidence from the selection or selections.
- The response is a somewhat complete answer to the question/prompt.
- The organization of the response is somewhat meaningful.
- The response maintains focus; ideas are linked to one another.
- The response has occasional errors in spelling, grammar, usage, and mechanics, and it is, for the most part, written neatly and legibly.

Score: 2
- The student has partial understanding of the question/prompt and uses some text evidence.
- The response is an incomplete answer to the question/prompt.
- The organization of the response is weak.
- The writing is careless; contains extraneous information and ineffective transitions.
- The response requires effort to read easily.
- The response has noticeable errors in spelling, grammar, usage, and mechanics, and it is written somewhat neatly and legibly.

Score: 1
- The student has minimal understanding of the question/prompt and uses little to no appropriate text evidence.
- The response is a barely acceptable answer to the question/prompt.
- The response lacks organization.
- The writing is erratic with little focus; ideas are not connected to each other.
- The response is difficult to follow.
- The response has frequent errors in spelling, grammar, usage, and mechanics, and it is written with borderline neatness and legibility.

Score: 0
- The student fails to compose a response.
- If a response is attempted, it is inaccurate, meaningless, or completely irrelevant.
- The response may be written so poorly that it is neither legible nor understandable.

Teacher Introduction

Evaluating Scores

The primary focus of each weekly assessment is to evaluate student progress toward mastery of previously-taught skills and strategies.

The expectation is for students to score 80% or higher on the assessment as a whole. Within this score, the expectation is for students to score 75% or higher on the items assessing Comprehension Skills; score 75% or higher on the items assessing the particular week's Vocabulary Strategy; and "3" or higher on the extended constructed response, if assigned.

For students who do not meet these benchmarks, assign appropriate lessons from the Tier 2 online PDFs. Refer to the weekly "Progress Monitoring" spreads in the Teacher's Editions of *Wonders* for specific lessons.

The Answer Keys in *Weekly Assessments* have been constructed to provide the information you need to aid your understanding of student performance, as well as individualized instructional and intervention needs. Further metadata is available in the online versions of the assessment, including specific test claims and targets.

This column lists the instructional content for the week that is assessed in each item.

Question	Correct Answer	Content Focus	CCSS	Complexity

This column lists alignment for each assessment item.

This column lists the Depth of Knowledge associated with each item.

Question	Correct Answer	Content Focus	CCSS	Complexity
7	B, E	Main Idea and Key Details	RI.4.2	DOK 2
8	D	Context Clues	L.4.4a	DOK 2
9A	C	Main Idea and Key Details	RI.4.2	DOK 2
9B	B	Main Idea and Key Details/Text Evidence	RI.4.2/RI.4.1	DOK 2

Although all items feature use of text evidence, this is explicitly mentioned in PART B EBSR items.

Comprehension 1A, 1B, 4, 5, 6, 7A, 7B, 10	/12	%
Vocabulary 2, 3A, 3B, 8, 9	/8	%
Total Weekly Assessment Score	/20	%

Scoring rows identify items associated with Reading and Language strands and allow for quick record keeping.

Read the passage "The Robin and the Vase" before answering Numbers 1 through 5.

The Robin and the Vase

Based on "The Crow and the Pitcher" from Aesop's Fables

A robin was flying south for the winter, and during his flight, he became thirsty. He knew that without water he would be too weak to continue his journey. He looked for a place to rest that was near water, but he did not see a drop anywhere.

Just when the robin was about to abandon all hope, he spotted a container on a picnic table. He was glad he had not given up trying to find water. The tall, thin vase was exactly what he needed. He landed on a tree branch near the table. "I know what that is used for!" the robin squawked excitedly. "I've seen people put flowers in these containers. Flowers need water. Maybe there is some water left in the bottom."

The robin flew quickly to the vase and perched on its edge. He saw that there was some water inside. Finally, he was relieved that he would be able to drink some water and quench his thirst. He was so grateful. Then he lowered his head and put his beak inside the vase.

The robin's joy quickly turned to despair when he discovered that his beak was not long enough to reach the water. Realizing the vase was too tall and narrow, the robin cried, "Now what am I going to do?"

As the robin perched on the edge of the vase, he thought about his problem. He needed water to stay alive. "My survival depends on getting water from this vase!" he shouted.

GO ON →

The water was so close yet so very far away. He could clearly see the liquid, but he could not get close enough to drink it. Somehow, he needed to raise the water. But how? Suddenly, the robin got an idea.

After looking around the yard, the robin spied a statue sitting among many small stones. He thought that if he could drop stones into the vase, the water level would rise.

So the robin flew toward the stones. He used his beak to pick up two small stones and then flew back to the vase. After dropping a few more stones into the vase he saw that the water was a little higher. This spurred him on and he felt hopeful. He kept telling himself, "You can do this!" The robin flew back and forth between the stones and the vase. Each time, he dropped a few small stones in the vase and watched as the water rose.

Finally the vase was full of stones, and the water was at the top. The robin took a long drink of water and satisfied his thirst. He was proud of himself for having such a clever idea.

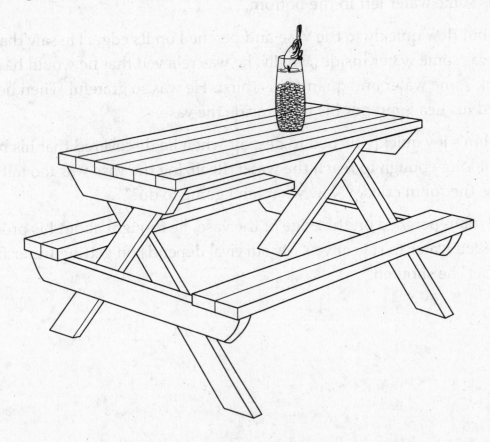

Now answer Numbers 1 through 5. Base your answers on "The Robin and the Vase."

1 This question has two parts. First, answer part A. Then, answer part B.

Part A: Read the following sentences from the passage.

Just when the robin was about to <u>abandon</u> all hope, he spotted a container on a picnic table. He was glad he had not given up trying to find water.

Which word means almost the **same** as <u>abandon</u> in the sentences above?

(A) find

(B) gain

(C) quit

(D) spot

Part B: Which words from the sentences help the reader understand the meaning of <u>abandon</u>?

(A) "spotted a container"

(B) "given up trying"

(C) "was glad"

(D) "trying to find"

2 What happens **after** the robin gets thirsty but **before** he collects the stones? Pick **two** choices.

(A) The robin sees a vase.

(B) The robin gets a drink of water.

(C) The robin puts stones in the vase.

(D) The robin watches the water rise.

(E) The robin had an idea.

GO ON →

3 Read the following sentences from the passage.

The robin's joy quickly turned to despair when he discovered that his beak was not long enough to reach the water.

Which word means almost the **same** as despair?

(A) anger

(B) fearlessness

(C) hopelessness

(D) joy

4 Mark the boxes in order of the sequence of events. Some columns may have more than one selection.

	This happened **first**.	This happened **next**.	This happened **last**.
The robin's hope faded.			
The robin was proud of himself.			
The robin looked for a place to rest.			
The robin dropped the stones in the vase.			

GO ON →

5 This question has two parts. First, answer part A. Then, answer part B.

Part A: Which event happens last in the passage?

(A) The robin is grateful to find water.

(B) The robin drinks from the vase.

(C) The robin spots a container.

(D) The robin thinks of a plan.

Part B: Which word lets the reader know this is the last event in the passage?

(A) clever

(B) finally

(C) proud

(D) water

GO ON →

Read the passage "What Did She Want?" before answering Numbers 6 through 10.

What Did She Want?

Dan studied the tracks on the ground. For the third night in a row, the adult bear had returned to visit the pen. Was she here because she was looking for food? Or was she here because of the cub locked in the pen? If that was the reason, what did she want with the little bear?

Dan thought about the cub. He knew there was a lot the cub could learn from an adult bear. He didn't want to interfere with the bears getting to know each other, and he was afraid to disturb a meeting between the adult bear and the cub. After all, the cub had been brought to him injured. As the cub's guardian, Dan had a responsibility to make sure it was safe. It was possible that the cub had been hurt by the adult bear. On the other hand, what if the adult bear was friendly? She could teach the cub things it had to learn so it could survive in the wilderness. Dan decided it was worth taking a chance. He would let the adult bear near the cub. But he had an idea about how to protect himself, just in case this turned out to be a mistake.

GO ON →

That night, Dan waited in the shadows near the pen with a big flashlight in his hand. If the adult bear tried to hurt the cub, he would try to scare her off with the light. If that did not work, he also had a loud horn with him. He thought the sudden noise from the horn would frighten the adult and drive her away.

Dan did not have to wait very long, because soon there was a rustling in the woods. Then the adult proclaimed her presence with a low growl. As she emerged from behind a tree, Dan saw that she was strong and healthy. Worried that he had made the wrong decision, he hoped she would scare easily.

As soon as the cub heard her growl, it perked up and started toward the fence in an awkward run. When the two bears met at the fence, the adult stood and put her front paws against it. The cub tried to do the same, but tottered and fell forward. The adult bear snorted, and Dan was not sure what the snort meant. Then the cub stuck its nose through the fence in a friendly greeting. How would the adult bear respond? Dan's heart raced as he raised the flashlight and the horn, ready to act.

The adult bear leaned forward and gently rubbed her nose against the cub's nose. Dan lowered the flashlight and released his grip on the horn. Everything was going to be just fine.

GO ON →

Now answer Numbers 6 through 10. Base your answers on "What Did She Want?"

6 Which events **most likely** happened **before** the passage takes place? Pick **two** choices.

- (A) The adult bear visits the cub.
- (B) The adult bear scares Dan.
- (C) The cub is put in a pen.
- (D) The cub leaves tracks.
- (E) The cub leaves with the adult bear.

7 Read the following sentences from the passage.

He knew there was a lot the cub could learn from an adult bear. He didn't want to interfere with the bears getting to know each other, and he was afraid to disturb a meeting between the adult bear and the cub.

Which word from the sentences has almost the **same** meaning as interfere?

- (A) learn
- (B) want
- (C) know
- (D) disturb

GO ON →

8 This question has two parts. First, answer part A. Then, answer part B.

Part A: Read the following sentences from the passage.

After all, the cub had been brought to him injured. As the cub's guardian, Dan had a responsibility to make sure it was safe. It was possible that the cub had been hurt by the adult bear.

Which word could the author use instead of guardian?

Ⓐ doctor

Ⓑ predator

Ⓒ protector

Ⓓ teacher

Part B: Which phrase supports your answer in Part B?

Ⓐ "brought to him injured"

Ⓑ "had a responsibility"

Ⓒ "had been hurt"

Ⓓ "was possible"

GO ON →

9 What happens at the **end** of the passage?

(A) The adult bear tracks are seen by Dan.

(B) Dan realizes that everything is fine.

(C) The cub is brought to Dan.

(D) Dan comes up with a plan.

10 Place the events into the correct sequence. Write *1* next to the first event and *2–6* next to the other events based on the sequence.

_____ Dan comes up with a plan.

_____ The cub is brought to Dan.

_____ The adult bear growls.

_____ Dan waits for the adult bear to return.

_____ Dan wonders what the adult bear wants.

_____ The bears rub noses.

STOP

Weekly Assessment • Unit 1, Week 1

Name: _____ Date: _____

Now answer Number 11. Base your answer on "The Robin and the Vase" and "What Did She Want?"

11 Explain how clever ideas help characters solve problems in the passages "The Robin and the Vase" and "What Did She Want?" Support your answer with clear text evidence from the passages.

_____

_____

_____

_____

_____

_____

_____

_____

_____

_____

_____

_____

_____

_____

Answer Key

Question	Correct Answer	Content Focus	CCSS	Complexity
1A	C	Context Clues: Synonyms	L.4.5c	DOK 2
1B	B	Context Clues: Synonyms/ Text Evidence	L.4.5c/ RL.4.1	DOK 2
2	A, E	Character, Setting, Plot: Sequence	RL.4.3	DOK 1
3	C	Context Clues: Synonyms	L.4.5c	DOK 2
4	see below	Character, Setting, Plot: Sequence	RL.4.3	DOK 1
5A	B	Context Clues: Synonyms	L.4.5c	DOK 2
5B	B	Context Clues: Synonyms/ Text Evidence	L.4.5c/ RL.4.1	DOK 2
6	A, C	Character, Setting, Plot: Sequence	RL.4.3	DOK 1
7	D	Context Clues: Synonyms	L.4.5c	DOK 2
8A	C	Context Clues: Synonyms	L.4.5c	DOK 2
8B	D	Context Clues: Synonyms/ Text Evidence	L.4.5c/ RL.4.1	DOK 2
9	B	Character, Setting, Plot: Sequence	RL.4.3	DOK 1
10	see below	Character, Setting, Plot: Sequence	RL.4.3	DOK 1
11	see below	Writing About Text	W.4.9a	DOK 4

Comprehension 2, 4, 6, 9, 10	/10	%
Vocabulary 1A, 1B, 3, 5A, 5B, 7, 8A, 8B	/10	%
Total Weekly Assessment Score	/20	%

4 Students should complete the chart with the following sequence:
- The robin looked for a place to rest.
- The robin's hope faded.
- The robin dropped the stones in the vase.
- The robin was proud of himself.

10 Students place the items into the following sequence:
- The cub is brought to Dan.
- Dan wonders what the adult bear wants.
- Dan comes up with a plan.
- Dan waits for the adult bear to return.
- The adult bear growls.
- The bears rub noses.

11 The following information should be included: The robin figured out how to get the water it needed to drink. Dan came prepared to protect himself and the cub. Some students may make the connection that both sets of clever ideas provided a means for survival.

Read the passage "One Act of Kindness" before answering Numbers 1 through 5.

One Act of Kindness

It was a bright, sunny Saturday morning, and the local grocery store was busy with many customers. The store manager was preparing for the day when she looked up from the service desk where she was working. She noticed a young boy was struggling to push his grandmother's wheelchair through the doors. The manager rushed over to give him a hand.

"Here," she said with a smile. "Let me help you with that." The manager helped the boy push the wheelchair through the door and into the store.

"Thank you for helping me," the boy said gratefully. He smiled as he turned and continued to push the wheelchair into the store. They passed a man reading the label on a box of cereal. While the man's back was turned, his groceries suddenly began tumbling from his cart.

"Oh, no!" the man exclaimed frowning at the groceries on the floor. "Now I'm in a pickle and I have quite a mess to clean up here!" There were cans and boxes lying all over the grocery aisle.

"Here," the boy said with a smile. "Let me help you pick up those groceries." Together they began picking up the fallen items and reloaded them back into the shopping cart.

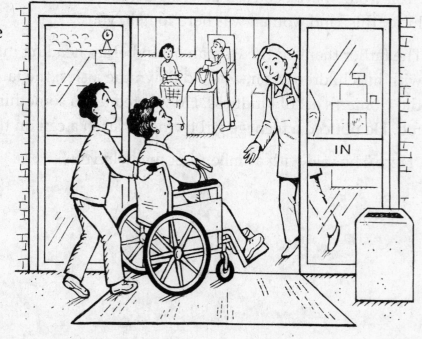

GO ON →

"Thank you, you are very thoughtful to stop and help me," the man said, grateful for the boy's help.

The boy grinned and thought, "Helping others sure is a piece of cake!"

The man beamed and turned away from the boy and his grandmother. He walked to the checkout lanes and he arrived at the same time as a woman. He noticed that she had only a few items in her basket while he had many, many items in his cart.

"You can go ahead of me," he said to the woman. "You only have two items, so you'll be done in a flash. It will take me much longer to check out."

The woman smiled and thanked him. After checking out she walked out of the store and into the parking lot. She saw a father with his two young children getting out of a car. The daughter stood next to the car and waited while the father worked to get his son out of a car seat.

The little girl spotted a feather on the ground a few feet in front of her. Suddenly the little girl darted away from her father to pick up the feather. The woman ran to the girl and stopped her, just as a bicycle zoomed by where the feather had been only moments before.

"Thank you!" the father cried to the woman, and to his daughter he said, "You would have been as flat as a pancake if that bike had hit you! We're lucky this kind woman was here to help you."

The father thanked the woman again before heading into the grocery store with his children. As he walked down the aisles, the father thought about the woman's act of kindness. He wanted to do something kind for someone, too. He noticed a teenage girl trying to reach a can on the top shelf.

"Here," he said with a smile. "Let me help you."

GO ON →

Name: _____ Date: _____

**Now answer Numbers 1 through 5. Base your answers on
"One Act of Kindness."**

1 This question has two parts. First, answer part A. Then, answer part B.

Part A: Read the following sentences from the passage.

"Oh, no!" the man exclaimed frowning at the groceries on the floor.
"Now I'm in a pickle and I have quite a mess to clean up here!" There
were cans and boxes lying all over the grocery aisle.

What does the phrase "in a pickle" mean in the sentences above?

Ⓐ to be dirty

Ⓑ to feel sour

Ⓒ to give up

Ⓓ to have a problem

Part B: Which action from the passage helps you understand
the phrase?

Ⓐ A boy helps pick up groceries.

Ⓑ A cashier helps push a wheelchair.

Ⓒ A woman keeps his daughter safe.

Ⓓ A man lets someone check out first.

GO ON →

2 Read the following sentences from the passage.

"You only have two items, so you'll be done <u>in a flash</u>. It will take me much longer to check out."

What does the phrase "in a flash" mean in the sentences above?

(A) brightly

(B) loudly

(C) quickly

(D) slowly

3 How does the woman solve the father's problem? Pick **two** choices.

(A) She pushes his wheelchair.

(B) She pick up his groceries.

(C) She gets his son out of his car seat.

(D) She stops his daughter from being hit by a bike.

(E) She reaches the can on the shelf.

(F) She notices his daughter is in danger.

GO ON →

4 Match the problem from the passage with the solution. Write the letter of the solution that matches the number of the problem.

Problem	Solutions
1. The bicycle was heading for the daughter.	A. The manager helped push the wheelchair.
2. The girl was unable to reach the can.	B. The woman moved the daughter out of the way.
3. The boy was pushing the wheelchair.	C. The boy helped pick up the groceries.
4. The man dropped his groceries.	D. The man got the can for the girl.

Correct Solution to Problem
1.
2.
3.
4.

5 This question has two parts. First, answer part A. Then, answer part B.

Part A: How is each character's problem solved in this passage?

(A) He or she is helped by a stranger.

(B) He or she finds a solution without any help.

(C) A wise grandmother solves all the problems.

(D) The problems are solved by the passing of time.

Part B: Which sentence from the passage supports your answer in Part A?

(A) "The grocery store was busy."

(B) "They passed a man reading the label on a box of cereal."

(C) "After checking out she walked out of the store."

(D) "He wanted to do something kind for someone, too."

GO ON →

Read the passage "Swing and a . . ." before answering Numbers 6 through 10.

Swing and a . . .

It was Gordon Dixon's first day on the baseball team. That by itself made him nervous,. but today his team was facing Billy Fallon, the best pitcher in the league. Fallon's fastball was legendary among league teams. Gordon's team had never won a game against Fallon and his team.

It seemed this game would be no different when Fallon struck out the first three players on Gordon's team. But in the second inning, the first batter managed to get on base with a single hit and the next batter hit another single. Now they had two runners on base!

Fallon struck out the next two batters. Then it was Gordon's turn at bat. This was his chance to help the team! But there were already two outs. Gordon felt the pressure to get a hit and bring in the two runners. He knew that if Fallon struck him out, the inning would be over.

"You might as well throw in the towel," the catcher muttered as Gordon walked up to the plate.

GO ON →

Gordon knew the catcher was trying to make him nervous. Even so, it seemed as though the catcher had read his mind. Gordon didn't think he could hit one of Fallon's fast pitches, but he was sure going to try. He decided that he would ignore the catcher's insult and put all of his attention on the ball.

Gordon swung the bat a few times to loosen up. Then he squared his shoulders, lifted his chin, and faced the pitcher. The first pitch came so fast that Gordon flinched. He did not even see the ball as it whizzed by. Standing on the mound, Fallon smiled confidently.

The second pitch blazed by so fast that it was in the catcher's glove almost before Gordon knew it had been thrown. "Fallon is on fire," the catcher said, snickering and taunting Gordon.

The players on the other team moved in from the outfield. This batter wasn't going to hit the ball and even if he did manage to hit the ball, it wasn't going to go very far.

With Fallon pitching, Gordon couldn't keep track of the ball. Gordon barely saw the third pitch, but something told him to swing hard. He felt the bat connect with the ball. Everyone in the stands gasped with wide eyes as the ball sailed over the fence.

Gordon had hit a home run! The score was three to zero! It was the best his team had ever done against Billy Fallon.

When the inning was over, an angry Fallon walked up to Gordon. Fallon was seeing red. "That was a fluke!" he hissed.

"Maybe it was," Gordon admitted. "But here's some food for thought. The next time you face me, you might not be so sure of yourself."

This time, it was Billy Fallon who flinched.

GO ON →

Now answer Numbers 6 through 10. Base your answers on "Swing and a . . ."

6 Which problems cause Gordon to feel nervous before he steps up to bat? Pick **two** choices.

(A) Fallon smiles at him.

(B) It is his first day on the team.

(C) Players move to the infield.

(D) He swings at the third pitch without seeing it.

(E) He is batting against the best pitcher in the league.

7 Read the following sentences from the passage.

Gordon knew the catcher was trying to make him nervous. Even so, it seemed as though the catcher had <u>read his mind</u>.

What does the phrase "read his mind" mean in the sentences above?

(A) knew the batter's average

(B) read a book about baseball

(C) guessed someone's thoughts

(D) told someone they were going to fail

GO ON →

Name: _____ Date: _____

8 This question has two parts. First, answer part A. Then, answer part B.

Part A: Read the following sentence from the passage.

"You might as well <u>throw in the towel</u>," the catcher muttered as Gordon walked up to the plate.

Which word means almost the **same** as the phrase "throw in the towel"?

(A) dry

(B) quit

(C) toss

(D) watch

Part B: Which sentence from the passage supports your answer in Part A?

(A) "Then it was Gordon's turn at bat."

(B) "This was his chance to help the team!"

(C) "Gordon felt the pressure to hit the ball and bring in the two runners."

(D) "He knew that if Fallon struck him out, the inning would be over."

GO ON →

9 This question has two parts. First, answer part A. Then, answer part B.

Part A: How was Gordon's problem solved in the passage?

Ⓐ Gordon got a hit.

Ⓑ The catcher made an error.

Ⓒ Fallon did not pitch well that day.

Ⓓ Gordon's team got two players on base.

Part B: Which sentence from the passage supports your answer in Part A?

Ⓐ "This batter wasn't going to hit the ball."

Ⓑ "The score was three to zero!"

Ⓒ "When the inning was over, an angry Fallon walked up to Gordon."

Ⓓ "This time, it was Billy Fallon who flinched."

10 Underline the sentence that reflects the **main** problem in the passage.

It was Gordon Dixon's first day on the baseball team. That by itself made him nervous. But today his team was facing Billy Fallon, the best pitcher in the league. Fallon's fastball was legendary. Gordon's team had never won a game against Fallon and his team.

Weekly Assessment • Unit 1, Week 2

**Now answer Number 11. Base your answer on "One Act of Kindness"
and "Swing and a . . ."**

11 Explain the way problems are solved in "One Act of Kindness" and
"Swing and a . . .." Support your answer with clear text evidence
from the passages.

_____

_____

_____

_____

_____

_____

_____

_____

_____

_____

_____

_____

_____

_____

Answer Key

Name: _____

Question	Correct Answer	Content Focus	CCSS	Complexity
1A	D	Figurative Language: Idioms	L.4.5b	DOK 2
1B	A	Figurative Language: Idioms/Text Evidence	L.4.5b/ RL.4.1	DOK 2
2	C	Figurative Language: Idioms	L.4.5b	DOK 2
3	D, F	Character, Setting, Plot: Problem and Solution	RL.4.3	DOK 2
4	see below	Character, Setting, Plot: Problem and Solution	RL.4.3	DOK 2
5A	A	Character, Setting, Plot: Problem and Solution	RL.4.3	DOK 2
5B	D	Character, Setting, Plot: Problem and Solution/Text Evidence	RL.4.3/ RL.4.1	DOK 2
6	B, E	Character, Setting, Plot: Problem and Solution	RL.4.3	DOK 2
7	C	Figurative Language: Idioms	L.4.5b	DOK 2
8A	B	Figurative Language: Idioms	L.4.5b	DOK 2
8B	D	Figurative Language: Idioms/Text Evidence	L.4.5b/ RL.4.1	DOK 2
9A	A	Character, Setting, Plot: Problem and Solution	RL.4.3	DOK 2
9B	B	Character, Setting, Plot: Problem and Solution/Text Evidence	RL.4.3/ RL.4.1	DOK 2
10	see below	Character, Setting, Plot: Problem and Solution	RL.4.3	DOK 2
11	see below	Writing About Text	W.4.9a	DOK 4

Comprehension 3, 4, 5A, 5B, 6, 9A, 9B, 10	/12	%
Vocabulary 1A, 1B, 2, 7, 8A, 8B	/8	%
Total Weekly Assessment Score	/20	%

4 Students should enter the following: 1-B; 2-D; 3-A; 4-C

10 Students should underline the following sentence:
   • Gordon's team had never won a game against Fallon and his team.

11 To receive full credit for the response, the following information should be included: The people in the grocery store have their problems solved when strangers help them out. Gordon solves his problem by taking a chance and getting lucky by hitting the ball.

Read the passage "All Shook Up" before answering Numbers 1 through 5.

All Shook Up

On August 23, 2011, an earthquake shook the eastern part of the United States. No major damage or injuries were reported.

The center of the earthquake was in Virginia. This quake had a magnitude of 5.8. Magnitude is a way to measure how strongly the ground shakes during an earthquake. The strongest quake ever documented had a magnitude of 9.5.

People near the center of the Virginia quake reported it sounded like a train roaring to a stop. The ground heaved, and buildings swayed. Farther away, people felt only a slight shaking of the ground.

The Recovery Begins

After the earthquake, there was a lot of work to be done. Everything needed to be checked for damage. Schools, government buildings, roads, and most bridges were closed. Train tracks and airports also needed to be inspected. Even a nuclear power plant was shut down until it was checked.

How Quakes Work

Earthquakes are caused by the shifting of huge rocks deep underground. These rocks are called *plates*. Sometimes these plates crack or break apart. The area where they separate is called a fault. When the plates move they grind together. This causes the ground above to shake. Sometimes the edges suddenly slip past each other. This also causes the earth to move.

There are faults all over the United States. However, some areas are more active than others. A long fault runs through most of California. This fault is very active, so earthquakes happen there more than in other parts of the country.

GO ON →

Different From Most Quakes

There are also faults near the area affected by the Virginia quake. This quake was unusual because it happened in the middle of a plate instead of along a fault.

The energy created by the Virginia quake traveled farther than most quakes in the West. This is because much of the rock under the East is solid and cold. When these rocks shift, the energy travels long distances. In the West, the rock is cracked and warm. These cracks prevent the energy from traveling as far.

Be Prepared

Earthquakes are dangerous. It is important to know what to do in an earthquake no matter where you live. If you ever find yourself in the middle of an earthquake:

- find shelter under a table, desk, or other sturdy object.
- stay away from windows or anything that might fall.
- cover your head until the shaking stops.
- don't go outside until it is over.
- don't use elevators.

GO ON →

Name: _____ Date: _____

Now answer Numbers 1 through 5. Base your answers on "All Shook Up."

1 Read the following sentences from the passage.

On August 23, 2011, an earthquake shook the eastern part of the United States. No <u>major</u> damage or injuries were reported.

Which meaning of <u>major</u> is the **same** one used above?

(A) important

(B) program

(C) officer

(D) serious

2 Read the paragraph from the passage.

The center of the earthquake was in Virginia. This quake had a magnitude of 5.8. Magnitude is a way to measure how strongly the ground shakes during an earthquake. The strongest quake ever documented had a magnitude of 9.5.

Why does the author use contrast in the paragraph? Pick **two** choices.

(A) to show how quakes are different

(B) to show how quakes are measured

(C) to show how quakes are unsafe

(D) to compare the damage of quakes

(E) to compare the strength of quakes

(F) to compare the temperature of quakes

GO ON →

3 This question has two parts. First, answer part A. Then, answer part B.

Part A: Read the following sentence from the passage.

The area where they separate is called a <u>fault</u>.

Which meaning of <u>fault</u> is the **same** one used in the sentence above?

(A) blame

(B) responsibility

(C) defect

(D) split

Part B: What evidence from the passage supports this meaning of <u>fault</u>?

(A) "Earthquakes are caused by the shifting of huge rocks deep underground."

(B) "Sometimes these plates crack or break apart."

(C) "When the plates move they grind together."

(D) "This also causes the earth to move."

4 Underline the sentence in this paragraph that uses compare or contrast to help the reader understand how quakes in the West are different from quakes in the East.

The energy created by the Virginia quake traveled farther than most quakes in the West. This is because much of the rock under the East is solid and cold. When these rocks shift, the energy travels long distances. In the West, the rock is cracked and warm. These cracks prevent the energy from traveling as far.

GO ON →

5 This question has two parts. First, answer part A. Then, answer part B.

Part A: How does the author show how earthquakes happen?

Ⓐ by describing the damage from different earthquakes

Ⓑ by explaining the effects of an earthquake

Ⓒ by comparing what happens underground in different earthquakes

Ⓓ by telling how to stay safe in an earthquake

Part B: What evidence from the passage supports your answer in Part A?

Ⓐ "There are also faults near the area affected by the Virginia quake."

Ⓑ "This quake was unusual because it happened in the middle of a plate instead of along a fault."

Ⓒ "The energy created by the Virginia quake traveled farther than most quakes in the West."

Ⓓ "When these rocks shift, the energy travels long distances."

GO ON →

Read the passage "The Importance of Precipitation" before answering Numbers 6 through 10.

The Importance of Precipitation

Have you ever seen a water wheel? These large wheels look like a tire made completely out of wood. The edge of the wheel is covered with buckets or slots. Some of these wheels turn when they are pushed by the force of a running river. Other water wheels spin when water is poured over the top and fills the buckets. The weight of the water forces the wheel to spin around.

A process similar to this happens on Earth every day. It is known as the water cycle. Heat from the sun warms water in lakes, rivers, and oceans. This heated water turns into vapor and rises into the air. The process of heated water turning into gas is called evaporation. Soon water droplets form and these droplets join together in the clouds. Eventually they get so heavy that the air cannot hold them any longer. When they fall from the clouds they become precipitation, and the process repeats.

Liquid precipitation is called rain. When the air is very cold, the water freezes in the clouds. We call these solid forms of precipitation snow, sleet, and ice.

The Good and Bad of Precipitation

The water cycle is very important. However, too much precipitation can have bad effects. When too much rain falls, it can cause problems. When water covers an area that is usually dry, a natural disaster called a flood occurs. Sometimes flooding happens in cities. When this happens, property can be destroyed and roads are closed.

Once the water drains away, the problems in cities can be fixed. The same is not true outside of cities. Property is damaged and roads are closed here, too. But floods also damage crops. This problem cannot be fixed quickly because soil is also usually ruined after a flood. This means new crops cannot be planted right away.

GO ON →

During winter, heavy snow, strong winds, and heavy precipitation often combine and cause blizzards. For these storms, roads close, schools shut down, and airports cancel flights. Entire cities come to a complete stop!

Precipitation affects what people wear, too. People use umbrellas to keep dry in the rain. They wear special clothing such as heavy coats, hats, and mittens to keep warm in the snow. Boots help people keep their feet dry and warm in both rain and snow.

Did you know precipitation does many good things, too? In the hot summer, precipitation helps to lower temperatures. It also cleans harmful things out of the air. Good or bad, we need precipitation. Whether it is a liquid, a solid, or a gas, precipitation is an important part of our lives.

GO ON →

Name: _____ Date: _____

Now answer Numbers 6 through 10. Base your answers on "The Importance of Precipitation."

6 Read the following sentences from the passage.

A process similar to this happens on Earth every day. It is known as the water <u>cycle</u>.

Which sentence uses <u>cycle</u> in the **same** way it is used in the sentences above?

Ⓐ This is the last book in a cycle of seven.

Ⓑ A baby being born is part of the life cycle.

Ⓒ Would you like to cycle over to the park?

Ⓓ What kind of cycle do you ride?

7 This question has two parts. First, answer part A. Then, answer part B.

Part A: Read the following sentence from the passage.

This heated water turns into <u>vapor</u> and rises into the air.

What is the meaning of <u>vapor</u> in the sentence above?

Ⓐ solid

Ⓑ liquid

Ⓒ gas

Ⓓ clouds

Part B: Which sentence from the passage **best** helps the reader understand this meaning of <u>vapor</u>?

Ⓐ "Heat from the sun warms water in lakes, rivers, and oceans."

Ⓑ "The process of heated water turning into gas is called evaporation."

Ⓒ "Soon water droplets form and these droplets join together in the clouds."

Ⓓ "Eventually they get so heavy that the air cannot hold them any longer."

GO ON →

8 Read this paragraph from the passage.

Once the water drains away, the problems in cities can be fixed. The same is not true outside of cities. Property is damaged and roads are closed here, too. But floods also damage crops. This problem cannot be fixed quickly because soil is also usually ruined after a flood. This means new crops cannot be planted right away.

Why did the author use contrast in this paragraph? Pick **two** choices.

(A) to show living outside the city is better

(B) to compare flooding inside and outside of cities

(C) to explain how flooding happens

(D) to describe soil erosion on farms

(E) to explain the different damages flooding causes

(F) to compare farms and crops outside cities

9 This question has two parts. First, answer part A. Then, answer part B.

Part A: Why does the author contrast rain and snow in the passage?

(A) to show what causes rain   (B) to show how they are different

(C) to show the effects of snow   (D) to show how they are formed

Part B: Which sentence from the passage best supports your answer in Part A?

(A) "The water cycle is very important. However, too much precipitation can have bad effects."

(B) "For these storms, roads close, schools shut down, and airports cancel flights. Entire cities come to a complete stop!"

(C) "People use umbrellas to keep dry in the rain. They wear special clothing such as heavy coats, hats, and mittens to keep warm in the snow."

(D) "It also cleans harmful things out of the air. Good or bad, we need precipitation."

GO ON →

10 A student took notes on this passage. Place a mark next to those notes which use compare and contrast. Choose as many as are correct.

	Compare/Contrast
Water wheels look like a wooden tire.	
The water cycle is important.	
Flooding in the cities is different from outside cities.	
Flooding can ruin soil, causing delays in planting.	
Snow can stop cities.	
People use umbrellas in the rain and heavy coats in the snow.	
Precipitation can be good and bad.	

STOP

Name: _____ Date: _____

Now answer Number 11. Base your answer on "All Shook Up" and "The Importance of Precipitation."

11 "All Shook Up" and "The Importance of Precipitation" both describe the effects natural disasters have on people. Explain how the authors structured the passages to compare and contrast these effects. Support your answer with clear text evidence from the passages.

_____

_____

_____

_____

_____

_____

_____

_____

_____

_____

_____

_____

_____

_____

_____

_____

Answer Key

Name: _____

Question	Correct Answer	Content Focus	CCSS	Complexity
1	D	Context Clues: Multiple-Meaning Words	L.4.4a	DOK 2
2	A, E	Text Structure: Compare and Contrast	RI.4.5	DOK 2
3A	D	Context Clues: Multiple-Meaning Words	L.4.4a	DOK 2
3B	B	Context Clues: Multiple-Meaning Words/Text Evidence	L.4.4a/ RI.4.1	DOK 2
4	see below	Text Structure: Compare and Contrast	RI.4.5	DOK 2
5A	C	Text Structure: Compare and Contrast	RI.4.5	DOK 2
5B	B	Text Structure: Compare and Contrast/ Text Evidence	RI.4.5/ RI.4.1	DOK 2
6	B	Context Clues: Multiple-Meaning Words	L.4.4a	DOK 2
7A	C	Context Clues: Multiple-Meaning Words	L.4.4a	DOK 2
7B	B	Context Clues: Multiple-Meaning Words/Text Evidence	L.4.4a/ RI.4.1	DOK 2
8	B,E	Text Structure: Compare and Contrast	RI.4.5	DOK 2
9A	B	Text Structure: Compare and Contrast	RI.4.5	DOK 2
9B	C	Text Structure: Compare and Contrast/ Text Evidence	RI.4.5/ RI.4.1	DOK 2
10	see below	Text Structure: Compare and Contrast	RI.4.5	DOK 2
11	see below	Writing About Text	W.4.9b	DOK 4

Comprehension 2, 4, 5A, 5B, 8, 9A, 9B, 10	/12	%
Vocabulary 1, 3A, 3B, 6, 7A, 7B, 8	/8	%
Total Weekly Assessment Score	/20	%

4 Students should underline the following sentence:
- The energy created by the Virginia quake traveled farther than most quakes in the West.

10 Students should select the following sentences:
- Water wheels look like a wooden tire.
- Flooding in the cities is different from outside cities.
- People use umbrellas in the rain and heavy coats in the snow.
- Precipitation can be good and bad.

11 **Structure:** The articles compare and contrast the effects of natural disasters.
Similarities: Both are natural disasters that cause/caused damage and scared people.
Differences: The Virginia quake caused minor damage and interfered with lives for a short time; Floods can affect areas outside of cities for a long time.

Read the passage "Pedal Power" before answering Numbers 1 through 5.

Pedal Power

Pedal faster! Pedal faster! What could be more fun than pedaling a bike? Did you know that the first bicycles had no pedals and no brakes? How do you suppose they stopped? Later, during the mid-1800s, bikes were built with pedals. One type of bike had a gigantic wheel at the front and one small wheel at the back. The rider sat on a seat above the front tire.

Roads today are smooth. In the past, roads were bumpy because they were made of stone, brick, or dirt. One early bicycle was called the boneshaker. It had a heavy frame and hard, wooden wheels. Imagine riding a bike with wooden wheels on a bumpy road. No wonder they called it the boneshaker!

Over time, bikes began to look like what we are used to seeing today. They had two rubber tires that were the same size. One tire was in the front and the other in the back. Riders sat on a seat near the middle of the bike where they could pedal to make the bike move.

Bikes today are lower to the ground than bikes of long ago. These modern bikes are also more comfortable. They are stronger and weigh less than bikes of the past. They are safer and go faster, too!

This bike was called a Penny-farthing because the tires reminded people of the British coins the penny and the farthing. It was also called a High Wheeler.

GO ON →

Have you ever wondered what makes a bike move? The pedals are attached to cranks. When the rider pedals, the cranks turn a sprocket. This wheel with metal teeth then pulls a chain that moves a gear. The gear turns the rear tire and the bike moves forward. This makes the front wheel turn. You could say that the energy created is called pedal power!

Although most bikes work in the same way, their parts can be different. For example, there are two kinds of pedals. Block pedals have rubber or plastic blocks that fit into a metal frame, and other pedals are all metal with tiny teeth along the edges. The teeth keep feet from slipping off the pedals by gripping onto the rider's shoes.

To stop a bike, foot or hand brakes are used. With foot brakes, the pedals are pushed backward to stop, and with hand brakes, a lever on the handlebars is squeezed to make the bike stop.

While most bikes are used for fun, some have different purposes. Touring bikes have a light frame and thin tires. Most have ten or more speeds. These bikes are designed for taking long, relaxing bike trips. Racing bikes are even lighter than touring bikes. They have skinny tires and low handlebars and are built to go fast in long road races.

Dirt bikes are small and strong. They have long handlebars and unlike the touring bike, they have only one speed. Dirt bikes are made for racing on bumpy dirt tracks. Like the dirt bike, the mountain bike has a strong frame with thick, wide tires. These bikes are used on rugged roads that are rough and uneven.

Bikes all have the same basic parts, but they can be so different. Whichever kind of bike you ride, just keep on pedaling.

GO ON →

Now answer Numbers 1 through 5. Base your answers on "Pedal Power."

1 This question has two parts. First, answer part A. Then, answer part B.

Part A: Read this paragraph from the passage.

Roads today are smooth. In the past, roads were bumpy because they were made of stone, brick, or dirt. One early bicycle was called the boneshaker. It had a heavy frame and hard, wooden wheels. Imagine riding a bike with wooden wheels on a bumpy road. No wonder they called it the boneshaker!

What is the effect of the author providing the nickname of a bike in this paragraph?

(A) It tells a funny story about bikes.

(B) It helps show what this bike was like to ride.

(C) It describes why this type of bike was popular.

(D) It explains how bones were used to make the bike.

Part B: What evidence from the paragraph supports your answer in Part A?

(A) "In the past, the roads were bumpy because they were made of stone, bricks, or dirt."

(B) "It had a heavy frame and hard, wooden wheels."

(C) "Imagine riding a bike a bike with wooden wheels on bumpy road."

(D) "Roads today are smooth."

GO ON →

2 Read the following sentences from the passage.

Bikes today are lower to the ground than bikes of long ago. These <u>modern</u> bikes are also more comfortable.

What does <u>modern</u> mean in the sentence above?

(A) from today

(B) from the past

(C) from the future

(D) from yesterday

3 Read the following sentences from the passage.

When the rider pedals, the cranks turn a <u>sprocket</u>. This wheel with metal teeth then pulls a chain that moves a gear.

How is <u>sprocket</u> restated in this sentence?

(A) a gear

(B) a pedal

(C) a crank that turns

(D) a wheel with teeth

GO ON →

4 Read the paragraph from the passage.

Although most bikes work in the same way, their parts can be different. For example, there are two kinds of pedals. Block pedals have rubber or plastic blocks that fit into a metal frame, and other pedals are all metal with tiny teeth along the edges. The teeth keep feet from slipping off the pedals by gripping onto the rider's shoes.

Why does the author describe metal pedals? Pick **two** choices.

(A) to show the problems caused by this type of pedal

(B) to compare the use of the pedals

(C) to describe how metal pedals are different

(D) to explain how this type of pedal helps the rider

(E) to show when this type of pedal was invented

(F) to explain when pedals were first used

5 Draw a line between the cause and its effect.

Cause	Effect
1. The gear turns the rear tire.	A. The rider's shoe is gripped.
2. The bike has wooden wheels.	B. The bike is nicknamed the boneshaker.
3. The pedals have metal teeth.	C. The bike stops.
4. The pedal are pushed backward.	D. The bike moves forward.

GO ON →

Read the passage "Wind Power" before answering Numbers 6 through 10.

Wind Power

People have been using wind power for a very long time. The earliest windmills had simple uses. In China they were used to pump water. Later, windmills were used to grind grain and saw wood. The Dutch used windmills to drain lakes and marshes. Over time, new machines were invented to do these same tasks, and windmills were used less and less.

Today, windmills have made a big comeback. Early windmills had four large sails that turned in the wind. Modern windmills, called turbines, usually have three blades. The blades are located at the top of a very tall tower. When the wind blows, it spins the blades on the turbine, and the turning blades run a generator. This machine creates electrical energy. The more the wind blows, the longer the blades turn, and this creates more electricity.

GO ON →

Wind turbines are often placed in groups called wind farms. These farms need to be built on certain sites where the wind blows frequently. Flat, open lands are good locations for wind farms. Many wind farms can be found in the Midwestern United States in the middle of farmland. They are also found in the deserts of the West and Southwest. Turbines are also located on the coasts of oceans and large lakes.

Land is not the only good location for wind farms. The wind is strong and steady over water. People are planning to build wind farms in the middle of oceans.

There are many benefits to wind farms. But they do cause problems. Birds may be hurt if they fly into the spinning blades. Some people think the turbines are hideous. They believe the towers spoil the look of the land. Some people worry that tourists might stop coming to the beaches if wind farms are built near the ocean. This could cause local businesses to lose money. Others complain that the turbines hum noisily as they spin.

Using wind power to make electricity has many advantages. Wind is free and it will never run out. Also, wind farms do not create pollution. This makes wind power good for the environment.

Wind power is becoming more popular in the United States. Over half of the fifty states have wind turbines. California is one of the highest producers of wind power. One wind farm in California has thousands of wind turbines.

One thing is for sure: wind energy has been useful to people for a very long time. The next time you feel the wind blowing on your face, think about all of the things that energy could do for you!

GO ON →

Now answer Numbers 6 through 10. Base your answers on "Wind Power."

6 Read the following sentence from the passage.

When the wind blows, it spins the blades on the turbine, and the turning blades run a <u>generator</u>.

What is a <u>generator</u>?

(A) a machine that turns blades on a turbine

(B) a machine that turns wind power into pollution

(C) a machine that turns electrical power into wind power

(D) a machine that turns wind power into electrical power

7 Read this paragraph from the passage.

Wind turbines are often placed in groups called wind farms. These farms need to be built on certain sites where the wind blows frequently. Flat, open lands are good locations for wind farms. Many wind farms can be found in the Midwestern United States in the middle of farmland. They are also found in the deserts of the West and Southwest. Turbines are also located on the coasts of oceans and large lakes.

How does the author organize this paragraph? Pick **two** choices.

(A) by using cause and effect

(B) by using compare and contrast

(C) by sequencing the location of wind farms

(D) by telling how location affects wind farms

(E) by comparing wind energy with other forms

(F) by discussing the problems with wind farms

GO ON →

8 This question has two parts. First, answer part A. Then, answer part B.

Part A: Read the following paragraph from the passage.

There are many benefits to wind farms. But they do cause problems. Birds may be hurt if they fly into the spinning blades. Some people think the turbines are <u>hideous</u>. They believe the towers spoil the look of the land. Some people worry that tourists might stop coming to the beaches if wind farms are built near the ocean. This could cause local businesses to lose money. Others complain that the turbines hum noisily as they spin.

What does <u>hideous</u> mean in the paragraph above?

(A) beautiful

(B) plain

(C) special

(D) ugly

Part B: Which sentence from the passage best supports your answer in Part A?

(A) "There are many benefits to wind farms."

(B) "Birds may be hurt if they fly into the spinning blades."

(C) "They believe the towers spoil the look of the land."

(D) "This could cause local businesses to lose money."

GO ON →

9 This question has two parts. First, answer part A. Then, answer part B.

Part A: Why does the author begin the passage with details about the history of windmills?

(A) to show the different types of windmills

(B) to explain that windmills are gaining popularity again

(C) to show that windmills are a new technology

(D) to tell why we should protect wind farms

Part B: Which sentence from the passage best supports your answer in Part A?

(A) People have been using wind power for a very long time.

(B) In China they were used to pump water.

(C) The Dutch used windmills to drain lakes and marshes.

(D) Today, windmills have made a big comeback.

10 Mark each note as either a cause or an effect.

	Cause	Effect
New machines were invented.		
People are planning to build wind farms in the ocean.		
Wind power is good for the environment.		
Wind power is becoming more popular in the United States.		

Weekly Assessment • Unit 1, Week 4

Name: _____ Date: _____

**Now answer Number 11. Base your answer on "Pedal Power"
and "Wind Power."**

11 Describe the overall structure of the passages. Explain how this helps
the reader understand ways energy is created. Support your answer
with clear text evidence from the passages.

_____

_____

_____

_____

_____

_____

_____

_____

_____

_____

_____

_____

_____

_____

Question	Correct Answer	Content Focus	CCSS	Complexity
1A	B	Text Structure: Cause and Effect	RI.4.5	DOK 2
1B	C	Text Structure: Cause and Effect/Text Evidence	RI.4.5/ RI.4.1	DOK 2
2	A	Context Clues: Definitions and Restatements	L.4.4a	DOK 2
3	D	Context Clues: Definitions and Restatements	L.4.4a	DOK 2
4	C, D	Text Structure: Compare and Contrast	RI.4.5	DOK 2
5	see below	Text Structure: Compare and Contrast	RI.4.5/ RI.4.1	DOK 2
6	D	Context Clues: Definitions and Restatements	L.4.4a	DOK 2
7	A, D	Text Structure: Cause and Effect	RI.4.5	DOK 2
8A	D	Context Clues: Definitions and Restatements	L.4.4a	DOK 2
8B	C	Context Clues: Definitions and Restatements/Text Evidence	L.4.4a/ RI.4.1	DOK 2
9A	B	Text Structure: Cause and Effect	RI.4.5	DOK 2
9B	D	Text Structure: Cause and Effect/Text Evidence	RI.4.5/ RI.4.1	DOK 2
10	see below	Text Structure: Cause and Effect	RI.4.5	DOK 2
11	see below	Writing About Text	W.4.9b	DOK 4

Comprehension 1A, 1B, 4, 5, 7, 9A, 9B, 10	/12	%
Vocabulary 2, 3, 6, 8A, 8B	/8	%
Total Weekly Assessment Score	/20	%

5 Students should match 1-D; 2-B; 3-A; 4-C

10 Students should mark the following sentences as causes:
- New machines were invented.
- Wind power is becoming more popular in the United States.

Students should mark the following sentences as effects:
- People are planning to build wind farms in the ocean.
- Wind power is good for the environment.

11 **Structure:** Both articles discuss the cause and effect of how these types of energy are created. **Reader's Understanding:** The reader is shown how each type of energy is created and the effects they have on people and the environment. The articles also address both positive and negative effects (such as pollution, noise, cost, etc.).

Read the passage "Open for Business" before answering Numbers 1 through 5.

Open for Business

Imagine that you have a pet turtle. You like to let him out of the terrarium so he can get some exercise. Sometimes you wonder if he gets lonely. Where could you take him to play with other turtles? There is no such thing as a turtle park. But what if you created one? You could charge a small fee and let other turtle owners bring their pets for exercise.

Many new businesses start just like this. Someone gets an idea for a product or service that meets a need or want. Most also hope to make a profit. This means they make more money than they spend running the business. Here are some examples of businesses that serve specific needs or wants.

Need a Lift?

Some businesses do work for charity. They donate things to people in need and do not try to make a profit. Take for example a bike shop that fixes up used bikes and gives them to people in need of transportation. New bicycles can be expensive. Many people cannot afford to buy them. This business helps those who cannot normally afford a bike to get one that is safe and working.

GO ON →

Fun for All

One day, a father noticed that his daughter's special needs prevented her from enjoying outdoor activities with other children. He wanted a fun place for her to play. He decided to provide a way for her and children of all abilities to have fun. He helped design a special amusement park. At this amusement park, everyone can enjoy the rides because they have seats that fit wheelchairs.

Trash to Treasure

Resale shops are another type of business that helps people. Resale shops sell everything from clothes to useful household items such as dishes and furniture. In this type of business, people donate or sell used items to the shop. The items are then sold to customers at a discounted price. Resale shops are open to anyone looking for a bargain.

Homework Help

Some businesses help students learn. These tutoring centers help students needing assistance with schoolwork. At these centers, tutors or teachers work with students individually or in small groups. Many students find that the extra practice improves their understanding.

A lot of planning must happen before starting any business. Owners must decide what type of business to open. Then lots of decisions need to be made. The owner has to find a location, set competitive prices, hire employees, and advertise. Starting a business can be very rewarding. What type of business would you like to start?

GO ON →

Now answer Numbers 1 through 5. Base your answers on "Open for Business."

1 Read this paragraph from the passage.

Many new businesses start just like this. Someone gets an idea for a product or service that meets a need or want. Most also hope to make a profit. This means they make more money than they spend running the business. Here are some examples of businesses that serve specific needs or wants.

Which sentence best explains what this passage is about?

(A) Making a profit is very important.

(B) Businesses can serve needs.

(C) It is difficult to start a new business.

(D) Products can fulfill a want.

2 Which section would **best** be supported by the following detail?

Reselling items keeps them out of landfills.

(A) **Need a Lift?**

(B) **Fun for All**

(C) **Homework Help**

(D) **Trash to Treasure**

GO ON →

3 Read the following sentences from the passage.

Then lots of decisions need to be made. The owner has to find a location, set competitive prices, hire employees, and advertise.

If *compete* means "to try to win," what does competitive mean in the sentences above?

(A) never competing

(B) unable to compete

(C) good for competition

(D) losing a competition

4 Read the following sentence from the passage.

Resale shops sell everything from clothes to useful household items such as dishes and furniture.

What does useful mean?

(A) quite old

(B) serves a purpose

(C) brightly colored

(D) costs a lot of money

GO ON →

5 This question has two parts. First, answer part A. Then, answer part B.

Part A: Which business in the passage helps people get around town?

(A) tutoring centers

(B) resale shops

(C) bike shops

(D) amusement parks

Part B: What evidence from the passage supports your answer in Part A?

(A) "This business helps those who cannot normally afford a bike to get one that is safe and working."

(B) "At this amusement park, everyone can enjoy the rides because they have seats that fit wheelchairs."

(C) "Resale shops sell everything from clothes to useful household items such as dishes and furniture."

(D) "At these centers, tutors or teachers work with students individually or in small groups."

GO ON →

Read the passage "Young Thomas Edison" before answering Numbers 6 through 10.

Young Thomas Edison

The name Thomas Edison has come to stand for inventions that greatly changed life. A look at his early life shows that even when he was young, Edison liked to make things and was always ready to start a new business venture.

Edison was born in 1847. His mother had been a teacher. Instead of sending Edison to school, she taught him at home. Judging by what he eventually accomplished, she did a very good job.

As a boy, Edison loved to read science books. The books made him ask questions. He wanted to know how things worked. He started to build models of things. He built a working sawmill and a working train engine. Both models ran on steam.

Young, clever Edison was a very active and enterprising boy who was far from lazy. Edison grew up on a farm. He grew vegetables and sold them in town. When he was 12 years old, he sold food and newspapers to passengers on trains. Then, to help his business grow, he had other people sell things for him. As a teen, the creative Edison started his own newspaper, which he called *The Weekly Herald*.

In his teenage years, Edison began to have problems with his hearing. As he grew older, his hearing would become worse and worse. Later in life, he had a lot of trouble hearing people unless they shouted. These problems were difficult for him. However, they did not stop him from constantly trying to improve the world around him.

GO ON →

When he was 15 years old, Edison saved a boy's life by pulling him out of the path of a train. The boy's father was a telegraph operator. As a reward for saving his son, the man taught Edison how to operate a telegraph. Edison kept at it and worked hard, and his persistence paid off. He got jobs working as a telegraph operator, sending and receiving messages.

Working as a telegraph operator was another learning opportunity for Edison. He sent messages to and received messages from people all over the country. He also took the opportunity to learn about the telegraph and how it worked. As he started doing his own experiments with telegraph equipment, he found ways to make it work better.

Later, he moved to Boston. Edison soon began making improvements to the telegraph. The hard-working boy had grown into a busy young man whose inventions, such as an early movie camera, would later change the world.

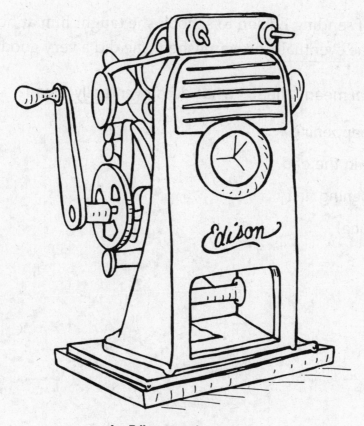

An Edison movie camera

GO ON →

Now answer Numbers 6 through 10. Base your answers on "Young Thomas Edison."

6 Which statement describes Thomas Edison as a child and as an adult? Pick **two** choices.

(A) He did not like science.

(B) He often forgot to do things.

(C) He was always building things.

(D) He never finished what he started.

(E) He was creative in many ways.

(F) He was not very active.

7 Read the following sentences from the passage.

Instead of sending Edison to school, she taught him at home. Judging by what he eventually accomplished, she did a very good job.

If *eventual* means "final," what does eventually mean?

(A) not happening

(B) done in the end

(C) happening first

(D) not final

8 This question has two parts. First, answer part A. Then, answer part B.

Part A: What is the **main** idea of the passage?

Ⓐ Edison's inventions changed how people live.

Ⓑ Edison wanted to know how things worked.

Ⓒ Edison liked to make and try new things.

Ⓓ Edison's newspaper was successful and popular.

Part B: Which sentence from the passage best supports your answer in Part A?

Ⓐ "A look at his early life shows that even when he was young, Edison liked to make things and was always ready to start a new business venture."

Ⓑ "As he started doing his own experiments with telegraph equipment, he found ways to make it work better."

Ⓒ "As a teen, the creative Edison started his own newspaper, which he called *The Weekly Herald*."

Ⓓ "The hard-working boy had grown into a busy young man whose inventions, such as an early movie camera, would later change the world."

GO ON →

9 What is the main idea of the last paragraph on page 54?

Ⓐ Not being able to hear is difficult.

Ⓑ People sometimes shouted at Edison.

Ⓒ Edison lost his hearing when he was older.

Ⓓ Edison had hearing problems for much of his life.

10 Read the words and the sentences from the passage. Write the word next to its matching definition below the chart.

Word	Sentence from Passage
1. greatly	"The name Thomas Edison has come to stand for inventions that <u>greatly</u> changed life."
2. creative	"As a teen, the <u>creative</u> Edison started his own newspaper, which he called *The Weekly Herald*."
3. constantly	"However, these problems did not stop Edison from <u>constantly</u> trying to improve the world around him."

_____ having orginal ideas

_____ in important ways

_____ done in a continuous way

Name: _____ Date: _____

Now answer Number 11. Base your answer on "Open for Business" and "Young Thomas Edison."

11 "Open for Business" and "Young Thomas Edison" discuss reasons businesses are started and how they help others. What are the key ideas that support this main idea? Support your answer with clear text evidence from the passages.

_____

_____

_____

_____

_____

_____

_____

_____

_____

_____

_____

_____

_____

_____

Answer Key

Question	Correct Answer	Content Focus	CCSS	Complexity
1	B	Main Ideas and Key Details	RI.4.2	DOK 2
2	D	Main Ideas and Key Details	RI.4.2	DOK 2
3	C	Suffixes: *-ly* and *-ive*	L.3.4b	DOK 2
4	B	Suffixes: *-ful*	L.3.4b	DOK 2
5A	C	Main Ideas and Key Details	RI.4.2	DOK 2
5B	A	Main Ideas and Key Details/ Text Evidence	RI.4.2/ RI.4.1	DOK 2
6	C, E	Main Ideas and Key Details	RI.4.2	DOK 2
7	B	Suffixes: *-ly* and *-ive*	L.3.4b	DOK 2
8A	C	Main Ideas and Key Details	RI.4.2	DOK 2
8B	A	Main Ideas and Key Details/ Text Evidence	RI.4.2/ RI.4.1	DOK 2
9	D	Main Ideas and Key Details	RI.4.2	DOK 2
10	see below	Suffixes: *-ly* and *-ive*	L.3.4b	DOK 2
11	see below	Writing About Text	W.4.9b	DOK 4

Comprehension 1, 2, 5A, 5B, 6, 7, 8A, 8B, 9		/12	%
Vocabulary 3, 4, 7, 8A, 8B, 10		/8	%
Total Weekly Assessment Score		/20	%

10 Students should complete the item with the following definitions:

- greatly: in important ways
- creative: having original ideas
- constantly: done in a continuous way

11 **Main Idea:** *Open for Business*: Some businesses help others. Some people want to help others do what they might not be able to accomplish by themselves. *Young Thomas Edison*: Edison's ideas helped people; he wanted to improve inventions to help others. **Key Details:** *Open for Business*: Some bicycle shops fix up used bikes and donate them to people in need. Resale shops help people buy items for less money. Some people make the world accessible to people of all abilities. *Young Thomas Edison*: Edison sold food and newspapers to people on trains. He made improvements to the telegraph to help people send messages.

Read the passage "Help, Please!" before answering Numbers 1 through 5.

Help, Please!

"I know what would taste really good right now," Raccoon said. "A warm, yummy baked apple!" Raccoon headed for the apple tree, but the apples on the ground were rotten and mushy. She spotted juicy apples hanging from the tree overhead. Sadly, Raccoon's old bones ached whenever she tried to climb trees.

Just then, Deer trotted past. "Deer, I'm so glad to see you," said Raccoon. "I want to make a baked apple. Is there a possibility that you could reach up and pick one of those nice apples for me?"

But Deer was already nearly out of sight. "Sorry, Raccoon!" he called over his shoulder. "I'm late...."

Raccoon sighed, but just then Bear padded by. "Bear," Raccoon said, "could you please reach up and pick one of those nice apples for me?"

"I'd be glad to, Raccoon," Bear said, "but I need to save my energy because it's almost time for my long winter nap."

As Bear lumbered into the woods, Raccoon started up the tree, gripping the trunk painfully with her claws. She was creeping along a branch and was almost to the apples when her back paws slipped! Raccoon hung by her front paws until she finally managed to pull herself back up on the branch.

GO ON →

"Whew! I better get two apples," Raccoon thought, "because I'm not doing this again!" Of course, holding two apples made it even harder to climb down. Raccoon fell the last few feet. She landed hard, but she wasn't hurt.

Now Raccoon needed sticks and twigs to make a fire to bake the apples. She gathered the sticks she could see, but the pile was too small for a good fire. Just then, Rabbit tiptoed into the clearing and asked, "Why are you looking in the bushes, Raccoon?"

"I want to build a fire so I can bake some apples," Raccoon explained. "Could you help me find more sticks?" Her smile was full of friendliness.

"I can't because I hurt my leg today," Rabbit said, holding up one front leg in a sorrowful way. Then he hopped off, using all four legs, Raccoon noticed.

Next, Raccoon spotted Mouse in the bushes. "Mouse," Raccoon begged, "would you help me gather sticks to make a fire? I want to bake some apples."

"Oh," Mouse whispered, "I'm so small that I couldn't even carry a twig." With that, Mouse scurried back into the bushes.

Then Bee buzzed by. Raccoon called, "Bee? Oh, never mind! You're too small to be of any help."

"Maybe not," Bee told her. "My mom always told me you are only as small as your ideas. What do you need?"

Raccoon explained the situation. Bee smiled and said, "I might be too small to gather twigs, but I have some very nice honey to sweeten your apples!"

With renewed energy, Raccoon found enough twigs to make a small fire. Soon, Raccoon and Bee were contentedly feasting on sweet, warm baked apples. Deer, Bear, Rabbit, and Mouse watched hungrily from the bushes. They were not too busy, tired, or small to help eat the apples, but now Raccoon and Bee didn't need help!

GO ON →

Name: _____ Date: _____

Now answer Numbers 1 through 5. Base your answers on "Help, Please!"

1 Read the sentence from the passage.

"Is there a <u>possibility</u> that you could reach up and pick one of those nice apples for me?"

If *possible* means "able to happen," what does <u>possibility</u> mean?

(A) something that could happen

(B) something that has happened

(C) something that cannot happen

(D) something that needs to happen

2 This question has two parts. First, answer part A. Then, answer part B.

Part A: What is the theme of this passage?

(A) Everyone needs friends.

(B) Learn from your mistakes.

(C) It takes a big idea to solve a problem.

(D) If you do not help, do not expect a reward.

Part B: Which key detail supports the theme of the passage?

(A) Raccoon needs twigs to make a fire.

(B) Raccoon asks other animals to help her.

(C) Only Raccoon and Bee share the apples.

(D) On the way down, Raccoon falls out of the tree.

GO ON →

3 Read the sentence from the passage.

Her smile was full of <u>friendliness</u>.

Which word has the **same** root word as <u>friendliness</u>?

(A) end

(B) fried

(C) friendly

(D) happiness

4 Which evidence from the text **best** supports the theme? Pick **two** choices.

(A) "Raccoon headed for the apple tree, but the apples on the ground were rotten and mushy."

(B) "'Bear,' Raccoon said, 'could you please reach up and pick one of those nice apples for me?'"

(C) "'Whew! I better get two apples,' Raccoon thought, 'because I'm not doing this again!'"

(D) "'Mouse,' Raccoon begged, 'would you help me gather sticks to make a fire?'"

(E) "Bee smiled and said, 'I might be too small to gather twigs, but I have some very nice honey to sweeten your apples!'"

(F) "They were not too busy, tired, or small to help eat the apples, but now Raccoon and Bee didn't need help!"

GO ON →

5 How does the text evidence below support the message of the passage? Write **two** statements from the box to complete the chart.

Text Evidence	How It Supports the Message of the Passage
"Soon, Raccoon and Bee were contentedly feasting on sweet, warm baked apples. Deer, Bear, Rabbit, and Mouse watched hungrily from the bushes."	

Statements:

It shows that Raccoon and Bee are very close friends.

It shows that Deer, Bear, Rabbit, and Mouse make a mistake.

It shows that baked apples taste better with honey.

It shows that Raccoon and Bee are rewarded for their hard work.

It shows that warm apples are difficult to make.

It shows that Deer, Bear, Rabbit, and Mouse cannot help Raccoon.

GO ON →

Read the passage "Visitors in the Woods" before answering Numbers 6 through 10.

Visitors in the Woods

Gwen and her father were spending the day in the state park a few miles from their house. Each time they saw an animal Gwen's father would stop and lower his voice while they watched it. As they rounded a curve in the trail, they heard a scuffling sound in the woods.

About 100 feet ahead, a deer and her fawn cautiously stepped onto the trail. Gwen's father immediately put his hand on her shoulder to prevent her from taking another step and whispered, "Look!"

"They are beautiful!" Gwen said softly.

The mother deer froze in her tracks and stared at them, almost as if she were eavesdropping and following their conversation. She also was paying close attention to her baby.

GO ON →

Gwen took a step toward the deer, but her father's voice stopped her in her tracks. "Keep your distance, Gwen." He continued speaking softly. "Don't get too close or you'll scare them."

Gwen knew her father's warning was logical, but she still wanted a better look at the deer. Would it really make a difference if she went a little closer? She was thinking of taking just one more step when she noticed that she was about to walk right on top of a jumble of twigs. The noise from the twigs would surely frighten the deer, so Gwen reacted by staying right where she was on the trail.

Just then, Gwen heard someone talking loudly behind them. It was a father and his son, who were laughing and joking around with each other. The mother deer watched them carefully and moved closer to her baby.

"Shhh," Gwen's father warned. "You'll frighten the deer."

"So what?" the father answered rudely as he rolled his eyes at Gwen's father. "Look, there are a lot of people in the park today. It's better to scare the deer away than have them on the trail while we're hiking." He spoke so loudly that Gwen thought he was deliberately trying to frighten the deer.

Sure enough, the mother bounded into the dense woods with the fawn at her heels. With her eyes full of longing, Gwen gazed after them wistfully. They had been so much fun to watch.

The father and son were completely unaffected by the incident. "They should be more careful when people are on the trail," the father said.

"No," replied Gwen's father courageously. "It's the other way around. The animals live here and we are the visitors."

GO ON →

Now answer Numbers 6 through 10. Base your answers on "Visitors in the Woods."

6 Read the sentence from the passage.

Gwen knew her father's warning was <u>logical</u>, but she still wanted a better look at the deer.

What does the root word *logic* explain about a <u>logical</u> action?

Ⓐ It is easy.

Ⓑ It is quick.

Ⓒ It is dangerous.

Ⓓ It is reasonable.

7 This question has two parts. First, answer part A. Then, answer part B.

Part A: What is the theme of this passage?

Ⓐ People should respect animals that live in nature.

Ⓑ People should be quiet when animals are around.

Ⓒ Animals are more important than people.

Ⓓ It is important to spend time outdoors.

Part B: Which evidence from the text **best** supports the theme of the passage?

Ⓐ "About 100 feet ahead, a deer and her fawn cautiously stepped onto the trail."

Ⓑ "'They are beautiful!' Gwen said softly."

Ⓒ "It was a father and his son, who were laughing and joking around with each other."

Ⓓ "'The animals live here and we are the visitors.'"

GO ON →

8 Read the sentence from the passage.

He spoke so loudly that Gwen thought he was <u>deliberately</u> trying to frighten the deer.

Which word has the **same** root word as <u>deliberately</u>?

(A) delicately

(B) deliberation

(C) lately

(D) rate

9 Underline **two** sentences in the paragraphs that support the theme of the passage.

The mother deer froze in her tracks and stared at them, almost as if she were eavesdropping and following their conversation. She also was paying close attention to her baby.

Gwen took a step toward the deer, but her father's voice stopped her in her tracks. "Keep your distance, Gwen." He continued speaking softly. "Don't get too close or you'll scare them."

GO ON →

10 How do the actions of Gwen's father support the theme of the passage? Pick **two** choices.

   Ⓐ He points out the deer to Gwen.

   Ⓑ He takes Gwen hiking in the park.

   Ⓒ He hears a scuffling noise on the trail.

   Ⓓ He tells the man not to frighten the deer.

   Ⓔ He lives only a few miles from the state park.

   Ⓕ He lowers his voice when animals are around.

Now answer Number 11. Base your answer on "Help, Please!" and "Visitors in the Woods."

11 What messages are presented in the passages? Support your answer with details from both passages.

_____

_____

_____

_____

_____

_____

_____

_____

_____

_____

_____

_____

_____

_____

Answer Key

Name: _____

Question	Correct Answer	Content Focus	CCSS	Complexity
1	A	Root Words	L.3.4c	DOK 2
2A	D	Theme	RL.4.2	DOK 3
2B	C	Theme/Text Evidence	RL.4.2/ RL.4.1	DOK 2
3	C	Root Words	L.3.4c	DOK 1
4	E, F	Theme	RL.4.2	DOK 2
5	see below	Theme	RL.4.2	DOK 3
6	D	Root Words	L.3.4c	DOK 1
7A	A	Theme	RL.4.2	DOK 3
7B	D	Theme/Text Evidence	RL.4.2/ RL.4.1	DOK 3
8	B	Root Words	L.3.4c	DOK 1
9	see below	Theme	RL.4.2	DOK 3
10	D, F	Theme	RL.4.2	DOK 3
11	see below	Writing About Text	W.4.9a	DOK 4

Comprehension 2A, 2B, 4, 5, 7A, 7B, 9, 10	/12	%
Vocabulary 1, 3, 6, 8	/8	%
Total Weekly Assessment Score	/20	%

5 Students should complete the chart with the following statements:

- It shows that Deer, Bear, Rabbit, and Mouse make a mistake.
- It shows that Raccoon and Bee are rewarded for their hard work.

9 Students should underline the following sentences:

- "Keep your distance, Gwen."
- "Don't get too close or you'll scare them."

11 To receive full credit, responses should highlight the fact that both passages stress the importance of showing consideration or respect for others. In "Help, Please!" none of the animals except for Bee is willing to help Raccoon. When Raccoon is able to make the baked apples, only Bee enjoys the treat. In "Visitors in the Woods," Gwen's father understands that people, not deer, are the real visitors and should acknowledge that when they encounter wildlife in the woods.

Read the passage "Little Red" before answering Numbers 1 through 5.

Little Red

Once upon a time, there was a young girl who lived in a big city. The girl and her granny liked to do things together. They rode bikes, ran in the park, did yoga, and danced. The two were always active, never idle. Since the girl had red hair like her granny, people called her Little Red.

Little Red took a backpack filled with food to Granny's apartment every Saturday, and they ate lunch together. A family of pigs lived in Granny's building, and the largest pig, named Piggy, was always hungry. "I think Little Red has sweet treats in her backpack," said Piggy. "I want to eat those cookies, cakes, and candies—yummers!"

Piggy planned to trick Little Red by dressing like Granny, who always wore comfortable, casual clothes. So Piggy put on a jogging suit, sneakers, and sunglasses, and he waited for Little Red outside on the steps.

"Hi, Granny," said Little Red. "I brought lunch!" Then, Little Red took another look. Everything seemed the same as usual, but Granny looked peculiar.

Little Red commented, "What funny hands you have, Granny."

"The better to hold the food you brought," said Piggy.

Little Red remarked, "What a big nose you have, Granny."

"The better to smell the food you brought," said Piggy.

Little Red exclaimed, "What a big mouth you have, Granny!"

"The better to eat all your food!" yelled Piggy as he reached for the backpack.

GO ON →

Little Red ducked and ran away from Piggy. The pleasure Piggy felt suddenly turned to discomfort, as Piggy was out of shape and had no energy to chase Little Red. With sweat dripping off his snout, he squealed, "I'm so tired that I can't move another step!" Piggy dropped to the sidewalk.

Little Red kindly went back to help Piggy as she said, "Piggy, you need to eat some healthy food."

"Yummers! Food! Do you have any fudge?" asked Piggy. "I would love some fudge right now."

"No, but I have corn and apples," said Little Red. "When you eat healthy foods like vegetables and fruit, you feel better. Don't devour it, but slowly eat a bit of this corn," she offered.

"You need to exercise, too," insisted Little Red. "Let's go to Granny's apartment and walk on the treadmill. Exercise gives you strength and energy so you can run and play! And please don't trick me again," she added. "Just join Granny and me for a healthy lunch."

"Yummers!" agreed Piggy.

GO ON →

Name: _____ Date: _____

Now answer Numbers 1 through 5. Base your answers on "Little Red."

1 This question has two parts. First, answer part A. Then, answer part B.

Part A: Which sentence **best** describes the theme of "Little Red"?

Ⓐ It is important to exercise and eat healthy foods.

Ⓑ Always carry food in case of emergency.

Ⓒ Visit your grandparents often.

Ⓓ Pigs are clever animals.

Part B: Which text evidence **best** supports the theme of the passage?

Ⓐ "'I brought lunch!'"

Ⓑ "'The better to smell the food you brought,' said Piggy."

Ⓒ "'Do you have any fudge?' asked Piggy."

Ⓓ "'When you eat healthy foods like vegetables and fruit, you feel better.'"

2 Read the sentence from the passage.

"Don't devour it, but slowly eat a bit of this corn," she offered.

Which word has the **opposite** meaning of devour?

Ⓐ destroy

Ⓑ gobble

Ⓒ nibble

Ⓓ smash

GO ON →

3 Read the sentences from the passage.

The pleasure Piggy felt suddenly turned to discomfort, as Piggy was out of shape and had no energy to chase Little Red. With sweat dripping off his snout, he squealed, "I'm so tired that I can't move another step!"

How does this text evidence support the theme?

(A) It tells what happens when you squeal.

(B) It tells why you need to wear sneakers.

(C) It tells how to bake and eat tasty baked goods.

(D) It tells the results of not exercising and unhealthy eating.

4 Which details from the passage **best** support the theme? Pick **two** choices.

(A) Piggy plans to trick Little Red.

(B) The largest pig is named Piggy.

(C) Exercise gives you strength and energy.

(D) Since Little Red was kind, she went back to help.

(E) Little Red and her granny like to do things together.

(F) Little Red is healthy and in very good physical shape.

GO ON →

5 Draw a line to match the underlined words in the sentences on the left with the words that have the **opposite** meaning on the right.

| The two were always active, never <u>idle</u>. | | normal |

| Piggy planned to trick Little Red by dressing like Granny, who always wore comfortable, <u>casual</u> clothes. | | busy |

| Everything seemed the same as usual, but Granny looked <u>peculiar</u>. | | formal |

GO ON →

Read the passage "The Three Little Mice" before answering Numbers 6 through 10.

The Three Little Mice

Once upon a time, in the dark of night, three little mice went out to build houses. The little mice had many friends in the forest, but they also had foes like the Big Bad Owl. The first little mouse wanted the mice to work together to build one small, safe house, but the other two mice wanted to have big houses of their own.

The second little mouse gathered dried grass to build his house. It was a flimsy house, not solid, but it had a gym where he could run. The little mouse thought, "Why work together? This house is all mine!"

The third little mouse built a house of twigs. It was not a strong house. He built it around a puddle so he had his own swimming pool. The little mouse thought, "When I work alone I get what I want."

While the others built houses of grass and twigs, the first little mouse searched and searched until he found a hollow log. "This will be my home for now," he thought. It was not a big, new house, but it was sturdy and safe.

As the second little mouse was running in his gym he heard a voice outside. "Whooo! Who will let me come in?" hooted the Big Bad Owl.

"Not a chancey-chance-chance," squeaked the little mouse.

GO ON →

"Then I'll flap, and I'll slap, and I'll knock your house down!" screeched the Big Bad Owl. So the owl flapped and slapped his wings and knocked the grass house down.

The second little mouse did not linger. He hurried away to the twig home of the third little mouse, who was drying off after a midnight swim. Both mice heard a voice outside. "Whooo! Who will let me come in?" hooted the Big Bad Owl.

"Not a chancy-chance-chance," squeaked the little mice.

"Then I'll flap, and I'll slap, and I'll knock your house down!" screeched the Big Bad Owl.

So the owl flapped and slapped his wings and demolished the twig house. The mice quickly scampered to the log home. Once inside, they admitted, "We made a big mistake by working alone!"

"Don't panic. Stay calm. You're safe now," said the first little mouse. The Big Bad Owl hooted and flapped for most of the night, but he could not move the log house. In the morning, the owl was asleep, so the three mice ran to the other side of the forest. This time, they worked together and they got the job done right. The three little mice dug a small, well-built burrow. Here they lived safely forever away from the Big Bad Owl.

GO ON →

Now answer Numbers 6 through 10. Base your answers on "The Three Little Mice."

6 This question has two parts. First, answer part A. Then, answer part B.

Part A: Which sentence **best** describes the theme of "The Three Little Mice"?

(A) Mice need big houses.

(B) It is best to build things at night.

(C) Working together gets the job done right.

(D) Never let the Big Bad Owl into your house.

Part B: Which text evidence **best** supports the theme of the passage?

(A) "The little mouse thought, 'When I work alone I get what I want.'"

(B) "'This will be my home for now,' he thought."

(C) "'Who will let me come in?' hooted the Big Bad Owl."

(D) "Once inside, they admitted, 'We made a big mistake by working alone!'"

7 Read the sentences from the passage.

The second little mouse did not <u>linger</u>. He hurried away to the twig home of the third little mouse, who was drying off after a midnight swim.

Which word means the **opposite** of <u>linger</u>?

(A) hurry

(B) laugh

(C) swim

(D) wait

GO ON →

8 Select **three** words that have to do with the message of the story. Write the words in the chart.

Theme of "The Three Little Mice"

Teamwork
Kindness
Sadness
Success
Mistakes
Loyalty

9 Read the sentence from the passage.

So the owl flapped and slapped his wings and <u>demolished</u> the twig house.

Which word has the **opposite** meaning of <u>demolished</u>?

(A) built

(B) destroyed

(C) visited

(D) wrecked

GO ON →

10 Read the sentences from the passage.

This time, they worked together and they got the job done right. The three little mice dug a small, well-built burrow.

How does this text evidence support the theme? Pick **two** choices.

(A) It tells what can happen when you work with others.

(B) It tells how long it takes to dig a well-built burrow.

(C) It tells that burrows are the best type of homes.

(D) It tells why mice live in burrows.

(E) It tells how to complete any job.

(F) It tells about fixing an error.

**Now answer Number 11. Base your answer on "Little Red" and
"The Three Little Mice."**

11 The themes of "Little Red" and "The Three Little Mice" show the
importance of decision-making. Use details from both passages to
show what the characters learned from their poor decisions.

_____

_____

_____

_____

_____

_____

_____

_____

_____

_____

_____

_____

_____

_____

Answer Key

Question	Correct Answer	Content Focus	CCSS	Complexity
1A	B	Theme	RL.4.2	DOK 3
1B	C	Theme/Text Evidence	RL.4.2/ RL.4.1	DOK 3
2	D	Context Clues: Antonyms	L.4.5c	DOK 2
3	D	Theme	RL.4.2	DOK 2
4	C, F	Theme	RL.4.2	DOK 2
5	see below	Context Clues: Antonyms	L.4.5c	DOK 2
6A	C	Theme	RL.4.2	DOK 3
6B	D	Theme/Text Evidence	RL.4.2/ RL.4.1	DOK 3
7	A	Context Clues: Antonyms	L.4.5c	DOK 2
8	see below	Theme	RL.4.2	DOK 3
9	A	Context Clues: Antonyms	L.4.5c	DOK 2
10	A, F	Theme	RL.4.2	DOK 2
11	see below	Writing About Text	W.4.9a	DOK 4

Comprehension 1A, 1B, 3, 4, 6A, 6B, 8, 10	/12		%
Vocabulary 2, 5, 7, 9	/8		%
Total Weekly Assessment Score	/20		%

5 Students should match the underlined words with their antonyms as follows:
- idle: busy
- casual: formal
- peculiar: normal.

8 Students should write the following words in the chart:
- Teamwork
- Success
- Mistakes

11 To receive full credit for the response, the following information should be included: Piggy learned that it is important to eat healthy food and to exercise to be healthy. The mice learned that working together gets the job done right.

Read the article "Life in the Forest" before answering Numbers 1 through 5.

Life in the Forest

Forests are home to many living things. Many types of forests cover parts of Earth. One kind of forest is the deciduous forest. In these forests, leaves on trees and shrubs change color and fall off in autumn. Deciduous forests are found in temperate climates with warm summers and cool winters. The mild weather in these forests helps many things grow and survive.

Deciduous forests have five different zones, and different types of living things can be found in each zone. The animals, plants, and other organisms in each zone have learned to survive together. Animals in these forests eat plants and sometimes each other. They also use the trees for shelter and sources of water. Forest plants get the nutrients needed for growth from the ground. Most plants also grow toward the sun to get the light they need.

GO ON →

The canopy is the highest layer in the forest and is home to the tallest trees. This area gets the most sunlight. It produces the most food. Birds, insects, and mammals that live here eat leaves and fruits that grow on trees.

The understory is found below the canopy. Two different types of trees are found in this zone: small trees and saplings. Small trees depend on the shade of the canopy to survive. Saplings are young, short trees that will eventually join the canopy. The understory in a deciduous forest can be thick, which helps animals find food and shelter.

The third zone is the shrub layer. Shrubs have many woody stems and do not grow as tall as trees. Many birds and insects live in the shrub layer.

Beneath the shrub layer is the herb zone. Ferns, grasses, and wildflowers live in this zone. It is home to ground animals such as snakes, mice, turtles, bears, and deer. These animals feed on the plants and small animals found in the herb zone.

The lowest zone is the forest floor. This layer is covered by waste materials including leaves, twigs, animal droppings, and dead plants and animals. Millions of creatures, such as earthworms, insects, and spiders, are found on the forest floor. These creatures, along with tiny living things called bacteria, help break down waste materials. Once broken down, this material goes back into the soil. Forest plants then take in nutrients from the soil. Plant-eating animals eat these plants. These animals become the food of meat-eating animals. New waste from these plants and animals goes back into the soil and the cycle continues.

The five zones in a deciduous forest are connected. All life in the forest depends on the energy it gets from other living things. Every living thing in the forest is equally important. Each has a role in helping the others survive.

GO ON →

Name: _____ Date: _____

Now answer Numbers 1 through 5. Base your answers on "Life in the Forest."

1 This question has two parts. First, answer part A. Then, answer part B.

Part A: Read the sentence from the article.

The animals, plants, and other <u>organisms</u> in each zone have learned to survive together.

What does the word <u>organisms</u> mean in this sentence?

(A) thick layers

(B) living things

(C) waste materials

(D) weather patterns

Part B: Which words in the sentence help to show the meaning of <u>organisms</u>? Pick **two** choices.

(A) animals

(B) plants

(C) zone

(D) learned

(E) survive

(F) together

2 Which living things can be found in the shrub layer?

(A) birds

(B) mice

(C) snakes

(D) turtles

GO ON →

3 Read the detail below.

Sunlight is very important to the canopy.

Circle the paragraph that is **best** supported by this detail.

Deciduous forests have five different zones, and different types of living things can be found in each zone. The animals, plants, and other organisms in each zone have learned to survive together. Animals in these forests eat plants and sometimes each other. They also use the trees for shelter and sources of water. Forest plants get the nutrients needed for growth from the ground. Most plants also grow toward the sun to get the light they need.

The canopy is the highest layer in the forest and is home to the tallest trees. This area gets the most sunlight. It produces the most food. Birds, insects, and mammals that live here eat leaves and fruits that grow on trees.

The understory is found below the canopy. Two different types of trees are found in this zone: small trees and saplings. Small trees depend on the shade of the canopy to survive. Saplings are young, short trees that will eventually join the canopy. The understory in a deciduous forest can be thick, which helps animals find food and shelter.

The third zone is the shrub layer. Shrubs have many woody stems and do not grow as tall as trees. Many birds and insects live in the shrub layer.

Beneath the shrub layer is the herb zone. Ferns, grasses, and wildflowers live in this zone. It is home to ground animals such as snakes, mice, turtles, bears, and deer. These animals feed on the plants and small animals found in the herb zone.

GO ON →

4 Read the sentence from the article.

The canopy is the highest layer in the forest and is home to the tallest trees.

What does canopy mean in the sentence above?

(A) forest

(B) home

(C) top

(D) zone

5 This question has two parts. First, answer part A. Then, answer part B.

Part A: Which sentence **best** explains what the article is about?

(A) All living things in a forest are connected.

(B) Trees provide food for birds and animals.

(C) All deciduous trees lose their leaves.

(D) Forests are found all over the world.

Part B: Which sentence from the article **best** supports the main idea?

(A) "Forests are home to many living things."

(B) "Many types of forests cover parts of Earth."

(C) "Every living thing in the forest is equally important."

(D) "Each has a role in helping the others survive."

GO ON →

Read the article "The Coral Reef" before answering Numbers 6 through 10.

The Coral Reef

Some people think a coral reef is a large rock under the surface of the water, but that is not true. Unlike a rock, coral is alive. It also is brittle and breaks easily. Many people are not aware that when they break a piece of live coral, the coral dies. Over time, if many pieces of coral are broken off a reef, the entire reef may eventually die.

Many coral reefs have fish near them. The fish and the reef form a partnership, working together as a team. Fish receive a great benefit from swimming near a reef. Fish eat the plants growing on the reef. The reef also provides the fish with a home.

The perfect conditions of the water near coral reefs make it fun to swim near them. It is exciting to explore the reef and study the coral. Some coral is very pretty. Other coral looks a lot like something alien from another planet. Some people like to swim near a reef and drift with the current. They can see many colorful fish swimming nearby. Sometimes it can be hard to decide what to look at first. Both the coral and the fish are spectacular and eye-catching.

GO ON →

Two different types of people visit a coral reef. The first group is people whose behavior causes damage to the reef. They think it is all right to break off pieces of coral to take home. They also stand on the reef, which can hurt the coral and the person standing on it. A person standing on or touching a reef can get cut or scratched by the coral. Because coral is alive, sometimes these cuts and scratches can be very serious.

The second group is made up of people who take the time to learn how to behave near the reef. These people learn what they can do on the reef. They also learn what they should not do. They make sure that both they and the coral will stay safe. It would be wonderful if everyone took the time to do this. It would help us all be able to enjoy coral reefs for a long time to come.

Name: _____ Date: _____

Now answer Numbers 6 through 10. Base your answers on "The Coral Reef."

6 Read the sentence from the article.

The fish and the reef form a <u>partnership</u>, working together as a team.

Which word from the sentence helps the reader figure out what <u>partnership</u> means?

(A) fish

(B) reef

(C) team

(D) working

7 This question has two parts. First, answer part A. Then, answer part B.

Part A: Which detail shows that coral is a living thing?

(A) Coral is brittle.

(B) Coral is just like a rock.

(C) Coral dies when it breaks.

(D) Coral is home to many creatures.

Part B: Which sentence from the article supports your answer in part A?

(A) "Some people think a coral reef is a large rock under the surface of the water, but that is not true."

(B) "Over time, if many pieces of coral are broken off a reef, the entire reef may eventually die."

(C) "The first group is people whose behavior causes damage to the reef."

(D) "It would help us all be able to enjoy coral reefs for a long time to come."

GO ON →

8 This question has two parts. First, answer part A. Then, answer part B.

Part A: Read this sentence from the article.

Other coral looks a lot like something <u>alien</u> from another planet.

What does the word <u>alien</u> mean?

(A) beautiful

(B) important

(C) strange

(D) unexciting

Part B: Which phrase from the sentence helps the reader figure out what <u>alien</u> means?

(A) "other coral"

(B) "looks a lot"

(C) "like something"

(D) "from another planet"

9 Which detail **best** supports the main idea of the last paragraph?

(A) Coral reefs are living things.

(B) Coral reefs can be home to small sharks.

(C) Coral reefs will be around for a long time to come.

(D) People can learn about coral reefs through research.

GO ON →

Name: _____ Date: _____

10 Complete the chart with the main idea of the article and **two** details that support the main idea. Write the correct sentences from the box. Not all sentences will be used.

Main Idea	Supporting Details

Sentences:

Plants grow on coral reefs.

Coral reefs are found in the ocean.

Coral reefs are full of living things.

People enjoy swimming near coral reefs.

Many coral reefs have colorful fish living nearby.

Name: _____ Date: _____

Now answer Number 11. Base your answer on "Life in the Forest" and "The Coral Reef."

11 Both articles discuss how things found in an environment are related to each other. Use details from the articles to explain the relationship between living things and their environments.

_____

_____

_____

_____

_____

_____

_____

_____

_____

_____

_____

_____

_____

Answer Key

Name: _____

Question	Correct Answer	Content Focus	CCSS	Complexity
1A	B	Context Clues: Sentence Clues	L.4.4a	DOK 2
1B	A, B	Context Clues: Sentence Clues/ Text Evidence	L.4.4a/ RI.4.1	DOK 2
2	A	Main Idea and Key Details	RI.4.2	DOK 1
3	see below	Main Idea and Key Details	RI.4.2	DOK 2
4	C	Context Clues: Sentence Clues	L.4.4a	DOK 2
5A	A	Main Idea and Key Details	RI.4.2	DOK 2
5B	D	Main Idea and Key Details/ Text Evidence	RI.4.2/ RI.4.1	DOK 2
6	C	Context Clues: Sentence Clues	L.4.4a	DOK 2
7A	C	Main Idea and Key Details	RI.4.2	DOK 1
7B	B	Main Idea and Key Details/ Text Evidence	RI.4.2/ RI.4.1	DOK 1
8A	C	Context Clues: Sentence Clues	L.4.4a	DOK 2
8B	D	Context Clues: Sentence Clues/ Text Evidence	L.4.4a/ RI.4.1	DOK 2
9	D	Main Idea and Key Details	RI.4.2	DOK 1
10	see below	Main Idea and Key Details	RI.4.2	DOK 2
11	see below	Writing About Text	W.4.9b	DOK 4

Comprehension 2, 3, 5A, 5B, 7A, 7B, 9, 10	/12	%
Vocabulary 1A, 1B, 4, 6, 8A, 8B	/8	%
Total Weekly Assessment Score	/20	%

3 Students should circle the following paragraph:
- The canopy is the highest layer in the forest and is home to the tallest trees. This area gets the most sunlight. It produces the most food. Birds, insects, and mammals that live here eat leaves and fruits that grow on trees.

8 Students should complete the chart as follows:
- Main Idea: Coral reefs are full of living things.
- Supporting Details: Plants grow on coral reefs. Many coral reefs have colorful fish living nearby.

11 To receive full credit for the response, the following information should be included: Living things have a dependent relationship with their environments. In a forest, animals use trees for shelter and food. Meanwhile, bacteria break down waste materials that then go back into the soil. This in turn provides food for the trees. In a coral reef, the reef provides needs such as shelter and food for fish.

Read the article "Swimming to Survive" before answering Numbers 1 through 5.

Swimming to Survive

If you could walk four miles in one hour, how many hours would it take for you to walk 100 miles? You would have to walk for 25 hours! Did you know that when humpback whales migrate they travel 100 miles at this speed without stopping? Some humpback whales migrate from Central America to Antarctica without stopping. That's more than 5,000 miles! Other humpbacks travel from Hawaii to Alaska, a distance of about 3,000 miles.

Whales live in all of Earth's oceans. Each group has its own migration route. The map below shows routes taken by humpbacks in the North Pacific Ocean.

From North to South

Why do humpbacks and other whales make this incredible journey? Whales spend the cold winter months in warm water, where they have babies called calves. As summer approaches, the whales head to colder waters. There, they feast on millions of tiny fish and shrimp called krill. Krill thrive in the icy waters near the Arctic and Antarctic.

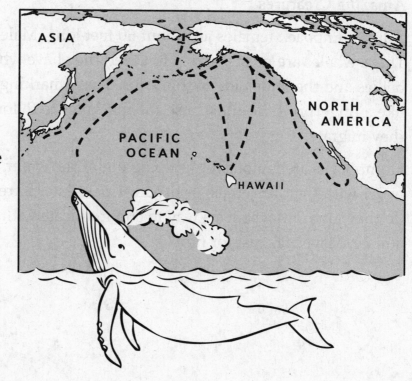

If the whales remained in the warmer water year-round they would not have enough to eat. One whale needs as much as 3,000 pounds of food a day. In fact, the whales fatten up on krill before leaving the cold waters. They eat very little on their long migration to warm waters. Instead, they live off the fat stored in their bodies.

How do whales know their migration routes? Scientists are unsure how the whales know which direction to head. Perhaps they learn the routes by traveling with older whales.

Protecting the Whales

Years ago, whales were killed for their blubber, or fat, and their meat. Most of the hunters were unaware of their effect on the whale population. In the North Pacific, only about 1,400 humpbacks remained in 1966. To preserve humpbacks, the whales were listed as an endangered species. It is illegal to kill a humpback whale. This has caused the number of whales to increase greatly. Today, about 21,000 humpbacks live in the North Pacific. As a precaution, humpbacks are still listed as endangered.

Amazing Creatures

Adult humpback females are about 60 feet long. Males are a little smaller. These whales are mostly gray. However, they have white markings on their bellies and the underside of their fins. These markings are one-of-a-kind, like a fingerprint. Scientists use the markings to follow specific whales as they migrate.

Humpbacks are famous for jumping out of the water. They also slap the water with their fins, tails, or heads. This creates a tremendous splash! Why do they jump? Maybe it's a way to communicate with other whales or attract a mate. Maybe it's just for fun!

GO ON →

Now answer Numbers 1 through 5. Base your answers on "Swimming to Survive."

1 Which details belong in a summary of the article? Underline **three** details in the list below.

Summary of "Swimming to Survive"

There are millions of krill in the ocean.

Humpbacks need a lot of food to survive.

People are working to protect humpbacks.

Only 1,400 humpbacks were alive in 1966.

Humpbacks migrate for important reasons.

Humpbacks can slap the water with their heads.

---

2 Read the sentence from the article.

Scientists are <u>unsure</u> how the whales know which direction to head.

If *sure* means "certain," what does <u>unsure</u> mean?

(A) not certain

(B) certain again

(C) always certain

(D) wanting to be certain

GO ON →

3 Choose **two** sentences that tell why whales migrate.

(A) They want to find food.

(B) They want to attract a mate.

(C) They need to escape hunters.

(D) They are going to have babies.

(E) They are visiting other whales.

(F) They need to get rid of their fat.

4 Read the sentence from the article.

As a precaution, humpbacks are still listed as endangered.

If *caution* means "a warning about a problem," what does precaution mean?

(A) a warning about a problem again

(B) in favor of warning about a problem

(C) a warning before a problem happens

(D) being against warning about problems

GO ON →

5 This question has two parts. First, answer part A. Then, answer part B.

Part A: Which sentence **best** describes the main idea of the article?

(A) Whales must swim to survive.

(B) Migration helps whales survive.

(C) We must save humpback whales.

(D) Whales travel thousands of miles.

Part B: Which sentence from the article **best** supports your answer in part A?

(A) "Other humpbacks travel from Hawaii to Alaska, a distance of about 3,000 miles."

(B) "As summer approaches, the whales head to colder waters."

(C) "If the whales remained in the warmer water year-round they would not have enough to eat."

(D) "They eat very little on their long migration to warm waters."

GO ON →

Read the article "Fireworms" before answering Numbers 6 through 10.

Fireworms

The fireworm lives in the tropical waters of the Atlantic and Pacific oceans. Most fireworms are three to four inches long, but some have grown as long as fourteen inches. These creatures are flat. They have tufts of white bristles along their sides. The tufts look like paint brushes, but they break easily if touched.

The size and shape of the fireworm are not the only things that set it apart. Another irregular fireworm trait is that it gives off light. Females use this light to attract males. The lighted female fireworms spin on the surface of the water. When the males see the light from the females, they flash their own lights. Then the males dart to the surface and bob up and down in the water. Scientists are able to predict exactly when this entire process will take place. On dark summer nights, the water glows green as the fireworms engage in this eerie dance.

Scientists believe that fireworms may also use the light to defend themselves. The light may be used to distract or mislead their predators.

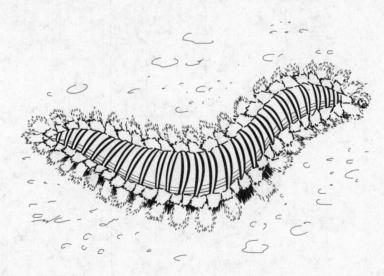

GO ON →

Fireworms also defend themselves with their bristles. This behavior keeps other creatures from getting too close. If a person touches a fireworm, the bristles will break off and stick into the person's skin. This releases poison into the wound that makes the area sore. It also causes an uncomfortable burning sensation on the skin. It is this reaction that gives the fireworm its name.

There are several ways to treat a wound from a fireworm. Covering the wound with tape helps remove the bristles. Washing the area with rubbing alcohol stops the burning sensation.

Fireworms would rather hide than fight. They are nonaggressive creatures. They often hide in areas covered with seagrass so they can get lost in the undergrowth. Unless you know where to look, you may never see a fireworm.

Once in a while, fireworms are found on objects that float onto shore. Some fireworms have even ended up in tanks at stores that sell tropical fish. Most fireworms live in coral reefs, but they would not live more than about 500 feet deep. Other fireworms live in the sea under stones. Some even live on mud bottoms. They eat shrimp, clams, and mussels, but their favorite food is coral.

Fireworms eat both soft and hard coral. When looking at a coral reef, it is easy to tell where fireworms have been eating. They eat coral down to its skeleton. Wherever fireworms feed, the coral is left with only the white tips of its bones showing.

GO ON →

Now answer Numbers 6 through 10. Base your answers on "Fireworms."

6 What happens when male fireworms see the light of female fireworms? Pick **two** choices.

(A) They glow green.

(B) They do an eerie dance.

(C) They flash their own light.

(D) They hurry toward the light.

(E) They stop flashing their own light.

(F) They move away from the flashing.

7 Read the sentence from "Fireworms."

The light may be used to distract or <u>mislead</u> their predators.

If *lead* means "to guide," what does <u>mislead</u> mean?

(A) lead again

(B) lead quickly

(C) lead in the wrong direction

(D) lead the wrong way on purpose

GO ON →

8 Underline the sentence that states the main idea of the paragraph below.

Fireworms also defend themselves with their bristles. This behavior keeps other creatures from getting too close. If a person touches a fireworm, the bristles will break off and stick into the person's skin. This releases poison into the wound that makes the area sore. It also causes an uncomfortable burning sensation on the skin. It is this reaction that gives the fireworm its name.

9 Read the sentence from the article.

They are <u>nonaggressive</u> creatures.

If *aggressive* means "ready to fight," what does <u>nonaggressive</u> mean?

Ⓐ not ready to fight

Ⓑ getting attacked

Ⓒ fighting again

Ⓓ feeling angry

GO ON →

Name: _____ Date: _____

10 This question has two parts. First, answer part A. Then, answer part B.

Part A: Which sentence **best** describes the main idea of the article?

Ⓐ Fireworms light up.

Ⓑ Fireworms eat coral.

Ⓒ Fireworms like to dance at night.

Ⓓ Fireworms are interesting creatures.

Part B: Which sentence from the article **best** supports your answer in part A?

Ⓐ "The size and shape of the fireworm are not the only things that set it apart."

Ⓑ "There are several ways to treat a wound from a fireworm."

Ⓒ "Unless you know where to look, you may never see a fireworm."

Ⓓ "Some fireworms have even ended up in tanks at stores that sell tropical fish."

Name: _____ Date: _____

Now answer Number 11. Base your answer on "Swimming to Survive" and "Fireworms."

11 Fireworms and humpback whales have adapted to survive in very different ways. Tell how these two animals survive and are protected. Support your answer with details from the articles.

_____

_____

_____

_____

_____

_____

_____

_____

_____

_____

_____

_____

_____

_____

_____

Answer Key

Name: _____

Question	Correct Answer	Content Focus	CCSS	Complexity
1	see below	Summarize	RI.4.2	DOK 2
2	A	Prefixes	L.4.4b	DOK 2
3	A, D	Main Idea and Key Details	RI.4.2	DOK 1
4	C	Prefixes	L.4.4b	DOK 2
5A	B	Main Idea and Key Details	RI.4.2	DOK 2
5B	C	Main Idea and Key Details/ Text Evidence	RI.4.2/ RI.4.1	DOK 2
6	C, D	Main Idea and Key Details	RI.4.2	DOK 1
7	C	Prefixes	L.4.4b	DOK 2
8	see below	Main Idea and Key Details	RI.4.2	DOK 1
9	A	Prefixes	L.4.4b	DOK 2
10A	D	Main Idea and Key Details	RI.4.2	DOK 2
10B	A	Main Idea and Key Details/ Text Evidence	RI.4.2/ RI.4.1	DOK 2
11	see below	Writing About Text	W.4.9b	DOK 4

Comprehension 1, 3, 5A, 5B, 6, 8, 10A, 10B	/12	%
Vocabulary 2, 4, 7, 9	/8	%
Total Weekly Assessment Score	/20	%

1 Students should underline the following details to include in a summary:
- Humpbacks need a lot of food to survive.
- People are working to protect humpbacks.
- Humpbacks migrate for important reasons.

8 Students should underline the following sentence:
- Fireworms also defend themselves with their bristles.

11 To receive full credit for the response, the following information should be included: Fireworms eat coral and small sea creatures that live in coral. They have natural defenses like tufts that inject poison if they are touched; they also glow to scare and confuse predators. Humpback whales migrate to have babies and to eat. They eat tons of food at a time and store it in their blubber. They don't protect themselves; people create laws to protect them.

Read the passage "Trouble with Poetry" before answering Numbers 1 through 5.

Trouble with Poetry

In shock, I listened as Mrs. True described our newest writing assignment. Did she actually think I could write a poem? My mind was spinning as fast as a top, and I shut my eyes and focused on listening to the rest of her directions.

"Anything can inspire a poem," Mrs. True was saying, "so you could write about things you see every day. Poets sometimes write about experiences they have had or emotions they have felt."

I glanced over at my friend Nate and tried not to groan. What could I write about? My life wasn't interesting or inspiring. No one wanted to read a poem about my messy room or about my little sister the pest, and there was no way I was writing about my feelings! Then, I realized Mrs. True was still talking.

"Take out your journals," she instructed. "We will be spending the next twenty minutes brainstorming ideas and writing rough drafts of our poems. Remember to include some of the poetry elements that we've talked about this week. Your poem must rhyme and have stanzas, and you should also use a few similes or metaphors."

"Great," I muttered under my breath. With a huge sigh, I dug my journal out of my desk, slapped it down, and opened it to the next clean page.

Mrs. True looked at me when she heard the slap and walked over to my backpack. "Is everything all right, Elan?" she asked.

GO ON →

"I just don't think I'm much of a poet, Mrs. True," I replied. "I don't know where to begin."

"Try thinking of things that make you happy," said Mrs. True. "It might be easier to write about something that makes you smile."

As she walked away, I thought of the things in my life that made me the happiest. Like a speeding train, Trouble crashed into my thoughts. You see, Trouble is the name of my dog. She got her name because she is always getting into trouble. I had millions of stories about her!

Suddenly, my hand was a jet flying across my paper. Trouble was great inspiration, and I quickly filled my page with great ideas for my poem. I turned to a clean page and started a rough draft of my poem.

> Trouble is the name of my dog,
> She hops and jumps like a frog.
> She tears up our shoes
> On sofas she chews.
> I wish she'd sit still like a log.
>
> She jumped through the back door screen.
> She licked my soup bowl clean.
> She barks at all cars.
> I'd send her to Mars
> For a break from this wild machine!
>
> But Trouble is loyal and true,
> She sticks to my side just like glue.
> I love every part
> Her big eyes and big heart,
> She cheers me when I am so blue.

I pushed back from my desk and grinned at my paper. Maybe writing poetry wouldn't be so bad after all. I had a great subject, who was sure to give me plenty of ideas for a long time to come.

GO ON →

Now answer Numbers 1 through 5. Base your answers on "Trouble with Poetry."

1 This question has two parts. First, answer part A. Then, answer part B.

Part A: Who is the narrator of the passage?

(A) Mrs. True

(B) Trouble

(C) Nate

(D) Elan

Part B: What does the point of view in the passage help the reader better understand?

(A) Elan's thoughts

(B) Nate's thoughts

(C) Trouble's thoughts

(D) Mrs. True's thoughts

2 Read the sentence from the passage.

My mind was spinning <u>as fast as a top</u>, and I shut my eyes and focused on listening to the rest of her directions.

Why does the author compare Elan's mind to a top?

(A) to show that Elan is rolling his head in circles

(B) to show that Elan is thinking of his new toy top

(C) to show that Elan has many thoughts going through his mind

(D) to show that Elan feels very dizzy while listening to the directions

GO ON →

3 Pick **three** sentences from the passage that show what Elan thinks about poetry.

(A) "I glanced over at my friend Nate and tried not to groan."

(B) "Then, I realized Mrs. True was still talking."

(C) "'Take out your journals,' she instructed."

(D) "'Great,' I muttered under my breath."

(E) "'I don't know where to begin.'"

(F) "You see, Trouble is the name of my dog."

4 Why does Elan love Trouble?

(A) Trouble jumps through screens.

(B) Trouble causes problems.

(C) Trouble chews on sofas.

(D) Trouble is a loyal dog.

GO ON →

5 Draw a line to match the underlined simile in each sentence on the left with the definition of the simile on the right.

Like a speeding train, Trouble crashed into my thoughts.	in a motionless way
She hops and jumps like a frog.	in a powerful way
I wish she'd sit still like a log.	in a busy way

GO ON →

Read the passage "A Visit to the Zoo" before answering Numbers 6 through 10.

A Visit to the Zoo

It was a beautiful spring day, and Raj and his sister, Adara, were visiting the zoo with their parents. The family loved the zoo, and they tried to come every few weeks for a visit.

Near every animal's home, there was a sign that told what kind of food it ate and where it lived in the wild. Today, the family noticed that the signs also had short poems about each animal."

Raj and Adara were excited by the new signs and couldn't wait to read all the poems. Adara wanted to know what was written about her favorite animals, the prairie dogs. She led her family to the prairie dog exhibit and read:

> Prairie dogs are funny clowns
> Popping up and popping down.
> As their heads rise through the ground
> They stare at you without a sound.

"That poem really explains how prairie dogs act," Adara said. She wondered what the other poems would say as they all approached the duck pond. Raj read the sign there.

GO ON →

The ducks are marching robots
Following their leader.
Two run, while one trots
Going to the feeder.

"That's exactly how they walk," laughed Raj.

Next, Adara and Raj led their parents to the reptile house. Inside, they visited the python. "It's your turn to read," Raj said to Adara. She read the sign.

Slithering, sliding all day long,
The python sings his snaky song.
He tells of adventures and glorious meals
While gliding silently toward your heels.

"Yikes!" Adara shuddered. "I have shivers from reading that one. I'm glad it can't get out of its habitat!"

Next, they walked to the monkey cages, where the monkeys screeched like sirens. Everyone plugged their ears as Raj shouted, "Let's skip the monkeys today! They're too loud!"

As they wandered past some peacocks, they noticed that one had his tail feathers fully opened. "Peacocks are so graceful," Adara said to Raj. "The markings on their feathers look like jeweled eyes keeping watch over the birds."

"You sound like a poet!" Raj replied. "Maybe we should think of our own poems for some of the animals."

At lunchtime the family talked about the animals they had seen. They tried composing a few poems of their own. Then, Raj and Adara played tag and ran until their legs turned to rubber.

Finally, it was time to go home. Exhausted, Raj and Adara walked to the car with smiles on their faces. It had been a wonderful day.

GO ON →

Name: _____ Date: _____

Now answer Numbers 6 through 10. Base your answers on "A Visit to the Zoo."

6 This question has two parts. First, answer part A. Then, answer part B.

Part A: Who is telling the story?

(A) an outside narrator

(B) Raj's father

(C) Adara

(D) Raj

Part B: Which sentence **best** shows who is telling the story?

(A) "It was a beautiful spring day, and Raj and his sister, Adara, were visiting the zoo with their parents."

(B) "Near every animal's home, there was a sign that told what kind of food it ate and where it lived in the wild."

(C) "'I have shivers from reading that one.'"

(D) "'Maybe we should think of our own poems for some of the animals.'"

GO ON →

7 Read the lines from a poem in the passage.

Prairie dogs <u>are funny clowns</u>
Popping up and popping down.

Why does the author compare prairie dogs to clowns?

(A) to show that prairie dogs are not very funny

(B) to show that prairie dogs are dressed like clowns

(C) to show that prairie dogs have cute little ears and noses

(D) to show that prairie dogs do things to make people laugh

8 Arrange the events from the passage in the correct sequence. Write the sentences in the correct order in the chart below.

1	
2	
3	
4	

Events:

Raj's family sees ducks.

Raj's family sees peacocks.

Raj's family sees prairie dogs.

Raj's family sees the python.

GO ON →

9 With which statements would the speaker of the python poem **most likely** agree? Pick **two** choices.

(A) Pythons are hard to find.

(B) Pythons are very sneaky.

(C) Pythons cannot be trusted.

(D) Pythons have many talents.

(E) Pythons are curious animals.

(F) Pythons make excellent pets.

10 Read the sentence from the passage.

Inside, the monkeys screeched like sirens.

What does the simile "screeched like sirens" explain about the monkeys?

(A) They were tired.

(B) They were being fed.

(C) They were very noisy.

(D) They were very dangerous.

Name: _____ Date: _____

**Now answer Number 11. Base your answer on "Trouble with Poetry"
and "A Visit to the Zoo."**

11 Explain how the poems in "Trouble with Poetry" and "A Visit to the
Zoo" help the reader understand the points of view of the characters
in the stories. Support your answer with details from the passages.

_____

_____

_____

_____

_____

_____

_____

_____

_____

_____

_____

_____

Answer Key

Name: _____

Question	Correct Answer	Content Focus	CCSS	Complexity
1A	D	Point of View	RL.4.6	DOK 2
1B	A	Point of View	RL.4.6	DOK 3
2	C	Figurative Language: Similes and Metaphors	L.4.5a	DOK 2
3	A, D, E	Point of View	RL.4.6	DOK 3
4	D	Point of View	RL.4.6	DOK 2
5	see below	Figurative Language: Similes and Metaphors	L.4.5a	DOK 2
6A	A	Point of View	RL.4.6	DOK 2
6B	A	Point of View/Text Evidence	RL.4.6/ RL.4.1	DOK 2
7	D	Figurative Language: Similes and Metaphors	L.4.5a	DOK 2
8	see below	Character, Setting, Plot: Sequence	RL.4.3	DOK 1
9	B, C	Point of View	RL.4.6	DOK 3
10	C	Figurative Language: Similes and Metaphors	L.4.5a	DOK 2
11	see below	Writing About Text	W.4.9a	DOK 4

Comprehension 1A, 1B, 3, 4, 6A, 6B, 8, 9	/12	%
Vocabulary 2, 5, 7, 10	/8	%
Total Weekly Assessment Score	/20	%

5 Students should match the similes with their definitions as follows:

- Like a speeding train—in a powerful way
- like a frog—in a busy way
- like a log—in a motionless way

8 Students should write the story events in the following sequence:

- 1 - Raj's family sees prairie dogs.
- 2 - Raj's family sees ducks.
- 3 - Raj's family sees the python.
- 4 - Raj's family sees peacocks.

11 To receive full credit for the response, the following information should be included:
The poems in both stories help to show how the characters feel about different animals. In "Trouble with Poetry," the poem about Elan's dog, Trouble, shows that Elan loves and feels happy around his dog. In "A Visit to the Zoo," the poems that Raj and Adara read reflect how they feel when they see the animals. The poems help the reader see how the characters react to the different zoo animals.

Read the passage "Welcome to a New School" before answering Numbers 1 through 5.

Welcome to a New School

I looked around at the other kids in the room. We were all members of the new student welcoming committee. Each member of the group was once a new kid at this school, and we knew what the first few days in a strange place were like. Then the advisor of the committee, Mrs. Campos, walked in.

I listened as Mrs. Campos said, "I am so excited to see all of you and to hear your ideas. Welcoming new students to our school is an important responsibility. Who wants to share the first idea?"

A few kids raised their hands, and Mrs. Campos called on Leah. "I think we should assign the new students a buddy," Leah offered, "The buddy could be the new kid's guide."

Then Jordan added, "The buddy could sit with the new kid at lunch because it's scary to eat alone."

I thought back to my first day at this school and remembered how nervous I felt. I had entered the lunchroom cautiously because I was so afraid that I would have to sit by myself.

GO ON →

I told Jordan that his idea was really good. Then I said, "And I have another idea. We could give new kids a tour of the building. It would have to be before school because the halls are too busy during the day."

I beamed with pleasure when Mrs. Campos said, "I really like that idea, Suwon. We would have to ask the principal for permission to have students in the building before school starts, but I am confident that he will like the idea. I know he wants new students to feel comfortable."

Then Mrs. Campos asked us for other ideas. Hunter shared his idea. "When I was a new student, I saw a lot of kids wearing shirts with the school's name on them. They wore them on school spirit day. I didn't have a shirt like that, and I felt really left out. I think we should give school shirts to new students."

I liked Hunter's idea but wondered how we would get the money to pay for these shirts. Mrs. Campos said, "I will talk to the school's parent group. They might be able to donate shirts for new students."

After hearing these fabulous ideas, I was really glad that I had volunteered to join this group. We had some wonderful plans to help new students feel welcome. I knew we had it in the bag! Now all we had to decide was where to start!

GO ON →

Now answer Numbers 1 through 5. Base your answers on "Welcome to a New School."

1 Read the paragraph from the passage.

I looked around at the other kids in the room. We were all members of the new student welcoming <u>committee</u>. Each member of the group was once a new kid at this school, and we knew what the first few days in a strange place were like. Then the advisor of the committee, Mrs. Campos, walked in.

What does the word <u>committee</u> mean in the paragraph?

(A) group

(B) member

(C) student

(D) teacher

2 This question has two parts. First, answer part A. Then, answer part B.

Part A: What does the point of view in the passage help to show about Suwon?

(A) the reasons why she did not like her new school

(B) the reasons why she came to a new school

(C) the reasons why she was nervous at lunch

(D) the reasons why she loves her old school

Part B: Which sentence from the passage **best** supports your answer in part A?

(A) "Then Jordan added, 'The buddy could sit with the new kid at lunch because it's scary to eat alone.'"

(B) "I had entered the lunchroom cautiously because I was so afraid that I would have to sit by myself."

(C) "'It would have to be before school because the halls are too busy during the day.'"

(D) "'When I was a new student, I saw a lot of kids wearing shirts with the school's name on them.'"

GO ON →

3 This question has two parts. First, answer part A. Then, answer part B.

Part A: Read the paragraph from the passage.

I beamed with pleasure when Mrs. Campos said, "I really like that idea, Suwon. We would have to ask the principal for permission to have students in the building before school starts, but I am <u>confident</u> that he will like the idea. I know he wants new students to feel comfortable."

What does the word <u>confident</u> mean in the paragraph?

- (A) comfortable
- (B) confined
- (C) satisfied
- (D) sure

Part B: Which phrase from the paragraph **best** supports your answer in part A?

- (A) "beamed with pleasure"
- (B) "ask the principal"
- (C) "before school starts"
- (D) "I know he wants"

4 Underline the sentence that **best** shows what Suwon thinks of Hunter's idea.

Then Mrs. Campos asked us for other ideas. Hunter shared his idea. "When I was a new student, I saw a lot of kids wearing shirts with the school's name on them. They wore them on school spirit day. I didn't have a shirt like that, and I felt really left out. I think we should give school shirts to new students."

I liked Hunter's idea but wondered how we would get the money to pay for these shirts. Mrs. Campos said, "I will talk to the school's parent group. They might be able to donate shirts for new students."

5 Pick **two** things the reader would know if the passage were written from Mrs. Campos's point of view.

Ⓐ how Jordan feels about Mrs. Campos

Ⓑ which idea Mrs. Campos likes the best

Ⓒ if Leah wants to be a new student buddy

Ⓓ if the parent group would pay for new shirts

Ⓔ how Suwon and Mrs. Campos know each other

Ⓕ what Mrs. Campos thinks about during the meeting

GO ON →

Read the passage "Sadie Says Hello" before answering Numbers 6 through 10.

Sadie Says Hello

Howard had been counting the days until today, the day of the big pet festival at his school. His pet snake, Sadie, was going to be in the festival, and he gently placed Sadie in a cardboard box for the occasion. He would use it to transport Sadie to the festival because it was just the right size and would accommodate her well. He could barely contain his excitement as he placed the box next to the front door. After checking to make sure that Sadie was comfortable, Howard waited for his mother to finish getting ready.

As Howard and his mother were just about to leave, the doorbell rang. Howard wondered why their neighbor Mrs. Brent was visiting now. He hoped she would not stay and talk to his mom for long.

Mrs. Brent was always nervous, and being around her made Howard nervous, too. Howard decided that this was an ideal opportunity to get a glass of juice, so he headed for the kitchen, leaving his mother and Mrs. Brent talking by the door.

When Howard returned from the kitchen, he peeked into Sadie's box. He could not believe it, but the box was empty! Then he saw a slight movement out of the corner of his eye. Sadie had slithered out of her box and was headed straight toward Mrs. Brent!

She had not seen Sadie yet, so maybe Howard could do something before it was too late. He rushed forward but not soon enough. Mrs. Brent felt something on her foot and looked down. "Oh, my goodness, a snake!" she screamed.

"Don't worry, Mrs. Brent. She's harmless," Howard said calmly. "Just keep still and she'll go away. She won't hurt you." Then he quickly scooped Sadie up and put her back in her box.

GO ON →

"No snake is harmless!" cried Mrs. Brent. "Did it bite me? Am I injured? Do I need to be taken to the hospital? Should we call an ambulance? Oh, I think I may faint!"

Howard knew that Sadie would not hurt Mrs. Brent, but by the look on her face, he saw that her fear was genuine and she really thought Sadie was dangerous.

"Please don't worry—everything is all right," Howard's mother assured her. "Howard has everything under control. Now Howard, please apologize to Mrs. Brent and tell her how sorry you are that this happened."

Howard was not quite sure why he should apologize, but one look at his mother told him he'd better do it. "I am very sorry, Mrs. Brent," he said. "I think Sadie just wanted to say hello."

"She wanted to say hello? How in the world does a snake say hello?" Mrs. Brent asked as she stepped closer to the door.

By curling around you, Howard thought to himself, but he decided it would be better if he did not say that to Mrs. Brent.

GO ON →

Now answer Numbers 6 through 10. Base your answers on
"Sadie Says Hello."

6 This question has two parts. First, answer part A. Then, answer part B.

Part A: Who is the narrator of the passage?

(A) Howard

(B) Mrs. Brent

(C) Howard's mother

(D) an outside observer

Part B: Which sentence from the passage **best** shows who the narrator is?

(A) "His pet snake, Sadie, was going to be in the festival, and he gently placed Sadie in a cardboard box for the occasion."

(B) "Howard decided that this was an ideal opportunity to get a glass of juice, so he headed for the kitchen, leaving his mother and Mrs. Brent talking by the door."

(C) "'Oh, my goodness, a snake!' she screamed."

(D) "'I think Sadie just wanted to say hello.'"

7 Read the paragraph from the passage.

When Howard returned from the kitchen, he peeked into Sadie's box. He could not believe it, but the box was empty! Then he saw a slight movement out of the corner of his eye. Sadie had slithered out of her box and was headed straight toward Mrs. Brent!

What does the word slithered mean, based on the paragraph clues?

(A) flew

(B) jumped

(C) slid

(D) stopped

GO ON →

8 Draw a line to match each problem on the left with its solution on the right.

Problem	Solution

Howard needs to get Sadie to the pet festival at his school.

Howard explains that Sadie is harmless.

Sadie gets out of the box.

Howard puts Sadie in a cardboard box.

Mrs. Brent gets upset when she sees Sadie.

Howard picks up Sadie.

9 How **most likely** would the passage be different if it were written from the mother's point of view? Pick **two** choices.

Ⓐ It would show that she does not like snakes.

Ⓑ It would show that she wants Mrs. Brent to feel better.

Ⓒ It would show that she feels the same way as Mrs. Brent.

Ⓓ It would show that the thinks Howard let Sadie go on purpose.

Ⓔ It would show that she does not want to argue with Mrs. Brent.

Ⓕ It would show that she likes Sadie even more than Howard does.

GO ON →

10 This question has two parts. First, answer part A. Then, answer part B.

Part A: Read the paragraph from the passage.

"Please don't worry—everything is all right," Howard's mother assured her. "Howard has everything under control. Now Howard, please apologize to Mrs. Brent and tell her how sorry you are that this happened."

Based on the paragraph clues, what does the word apologize mean?

Ⓐ give an excuse

Ⓑ repeat a question

Ⓒ ask for forgiveness

Ⓓ explain your reasons

Part B: Which phrase in the paragraph **best** explains the meaning of apologize?

Ⓐ "don't worry"

Ⓑ "everything under control"

Ⓒ "how sorry you are"

Ⓓ "this happened"

Name: _____ Date: _____

Now answer Number 11. Base your answer on "Welcome to a New School" and "Sadie Says Hello."

11 "Welcome to a New School" and "Sadie Says Hello" are written from different points of view. Explain how each point of view shows the characters thoughts and feelings. Support your answer with details from both texts.

_____

_____

_____

_____

_____

_____

_____

_____

_____

_____

_____

_____

Question	Correct Answer	Content Focus	CCSS	Complexity
1	A	Context Clues: Paragraph Clues	L.4.4a	DOK 2
2A	C	Point of View	RL.4.6	DOK 3
2B	B	Point of View/Text Evidence	RL.4.6/ RL.4.1	DOK 3
3A	D	Context Clues: Paragraph Clues	L.4.4a	DOK 2
3B	D	Context Clues: Paragraph Clues/ Text Evidence	L.4.4a/ RL.4.1	DOK 2
4	see below	Point of View	RL.4.6	DOK 2
5	B, F	Point of View	RL.4.6	DOK 3
6A	D	Point of View	RL.4.6	DOK 3
6B	B	Point of View/Text Evidence	RL.4.6/ RL.4.1	DOK 3
7	C	Context Clues: Paragraph Clues	L.4.4a	DOK 2
8	see below	Character, Setting, Plot: Problem and Solution	RL.4.3	DOK 2
9	B, E	Point of View	RL.4.6	DOK 3
10A	C	Context Clues: Paragraph Clues	L.4.4a	DOK 2
10B	C	Context Clues: Paragraph Clues/ Text Evidence	L.4.4a/ RL.4.1	DOK 2
11	see below	Writing About Text	W.4.9a	DOK 4

Comprehension 2A, 2B, 4, 5, 6A, 6B, 8, 9	/12	%
Vocabulary 1, 3A, 3B, 7, 10A, 10B	/8	%
Total Weekly Assessment Score	/20	%

4 Students should underline the following sentence:
- I liked Hunter's idea but wondered how we would get the money to pay for these shirts.

8 Students should draw lines to make the following matches of problems to solutions:
- Howard needs to get Sadie to the pet festival at his school.—Howard puts Sadie in a cardboard box.
- Sadie gets out of the box.—Howard picks up Sadie.
- Mrs. Brent gets upset when she sees Sadie.—Howard explains that Sadie is harmless.

11 To receive full credit for the response, the following information should be included: "Welcome to a New School" has a first-person point of view; the characters directly tell the reader what they think and feel through the use of "I." "Sadie Says Hello" has a third-person point of view; the narrator tells the reader what the characters think and feel.

Read the passage "Bingo" before answering Numbers 1 through 5.

Bingo

"Wow, they're using dogs to help find people after the earthquake," I called while reading the newspaper. I wished I could go and help, but what were the chances of my parents letting me go to South America?

I slumped on the couch in discouragement. It wasn't fair because I'd already spent many hours picking up trash in parks and collecting food for hungry families. Now I wanted to do something grand, something spectacular enough to be on the news.

"Jacob," Mom called, "it's time to go!" Great! Instead of becoming famous, I was going with Mom to visit Great Aunt Beth at the nursing home.

Aunt Beth had pneumonia, an illness that affects your lungs, a few weeks ago, but she was feeling better now and breathing easily. Thankfully, she would be going home soon. Now, I love my aunt, but I still don't want to spend all Saturday morning at the nursing home.

When we arrived at the nursing home, we found Aunt Beth in the dining hall playing bingo. "Mom," I whispered, "I don't want to play."

"Jacob!" Aunt Beth cried happily as she waved me over. I sighed and walked over to my aunt as she pulled out a chair for me and gave me one of her bingo cards.

"No cheating, young man!" someone shouted accusingly. A frowning, grumpy man sat on the other side of Aunt Beth. Was he blaming me for not playing fair? The game hadn't even started yet! "Anyway," the man bellowed, "you'll soon be bored to death here since we don't have those fancy gadgets you young ones use all the time."

"Don't mind Dave," Aunt Beth whispered. "He's hard of hearing." Still, I did NOT appreciate what Dave had said! I didn't like his comments, so I was not at all happy, and I wanted to shout back that I do NOT cheat at games. Besides, I don't even have a cell phone!

GO ON →

Wait, I'd show that guy! "Can I have another Bingo card, please?" I asked my aunt. The old man grumbled something about cards costing a quarter, and Aunt Beth fished a dollar out of her pocket to buy more cards. Soon I was playing five Bingo cards. I was determined to beat him—without cheating!

At last the caller said O-62, and I happily yelled, "Bingo!"

Dave turned to the man sitting next to him and yelled, "You know, I kind of like this boy!" My mouth dropped open. Then Dave leaned over to me and said, "So, do you think you could beat me at a more challenging game, like chess?"

"I have never played chess," I mumbled.

"I could teach you," Dave said with a wink.

"Umm, Aunt Beth is going home the day after tomorrow," I told him, "and I won't be coming here anymore."

"You don't think you could learn chess, huh?" Dave asked, raising one eyebrow.

I thought for a second and then said, "I could ride my bike here since it's not that far." Mom smiled at me.

"Okay, then," Dave said, "I'll see you next Saturday, same time, same place!"

As Mom and I left, Dave couldn't stop smiling. Neither could I, even though I wouldn't be on the evening news.

GO ON →

Now answer Numbers 1 through 5. Base your answers on "Bingo."

1 Read the sentence from the passage.

Aunt Beth had <u>pneumonia</u>, an illness that affects your lungs, a few weeks ago, but she was feeling better now and breathing easily.

According to the sentence, what type of illness is <u>pneumonia</u>?

Ⓐ one that is like a cold

Ⓑ one that affects breathing

Ⓒ one that usually causes death

Ⓓ one that is caused by ammonia

2 This question has two parts. First, answer part A. Then, answer part B.

Part A: Which sentence **best** describes the theme of the passage?

Ⓐ It is necessary to learn the rules of any game.

Ⓑ Friends make the world a more interesting place.

Ⓒ Playing games can be important when you are growing up.

Ⓓ There are simple ways to make a difference in the lives of others.

Part B: Which detail **best** supports the theme of the passage?

Ⓐ Jacob wins a game of Bingo.

Ⓑ Dave tells Jacob no cheating.

Ⓒ Dave is happy that Jacob will play chess with him.

Ⓓ Jacob does not want to play a game at the nursing home.

GO ON →

3 This question has two parts. First, answer part A. Then, answer part B.

Part A: Read the paragraph from the passage.

"No cheating, young man!" someone shouted accusingly. A frowning, grumpy man sat on the other side of Aunt Beth. Was he blaming me for not playing fair? The game hadn't even started yet! "Anyway," the man <u>bellowed</u>, "you'll soon be bored to death here since we don't have those fancy gadgets you young ones use all the time."

What does the word <u>bellowed</u> mean?

Ⓐ questioned

Ⓑ pointed out

Ⓒ noticed quietly

Ⓓ spoke in a loud voice

Part B: Which phrase in the paragraph restates the meaning of <u>bellowed</u>?

Ⓐ "shouted accusingly"

Ⓑ "on the other side"

Ⓒ "not playing fair"

Ⓓ "bored to death"

GO ON →

4 Underline the sentence that **best** shows how Jacob's feelings about Dave change.

"You don't think you could learn chess, huh?" Dave asked, raising one eyebrow.

I thought for a second and then said, "I could ride my bike here since it's not that far." Mom smiled at me.

"Okay, then," Dave said, "I'll see you next Saturday, same time, same place!"

As Mom and I left, Dave couldn't stop smiling. Neither could I, even though I wouldn't be on the evening news.

5 If the passage were written from Dave's point of view, what would **most likely** be explained? Pick **two** choices.

(A) how to play chess

(B) how to play Bingo

(C) whether Jacob likes Dave

(D) why Dave wants to play chess

(E) what Dave thinks about Jacob

(F) whether Aunt Beth likes Dave

GO ON →

Read the passage "Tomorrow" before answering Numbers 6 through 10.

Tomorrow

Teresa was wide awake again as she lay in bed listening to the adults talk in the next room. She had been doing the same thing for the last two nights and overheard them talking in low, solemn voices. Teresa did not understand why everyone sounded so serious.

Teresa did not understand everything she heard, either. If the adults had been speaking in English, she would have understood even less. But, like her family, they had come from Mexico to live in the United States. They came in search of possible work prospects, or chances for jobs in America. Many of them spoke very little English, so they spoke to each other in Spanish.

The adults were talking about something called a union. Teresa was not sure what unions were, but she knew that a union could make their lives better. She had heard workers in the fields talk about how a union could help the people in their community.

GO ON →

Tonight, a stranger named Mr. Ramirez was doing most of the talking. Teresa did not know who he was, but she heard someone say he had become a citizen of the United States. Teresa had heard her parents use that word before. When they spoke the word *citizen*, there was always hope and longing in their voices. They had strong feelings about wanting to become Americans.

In the next room, Mr. Ramirez was talking about a possible strike. Teresa knew what a strike was. It meant that everyone would stop working until they got things they wanted. Mr. Ramirez talked about other strikes. He said that some strikes had been successful, while others had not. He explained that strikes often resulted in some very favorable, or positive, effects in the communities where they happened. He also said that some strikes went on for a long time.

Mr. Ramirez answered questions about strikes, and then he started talking about something called a boycott. Teresa didn't know what that was, so she was glad when someone else asked. Mr. Ramirez explained that if there was a boycott, the public would be asked to stop buying melons. Teresa's father and many of their friends had jobs picking melons.

Mr. Ramirez answered a few more questions. Then Teresa could tell that the meeting was coming to an end. Finally, Mr. Ramirez said that tomorrow all the workers were going to vote on whether there would be a strike or not. He told them to think about everything he had said, because tomorrow was going to be a very important day.

After everyone left, Teresa lay in bed, still unable to fall asleep. She was thinking about tomorrow.

GO ON →

Now answer Numbers 6 through 10. Base your answers on "Tomorrow."

6 This question has two parts. First, answer part A. Then, answer part B.

Part A: Who is the narrator of the passage?

- (A) Teresa
- (B) Mr. Ramirez
- (C) Teresa's dad
- (D) an outside observer

Part B: Which statement **best** describes the point of view of the passage?

- (A) A narrator tells how a character feels.
- (B) A character tells how many characters feel.
- (C) A character tells describes her own feelings.
- (D) A narrator describes the feelings of the reader.

7 Which information would be known if the passage were told from the point of view of Teresa's mom? Pick **two** choices.

- (A) what it feels like to be a U.S. citizen
- (B) why Mr. Ramirez is at Teresa's home
- (C) how Teresa will feel if the workers decide to strike
- (D) why Teresa is listening to the adults as she lies in bed
- (E) more details about what the adults plan to do tomorrow
- (F) what Mr. Ramirez did before he came to Teresa's home

GO ON →

8 This question has two parts. First, answer part A. Then, answer part B.

Part A: Read the sentence from the passage.

They came in search of possible work <u>prospects</u>, or chances for jobs in America.

What are <u>prospects</u>?

(A) families

(B) opportunities

(C) results

(D) work

Part B: Which word in the sentence restates the meaning of <u>prospects</u>?

(A) search

(B) possible

(C) chances

(D) jobs

GO ON →

9 Use the list to fill in the chart. Write **two** words that show how Teresa feels in the passage. Then write the number of the text evidence that supports each choice.

How Teresa Feels	Text Evidence

How Teresa Feels:

angry

bored

confused

excited

Text Evidence:

1 – "Teresa did not understand why everyone sounded so serious."

2 – "Teresa had heard her parents use that word before."

3 – "Teresa knew what a strike was."

4 – "After everyone left, Teresa lay in bed, still unable to fall asleep."

10 Read the sentences from the passage.

Mr. Ramirez explained that if there was a boycott, the public would be asked to stop buying melons. Teresa's father and many of their friends had jobs picking melons.

What is a boycott?

(A) a choice to not buy something

(B) a choice to talk to someone

(C) a choice to not eat fruit

(D) a choice to work

Name: _____ Date: _____

Now answer Number 11. Base your answer on "Bingo" and "Tomorrow."

11 "Bingo" and "Tomorrow" are told from different points of view. Identify the point of view of each passage and tell how each type shares information about the characters. Support your answer with details from both texts.

_____

_____

_____

_____

_____

_____

_____

_____

_____

_____

_____

_____

_____

_____

Question	Correct Answer	Content Focus	CCSS	Complexity
1	B	Context Clues: Definitions and Restatements	L.4.4a	DOK 2
2A	D	Theme	RL.4.2	DOK 3
2B	C	Theme/Text Evidence	RL.4.2/ RL.4.1	DOK 3
3A	D	Context Clues: Definitions and Restatements	L.4.4a	DOK 2
3B	A	Context Clues: Definitions and Restatements/Text Evidence	L.4.4a/ RL.4.1	DOK 2
4	see below	Point of View	RL.4.6	DOK 3
5	D, E	Point of View	RL.4.6	DOK 3
6A	D	Point of View	RL.4.6	DOK 2
6B	A	Point of View	RL.4.6	DOK 2
7	B, E	Point of View	RL.4.6	DOK 3
8A	B	Context Clues: Definitions and Restatements	L.4.4a	DOK 2
8B	C	Context Clues: Definitions and Restatements/Text Evidence	L.4.4a/ RL.4.1	DOK 2
9	see below	Point of View	RL.4.6	DOK 3
10	A	Context Clues: Definitions and Restatements	L.4.4a	DOK 2
11	see below	Writing About Text	W.4.9a	DOK 4

Comprehension 2A, 2B, 4, 5, 6A, 6B, 7, 9	/12	%
Vocabulary 1, 3A, 3B, 8A, 8B, 10	/8	%
Total Weekly Assessment Score	/20	%

4 Students should underline the following sentence:
  • Neither could I, even though I wouldn't be on the evening news.

9 Students should write the following text in the chart:
  • How Teresa Feels: confused; Text Evidence: 1 – "Teresa did not understand why everyone sounded so serious."
  • How Teresa Feels: excited; Text Evidence: 4 – "After everyone left, Teresa lay in bed, still unable to fall asleep."

11 To receive full credit for the response, the following information should be included: "Bingo" is told in the first person and is narrated by the main character, Jacob. "Tomorrow" is told in the third person and is narrated by someone outside of the story, not a character. First-person point of view helps the reader learn more about a particular character's feelings and opinions. Third-person point of view generally narrates the action and what all the characters are thinking and feeling, rather than focusing on just one.

Read the article "School Strike" before answering Numbers 1 through 5.

School Strike

John Stokes wanted to learn, but he hated his school. The year was 1951, and John was a senior at Moton High School in Virginia. This school had been built for 180 students. Now more than 450 African American students crowded into the school.

The students and their parents protested the disgraceful conditions. In response, the school board added three temporary classrooms. These classrooms were not meant to last long. The school had no gym, no cafeteria, and no lockers. Just blocks away, white students attended classes in a modern brick building.

On April 23, 1951, John and other student leaders decided to act. They marched from the school to the county courthouse. They wanted to raise the community's consciousness of the dreadful conditions at their high school.

The county, however, argued that it was providing a separate but equal school for African American students. According to a United States Supreme Court ruling, this was all the county was required to do.

Yet the schools were not equal. As part of a campaign, or fight for fairness, students from Moton went on strike. For two weeks, they stayed away from their pitiful school. People from the National Association for the Advancement of Colored People (NAACP) heard about the strike.

GO ON →

The NAACP convinced the students at Moton and their parents to join a lawsuit. Four other groups from across the South were already a part of this lawsuit. Like Moton, these other schools were old and overcrowded, and some had no indoor plumbing or heating.

The lawsuit reached the Supreme Court in 1954. The judges listened to both sides of the dispute. Then the court reversed its earlier ruling. The times, indeed, were changing, and the court decided that separate but equal schools were not fair. All children should be educated together. However, the school board refused to allow African American students to attend white schools. Instead, it closed all of the schools! The school board was angry. It wanted the Supreme Court out of its school system.

Without schools, most white families found ways to educate their children. Private academies for white students were opened. Some African American children were taught in church basements or in homes. Unfortunately, not all African American students had the opportunity to attend these schools. As a result, many African American children did not attend school for more than four years.

In 1964, the courts finally forced the school district to reopen the schools and admit all students. In 2003, the State of Virginia apologized to the students who lost years of education in the battle for civil rights.

In time, John Stokes became a teacher and a principal. Today, he visits schools. He wants to make sure all students understand and appreciate being educated together. Stokes also tells them to never feel powerless. He points out that he and the other student leaders are proof that a small group can make a huge difference. In fact, Stokes tells them, "You can change the world!"

GO ON →

Now answer Numbers 1 through 5. Base your answers on "School Strike."

1 This question has two parts. First, answer part A. Then, answer part B.

Part A: What is the author's point of view of African American schools?

(A) They were very popular.

(B) They were misunderstood.

(C) They were in poor condition.

(D) They were bigger than other schools.

Part B: Which evidence from the text **best** supports the author's point about African American schools?

(A) African American students went on strike.

(B) White students had a modern brick building.

(C) The school board added three temporary classrooms.

(D) Moton High School was crowded with too many students.

2 Which statements show that the students were determined to improve their school? Pick **two** choices.

(A) The students went on strike.

(B) The county closed its schools.

(C) The school had no gym or cafeteria.

(D) The students wanted to receive an education.

(E) The students marched to the county courthouse.

(F) Most students did not attend school for four years.

GO ON →

3 Read the points that the author makes in the passage. Select the text evidence that supports each point and write it in the chart.

Author's Point of View	Text Evidence
Many people were angry about the conditions at the African American schools.	
African American families valued education.	
"the times, indeed, were changing"	

Text Evidence:

The Supreme Court decided that separate is not equal.

Families from four communities across the South joined the lawsuit.

African American children were taught in church basements or in homes.

GO ON →

4 Read the sentences from the article.

The lawsuit reached the Supreme Court in 1954. The judges listened to both sides of the <u>dispute</u>.

Which word has almost the **same** meaning as <u>dispute</u>?

(A) argument

(B) contract

(C) discussion

(D) issue

5 This question has two parts. First, answer part A. Then, answer part B.

Part A: Read the sentence from the article.

Unfortunately, not all African American students had the opportunity to <u>attend</u> these schools.

What does the word <u>attend</u> mean?

(A) go to

(B) leave

(C) compare

(D) talk about

Part B: Which word or phrase means the **opposite** of <u>attend</u>?

(A) join

(B) arrive

(C) not go

(D) not leave

GO ON →

Read the article "Standing Up to Segregation" before answering Numbers 6 through 10.

Standing Up to Segregation

Many believe that Rosa Parks helped initiate the civil rights movement. She did this in a very simple way, by refusing to give up her seat on a bus.

In 1955, segregation was a way of life in the American South. Segregation meant that people of different races were separated from each other. Under segregation, black people could not go to the same hospitals as white people nor eat in the same restaurants. They could not use the same water fountains. Black children could not attend the same schools as white children nor use the same playgrounds.

Segregation also meant that black people had to ride in the back of public buses. In Montgomery, Alabama, even if a black person was seated in the back of the bus, he or she may have had to surrender that seat. If the front seats were taken and a white person wanted to sit down, a black person had to give up his or her seat. Black people followed these rules every day. But one day, Rosa refused. When she did not give her seat to a white man, Rosa was arrested.

Such treatment of black people had been going on for hundreds of years. This unfairness began when their ancestors were enslaved. Some people saw the injustice of segregation while others did not. There were numerous challenges in court, but Southern states did not change the laws.

The bus driver ordered Rosa to give up her seat. The official charge against her was "refusing to obey the orders of a bus driver." Rosa's challenge was not meant to result in a court case. That day on the bus, the other riders probably had little idea that they were watching history being made. They were unsuspecting of what her actions would lead to.

Soon, black leaders in Montgomery organized a boycott of the city bus system. This boycott was led by Dr. Martin Luther King, Jr.

For 382 days, black people refused to ride the Montgomery buses. They found other ways to get to work and school. They walked and rode bicycles. They rode with people who had cars. As the boycott went on, it grew bigger. Finally, the Alabama Supreme Court said that segregated seating on buses violated the Constitution.

Rosa continued her civil rights work for the rest of her life. She became a well-known activist who spoke out for the rights of African Americans. In 1999, she was awarded a Congressional Gold Medal of Honor. That is the highest award given by the government of the United States.

GO ON →

Now answer Numbers 6 through 10. Base your answers on "Standing Up to Segregation."

6 Draw a line to match each underlined word in the sentences on the left with the word that has the **opposite** meaning on the right.

Many believe that Rosa Parks helped initiate the civil rights movement.		fight for

In Montgomery, Alabama, even if a black person was seated in the back of the bus he or she may have had to surrender that seat.		freed

When she did not give her seat to a white man, Rosa was arrested.		finish

7 Which point does the author support by providing details about Rosa's actions on the bus?

(A) Rosa was a quiet person and hard to understand.

(B) Rosa was well-liked by most people she met.

(C) Rosa had no choice but to do what she did.

(D) Rosa was an important person in history.

8 This question has two parts. First, answer part A. Then, answer part B.

Part A: What point does the author make about segregation?

Ⓐ It was illegal and wrong.

Ⓑ It was accepted by everyone.

Ⓒ It hurt both white and black people.

Ⓓ It was just beginning to become popular.

Part B: Which text evidence does the author use to support the point in part A?

Ⓐ facts about segregation in education

Ⓑ the events that led to the arrest of Rosa Parks

Ⓒ details about how badly black people were treated in America

Ⓓ the court ruling that segregation on buses violated the Constitution

9 Which evidence does the author use to **best** show that Rosa was a successful activist? Pick **two** choices.

Ⓐ her arrest on the bus

Ⓑ an explanation for segregation

Ⓒ the official charge that was brought against her

Ⓓ a description of what life was like in the South

Ⓔ details about the Congressional Gold Medal of Honor

Ⓕ the boycott of the city bus system that resulted from her actions

GO ON →

Name: _____ Date: _____

10 Read the sentence from the article.

Some people saw the <u>injustice</u> of segregation while others did not.

Which word has almost the **same** meaning as <u>injustice</u>?

(A) belief

(B) argument

(C) correction

(D) unfairness

Name: _____ Date: _____

Now answer Number 11. Base your answer on "School Strike" and "Standing Up to Segregation."

11 Both articles are secondhand accounts. How would the focus and information in "School Strike" and "Standing Up to Segregation" change if they were written as firsthand accounts? Support your answer with details from both texts.

_____

_____

_____

_____

_____

_____

_____

_____

_____

_____

_____

_____

_____

_____

Answer Key

Name: _____

Question	Correct Answer	Content Focus	CCSS	Complexity
1A	C	Author's Point of View	RI.4.8	DOK 3
1B	D	Author's Point of View/Text Evidence	RI.4.8/ RI.4.1	DOK 3
2	A, E	Main Idea and Key Details	RI.4.2	DOK 2
3	see below	Author's Point of View	RI.4.8	DOK 3
4	A	Context Clues: Synonyms	L.4.5c	DOK 2
5A	A	Context Clues: Antonyms	L.4.5c	DOK 2
5B	C	Context Clues: Antonyms	L.4.5c	DOK 2
6	see below	Context Clues: Antonyms	L.4.5c	DOK 2
7	D	Author's Point of View	RI.4.8	DOK 3
8A	A	Author's Point of View	RI.4.8	DOK 3
8B	D	Author's Point of View/Text Evidence	RI.4.8/ RI.4.1	DOK 3
9	E, F	Author's Point of View	RI.4.8	DOK 3
10	D	Context Clues: Synonyms	L.4.5c	DOK 2
11	see below	Writing About Text	W.4.9b	DOK 4

Comprehension 1A, 1B, 2, 3, 7, 8A, 8B, 9	/12	%
Vocabulary 4, 5A, 5B, 6, 10	/8	%
Total Weekly Assessment Score	/20	%

3 Students should complete the chart as follows:

- Author's Point of View—Many people were angry about the conditions at the African American schools; Text Evidence—Families from four communities across the South joined the lawsuit.
- Author's Point of View—African American families valued education; Text Evidence—African American children were taught in church basements or in homes.
- Author's Point of View—"the times, indeed, were changing"; Text Evidence—The Supreme Court decided that separate is not equal.

6 Students should draw lines to make the following matches:

- initiate—finish
- surrender—fight for
- arrested—freed

11 To receive full credit for the response, the following information should be included: Both articles would likely include more details about the authors' personal experiences and perhaps fewer facts related to the events described. The articles might also include more emotion, such as anger or pride regarding the events.

Read the article "Hybrid or Electric?" before answering Numbers 1 through 5.

Hybrid or Electric?

These days, many people want to "go green." They know that burning gasoline causes pollution. Because of this, they are giving serious consideration to buying an electric or hybrid car.

Here is how electric cars work. Electric cars have large, powerful batteries that send electricity to an electric motor. The motor turns the wheels. When the batteries run low on energy, they must be plugged in to recharge.

There are two types of hybrid cars. Both use gasoline and electricity in order to work. One type relies mostly on electric power. For this type, an electric motor turns the wheels, and a gasoline engine generates electricity. This car must be plugged in to receive a full recharge.

The second type of hybrid car gets its power mostly from a small gasoline engine. An electric motor serves as a backup. Electricity runs the car when it is moving slowly. The electric motor also helps the car build up speed. This car recharges itself while it is running. When the driver brakes, that energy is captured and stored in the battery.

Neither the electric nor the hybrid car is a new invention. In fact, the electric car has been around since the 1880s. Today, the cost of gas continues to rise, and more people are concerned about pollution, as well. That's why more electric and hybrid car models are offered for sale every year.

Advantages of an Electric Car

An electric car costs little to recharge and produces almost no pollution. This type of car is often called a "neighborhood car" because it cannot travel very far without needing to be charged. Older models only run about 40 miles (64 kilometers) on a charge. Newer cars can run for up to 200 miles (322 kilometers) on a single charge.

GO ON →

Electric cars can be recharged using any electrical outlet. Drivers can even run an extension cord from their house to their car! However, charging a car this way can take up to 24 hours. Charging stations have been built in some cities, and recharging is much faster at one of these stations.

Electric cars run very quietly. They also cost less to maintain because they have fewer parts. That makes the car more dependable. However, batteries have to be replaced every 10–15 years. These batteries are very expensive. Some cost as much as $10,000!

Advantages of Hybrid Cars

Hybrid cars can refuel at any gas station. If the batteries cannot be recharged, hybrids can run on gas for as long as necessary. However, their gas-powered engines require upkeep. Also, the batteries wear out in time.

Electric and hybrid cars have one similarity. Right now, both cost more than gas-powered cars. However, that cost will come down as more carmakers enter the market.

When choosing one of these cars, drivers must consider which type will work best for them and their budget. If drivers need a car for short trips, an electric car is perfect. If drivers travel far from home and won't be able to charge a car, a hybrid would be the right choice.

Electric charging stations like this one "refuel" both electric and hybrid cars.

GO ON →

Name: _____ Date: _____

Now answer Numbers 1 through 5. Base your answers on "Hybrid or Electric?"

1 This question has two parts. First, answer part A. Then, answer part B.

Part A: Read the paragraphs from the article.

There are two types of hybrid cars. Both use gasoline and electricity in order to work. One type relies mostly on electric power. For this type, an electric motor turns the wheels, and a gasoline engine generates electricity. This car must be plugged in to receive a full recharge.

The second type of hybrid car gets its power mostly from a small gasoline engine. An electric motor serves as a backup. Electricity runs the car when it is moving slowly. The electric motor also helps the car build up speed. This car recharges itself while it is running. When the driver brakes, that energy is captured and stored in the battery.

How are the paragraphs organized?

Ⓐ by sequencing the development of hybrid cars

Ⓑ by showing the effect hybrid cars have on travel

Ⓒ by discussing the problems gas-powered cars cause

Ⓓ by comparing and contrasting electric and hybrid cars

Part B: Which sentence **best** supports your answer in part A?

Ⓐ "Both use gasoline and electricity in order to work."

Ⓑ "This car must be plugged in to receive a full recharge."

Ⓒ "An electric motor serves as a backup."

Ⓓ "The electric motor also helps the car build up speed."

GO ON →

2 The author explains that electric cars have advantages. Choose **three** details about electric cars that support the author's point.

(A) They are sold every year.

(B) They cost little to recharge.

(C) They are very quiet to drive.

(D) Their batteries do not last long.

(E) Their batteries need to be charged.

(F) They produce almost no pollution.

3 This question has two parts. First, answer part A. Then, answer part B.

Part A: Read the sentence from the article.

That makes the car more dependable.

The suffix -*able* means "capable of." What does it mean if something is dependable?

(A) You can trust it.

(B) You should sell it.

(C) You easily forget it.

(D) You will likely avoid it.

Part B: Which other word includes the suffix -*able*?

(A) cable

(B) fable

(C) payable

(D) table

4 Read the sentence from the article.

Electric and hybrid cars have one <u>similarity</u>.

The suffix *-ity* means "state or quality of being." If two things have a <u>similarity</u>, what are they?

(A) exactly the same

(B) alike in some way

(C) not anything alike

(D) different in some way

5 The author makes the point that drivers must think of their needs when choosing between an electric car and a hybrid car. Underline **two** sentences that the author includes in the article to support this point.

Hybrid cars can refuel at any gas station. If the batteries cannot be recharged, hybrids can run on gas for as long as necessary. However, their gas-powered engines require upkeep. Also, the batteries wear out in time.

Electric and hybrid cars have one similarity. Right now, both cost more than gas-powered cars. However, that cost will come down as more carmakers enter the market.

When choosing one of these cars, drivers must consider which type will work best for them and their budget. If drivers need a car for short trips, an electric car is perfect. If drivers travel far from home and won't be able to charge a car, a hybrid would be the right choice.

GO ON →

Read the article "Nuclear Power: The Key to the Future" before answering Numbers 6 through 10.

Nuclear Power: The Key to the Future

People all over the world use nuclear energy to make electrical power. Most people would agree that nuclear energy is a workable source of electricity.

We have come a long way since nuclear energy was first used in the 1900s. We have learned how to better control nuclear energy. In the future, we may learn even more ways to control it.

Many groups speak in favor of nuclear energy. Actors, athletes, and other famous people have been ambitious in promoting its use. Many of these people have been tireless in their efforts. They have received criticism from people who question its safety.

Some people believe that using nuclear energy could have negative effects on the environment. It is possible, if we are not careful. However, nuclear energy saves natural resources. It gives us more heat and power than other energy sources. Uranium is used to create nuclear energy, which then becomes electricity. Another way to make electricity is by burning coal. One pound of uranium produces more energy than three million pounds of coal. This means fewer resources are used. Also, burning fuels like coal causes air pollution while using uranium to make electricity does not cause pollution.

GO ON →

One problem with nuclear energy still needs to be solved. What do we do with the uranium when it can no longer be used to make electricity? Uranium gives off radiation, or dangerous energy waves for a long time after it is removed from a power plant. It takes thousands of years before this nuclear material is fully decayed. When all the uranium has wasted away, it is safe. Until then, nuclear material must be handled with care. However, it is possible that we will find a safe way to store used nuclear material.

Indeed, we have little choice, because we will not have huge amounts of natural resources such as coal and oil forever. We must find other ways to create energy. People need to share the same vision of how we will get our energy. Nuclear energy is the key to the future!

GO ON →

Name: _____ Date: _____

Now answer Numbers 6 through 10. Base your answers on "Nuclear Power: The Key to the Future."

6 This question has two parts. First, answer part A. Then, answer part B.

Part A: Read the sentence from the article.

Actors, athletes, and other famous people have been <u>ambitious</u> in promoting its use.

The suffix -*ous* means "full of" or "having." What does it mean if someone is <u>ambitious</u>?

(A) That person has respect for other people.

(B) That person has many fears to overcome.

(C) That person is determined to succeed.

(D) That person lies to get his or her way.

Part B: Which other word includes the suffix -*ous*?

(A) hours

(B) houses

(C) joust

(D) joyous

7 Read the sentence from the article.

They have received <u>criticism</u> from people who question its safety.

A *critic* can point out what is wrong. What does it mean to receive <u>criticism</u>?

(A) to be judged

(B) to be praised

(C) to be welcomed

(D) to be encouraged

GO ON →

Weekly Assessment • Unit 3, Week 4

8 This question has two parts. First, answer part A. Then, answer part B.

Part A: Which statement **best** describes a point the author makes about nuclear energy?

(A) Nuclear energy needs to be handled carefully because it can be dangerous.

(B) Nuclear energy was once dangerous, but it is now completely safe to use.

(C) Nuclear energy is only dangerous at certain times of the day.

(D) Nuclear energy never involved any danger at all.

Part B: Which evidence from the text **best** supports your answer in part A?

(A) It is possible to find a safe way to store nuclear material.

(B) Uranium gives off radiation, or dangerous energy waves.

(C) Many groups are in favor of using nuclear energy.

(D) Burning coal is another way to produce energy.

9 Which conclusions can be made about the author's point of view of nuclear energy? Pick **two** choices.

(A) Its widespread use is a very long way off.

(B) It is the answer to our future energy needs.

(C) It still has problems that need to be solved.

(D) It will be most successful in the United States.

(E) It is the best source of energy we will ever have.

(F) It will have mostly negative effects on the environment.

GO ON →

Name: _____ Date: _____

10 The author makes the point that nuclear energy will continue to improve in the future. Write **two** details from the list that support this point.

Author's Point of View	Nuclear energy will continue to improve.
Details	

Details:

Burning fuel like coal causes air pollution.

People have different opinions about using nuclear energy.

We have learned to control nuclear energy so that it is safer.

It takes thousands of years for uranium to completely decay.

Energy resources are decreasing and nuclear energy is needed more than ever.

Name: _____ Date: _____

Now answer Number 11. Base your answer on "Hybrid or Electric?" and "Nuclear Power: The Key to the Future."

11 What is similar about the authors' points of view in "Hybrid or Electric?" and "Nuclear Power: The Key to the Future"? What reasons do the authors use to convince readers to make a change? Support your answer with details from both texts.

_____

_____

_____

_____

_____

_____

_____

_____

_____

_____

_____

_____

_____

Answer Key

Name: _____

Question	Correct Answer	Content Focus	CCSS	Complexity
1A	D	Text Structure: Compare and Contrast	RI.4.5	DOK 2
1B	A	Text Structure: Compare and Contrast/ Text Evidence	RI.4.5/ RI.4.1	DOK 2
2	B, C, F	Author's Point of View	RI.4.8	DOK 2
3A	A	Latin and Greek Suffixes	L.4.4b	DOK 2
3B	C	Latin and Greek Suffixes	L.4.4b	DOK 2
4	B	Latin and Greek Suffixes	L.4.4b	DOK 2
5	see below	Author's Point of View	RI.4.8	DOK 2
6A	C	Latin and Greek Suffixes	L.4.4b	DOK 2
6B	D	Latin and Greek Suffixes	L.4.4b	DOK 2
7	A	Latin and Greek Suffixes	L.4.4b	DOK 2
8A	A	Author's Point of View	RI.4.8	DOK 3
8B	B	Author's Point of View/Text Evidence	RI.4.8/ RI.4.1	DOK 3
9	B, C	Author's Point of View	RI.4.8	DOK 3
10	see below	Author's Point of View	RI.4.8	DOK 2
11	see below	Writing About Text	W.4.9b	DOK 4

Comprehension 1A, 1B, 2, 5, 8A, 8B, 9, 10	/12	%
Vocabulary 3A, 3B, 4, 6A, 6B, 7	/8	%
Total Weekly Assessment Score	/20	%

5 Students should underline the following sentences:
- If drivers need a car for short trips, an electric car is perfect.
- If drivers travel far from home and won't be able to charge a car, a hybrid would be the right choice.

10 Students should complete the chart with the following details:
- We have learned to control nuclear energy so that it is safer.
- Energy resources are decreasing and nuclear energy is needed more than ever.

11 To receive full credit for the response, the following information should be included: Both authors are concerned about the environment. They encourage the use of nuclear power or electric/hybrid cards to reduce use of gasoline and other fossil fuels, and thus reduce pollution.

Read the article "Intensive Farming: We Can Feed the World" before answering Numbers 1 through 5.

Intensive Farming: We Can Feed the World

Feeding the world is a big challenge. Everyone should get involved. It is our responsibility. The world's population is increasing every day, and every person on Earth needs food to survive.

To help meet this growing need for food, people have turned to a special method of farming called intensive farming, which is done on very large farms. Crops are grown in huge fields and are then sold. Intensive farming produces food more quickly and more cheaply than ever before. It is the best way to meet the challenge of feeding our world.

With a quick look around a farm using intensive farming you would notice there are not many workers. These large farms are mechanized. People and work animals have been replaced by modern machines. These machines do the jobs of a team of workers. Farmers use sophisticated machines such as combine harvesters. Farming is easier because these large machines can easily cover a large area of geography in a shorter amount of time. Many of the machines have more than one purpose. For example, one machine can harvest, separate, and load crops. This saves farmers time and money.

This combine is harvesting, separating, and loading crops.

GO ON →

In intensive farming, a large amount of food is grown by a few people. This makes the food less expensive than food sold by smaller farms. Lower prices means more people can afford it.

With intensive farming, a field that once grew food for ten people can now feed one hundred. This scientific data points out that intensive farming is a valuable method of producing food.

Farmers on these large farms often use new varieties of plants. Scientists have developed plants that can produce more food. One example is corn plants that grow more corncobs. Some plants have been created so that they do not spoil quickly. These plants can be shipped long distances and stay fresh.

As plants grow, they get materials they need from the soil. This happens naturally over time. But this is too slow for large farms. Scientists developed fertilizers that have the correct amount of chemical nutrients for plants to grow well. This allows farmers to plant the same crop every year in the same soil. Scientists also generated new ideas that help farmers protect their crops. They developed a wide variety of pesticides that kill insects that eat crops. Herbicides were also developed to kill weeds growing among the crops. These advances in science help meet the goal of growing more food.

There are many people to feed on our planet. There will be even more people in the future. Thanks to intensive farming, more affordable food is available. Intensive farming is the best way to be certain that each and every person gets enough to eat.

GO ON →

Now answer Numbers 1 through 5. Base your answers on "Intensive Farming: We Can Feed the World."

1 Read the paragraphs. Underline the sentence that states the main idea of the article.

Feeding the world is a big challenge. Everyone should get involved. It is our responsibility. The world's population is increasing every day, and every person on Earth needs food to survive.

To help meet this growing need for food, people have turned to a special method of farming called intensive farming, which is done on very large farms. Crops are grown in huge fields and are then sold. Intensive farming produces food more quickly and more cheaply than ever before. It is the best way to meet the challenge of feeding our world.

2 Read the sentence from the article.

Farmers use <u>sophisticated</u> machines such as combine harvesters.

The root of <u>sophisticated</u> means "no longer simple." What does this suggest about a <u>sophisticated</u> machine?

Ⓐ It is always available.

Ⓑ It is in need of repair.

Ⓒ It is complicated.

Ⓓ It is brand new.

GO ON →

3 In the article, the author states that new varieties of plants can be helpful in feeding the world. Which **two** sentences from the article **best** support this point?

Ⓐ "Crops are grown in huge fields and are then sold."

Ⓑ "For example, one machine can harvest, separate, and load crops."

Ⓒ "Scientists have developed plants that can produce more food."

Ⓓ "Some plants have been created so that they do not spoil quickly."

Ⓔ "As plants grow, they get materials they need from the soil."

Ⓕ "This allows farmers to plant the same crop every year in the same soil."

4 Read the sentence from the article.

Scientists also <u>generated</u> new ideas that help farmers protect their crops.

The Greek root of <u>generated</u> means "to create." What does <u>generated</u> mean?

Ⓐ planted

Ⓑ produced

Ⓒ shipped

Ⓓ stopped

GO ON →

5 This question has two parts. First, answer part A. Then, answer part B.

Part A: What **most likely** is the author's point of view about bugs?

(A) They can be damaging to plants.

(B) They work against advances in science.

(C) They are necessary to create herbicides.

(D) They can be helpful for intensive farming.

Part B: Which sentence from the article **best** supports this point?

(A) "Scientists developed fertilizers that have the correct amount of chemical nutrients for plants to grow well."

(B) "They developed a wide variety of pesticides that kill insects that eat crops."

(C) "Herbicides were also developed to kill weeds growing among the crops."

(D) "These advances in science help meet the goal of growing more food."

GO ON →

Read the article "Stop Intensive Farming" before answering Numbers 6 through 10.

Stop Intensive Farming

What is the best way to feed the world? Some people argue that intensive farming is the answer. Intensive farming grows crops in a big way. Modern machines are used on enormous farms that produce large amounts of food, both quickly and cheaply. Yet, is it worth the harm that intensive farming is doing to our environment? No! It is important to stop intensive farming now to protect our Earth.

There are many problems with intensive farming. Some have to do with the chemicals scientists have developed, such as fertilizers. The same crop is grown year after year on the same field. These plants eventually drain the soil of nutrients, the food plants need to grow. Then farmers must feed the soil in their fields with fertilizers.

Over time, some of the fertilizers seep through the soil and end up in our water sources. Fertilizers can promote the growth of tiny plants and bacteria. These plants and bacteria use up most of the oxygen in the water. Fish and other creatures die because they cannot breathe. This is pathetic and unacceptable.

To prevent this, farmers might use other scientific advances. For example, they could use thermal imaging cameras. These cameras take aerial photographs of crops as they ripen. Healthy and diseased crops show up different colors. With this information, farmers know exactly where to use fertilizer. They can use small amounts on the parts of the fields that need it. This won't purify our water sources, but it is a start.

On large farms, insects can spread quickly across fields, destroying crops as they feed. To keep insects away, many farmers spray chemicals called pesticides on their fields. Traces of these chemicals are often found in our food and water. Researchers conducted a ten-year study and found that ninety-seven percent of water samples showed small amounts of one or more pesticides. It is plain to see that these chemicals are bad for the environment, and bad for our health, too!

GO ON →

Farmers should find other ways to control pests. They could use pesticides that break down into harmless substances. Onions and marigolds have strong smells that many insects do not like. Farmers could grow these common plants between their crops to get rid of pests naturally.

Intensive farming may work for a while, but it cannot last forever. Over time, intensive farming destroys the environment. We need to find a better way to feed our world. Stop intensive farming now, before it is too late!

GO ON →

Now answer Numbers 6 through 10. Base your answers on "Stop Intensive Farming."

6 This question has two parts. First, answer part A. Then, answer part B.

Part A: Which **best** states the author's point of view about the use of chemicals in farming?

(A) They are helpful.

(B) They are harmful.

(C) They are expensive.

(D) They are necessary.

Part B: Which evidence from the article **best** supports this point?

(A) Some pesticides break down into harmless substances.

(B) Thermal image cameras take photos of diseased crops.

(C) Fertilizers and pesticides end up in our water supplies.

(D) Farmers must feed soil the nutrients that are missing.

7 Read the sentences from the article.

Fish and other creatures die because they cannot breathe. This is <u>pathetic</u> and unacceptable.

The root of <u>pathetic</u> means "to suffer." What does this suggest about something <u>pathetic</u>?

(A) It seeks out happiness.

(B) It is easy to remember.

(C) It is very noisy.

(D) It is very sad.

GO ON →

8 Read the sentence from the passage.

These cameras take <u>aerial</u> photographs of crops as they ripen.

The root of <u>aerial</u> means "air." From what would <u>aerial</u> spraying be done?

(A) a plane

(B) a truck

(C) a train

(D) a ship

9 Pick **two** types of evidence that the author uses to support the point that pesticides are found in our water supplies.

(A) videos

(B) research

(C) interviews

(D) experiments

(E) photographs

(F) personal experience

GO ON →

10 The author makes several points about intensive farming. Draw a line to match each point on the left with the text evidence that supports it on the right.

| Farmers can control pests naturally. | "Traces of these chemicals are often found in our food and water." |

| Intensive farming damages the earth. | "Onions and marigolds have strong smells that many insects do not like." |

| Pesticides are used too much on large farms. | "These plants eventually drain the soil of nutrients, the food plants need to grow." |

Name: _____ Date: _____

Now answer Number 11. Base your answer on "Intensive Farming: We Can Feed the World" and "Stop Intensive Farming."

11 The articles "Intensive Farming: We Can Feed the World" and "Stop Intensive Farming" discuss the same topic from different points of view. Explain how each point of view is presented and supported. Support your answer with details from both texts.

_____

_____

_____

_____

_____

_____

_____

_____

_____

_____

_____

_____

_____

Answer Key   Name: _____

Question	Correct Answer	Content Focus	CCSS	Complexity
1	see below	Main Idea and Key Details	RI.4.2	DOK 2
2	C	Greek Roots	L.4.4b	DOK 2
3	C, D	Author's Point of View	RI.4.8	DOK 3
4	B	Greek Roots	L.4.4b	DOK 2
5A	A	Author's Point of View	RI.4.8	DOK 3
5B	B	Author's Point of View/Text Evidence	RI.4.8/ RI.4.1	DOK 3
6A	B	Author's Point of View	RI.4.8	DOK 3
6B	C	Author's Point of View/Text Evidence	RI.4.8/ RI.4.1	DOK 3
7	D	Greek Roots	L.4.4b	DOK 2
8	A	Greek Roots	L.4.4b	DOK 2
9	B, D	Author's Point of View	RI.4.8	DOK 3
10	see below	Author's Point of View	RI.4.8	DOK 3
11	see below	Writing About Text	W.4.9b	DOK 4

Comprehension 1, 3, 5A, 5B, 6A, 6B, 9, 10	/12	%
Vocabulary 2, 4, 7, 8	/8	%
Total Weekly Assessment Score	/20	%

1 Students should underline the following sentence:
- It is the best way to meet the challenge of feeding our world.

10 Students should match the author's points with text evidence as follows:
- Farmers can control pests naturally.— "Onions and marigolds have strong smells that many insects do not like."
- Intensive farming damages the earth.— "These plants eventually drain the soil of nutrients, the food plants need to grow."
- Pesticides are used too much on large farms.— "Traces of these chemicals are often found in our food and water."

11 To receive full credit for the response, the following information should be included: "Intensive Farming: We Can Feed the World" is pro-intensive farming. This article states that large farms are the best way to meet the goal of feeding everyone in the world. Intensive farming uses modern machines and new kinds of plants to produce more food, more quickly, and more cheaply than ever before. "Stop Intensive Farming" is anti-intensive farming. This article states that intensive farming is destroying the environment and should be stopped. The fertilizers and pesticides used in intensive farming are ruining food and water supplies.

Read the article "Three Levels of Government" before answering Numbers 1 through 5.

Three Levels of Government

The United States has a system of rules or laws that protects the lives of its citizens. These laws provide citizens with personal liberties, or freedoms. They make sure that everyone is treated equally and fairly.

Three levels of government share the responsibility for making laws. At the national level, laws are made for the entire country. For example, the freedom to practice any religion is a national law.

State laws only apply to people in a particular state. Most states have laws requiring everyone to wear a seatbelt.

Local governments control communities, such as deciding which areas of the community are set up for businesses.

Each level of government has a court system that makes sure laws are followed. If a person has been accused of breaking a law, a judge or a jury decides if the person is guilty and what the punishment should be. A jury is a group of people chosen to find the truth. It listens to all the evidence and then decides if a person is innocent or guilty.

GO ON →

The government also provides services to people. At the national level, government workers check that food is safe to eat. They make sure food safety laws are followed so that no spoiled or unsafe food is sold. The national government also makes sure the air is safe to breathe and the water is safe to drink. Government workers also check everyone who wants to get on an airplane. People cannot take anything that is harmful on planes. The national government provides a military to protect the nation. The military defends the country from enemies. The national government also takes care of national parks and forests.

State governments build and maintain state roads. Roads must be kept in good repair so cars and trucks can transport goods and people. State governments provide money for public education. They offer programs that help keep people healthy. They also provide a National Guard to protect the people in the state. The Guard also supports the national military.

Local governments make sure trash is collected. Without this service, trash would gather in the streets or on sidewalks. Local governments provide police and firefighters to protect the people. They repair local streets and plow them after it snows. Local governments take care of libraries and public parks.

All levels of government collect taxes. People pay national, state, and local taxes. Tax money pays for services. The laws and services provided at each level of government allow citizens to have better lives.

GO ON →

Name: _____ Date: _____

Now answer Numbers 1 through 5. Base your answers on "Three Levels of Government."

1 Which statements describe effects of a law made by government? Pick **three** choices.

- (A) Seatbelts must be worn.
- (B) Water is checked for safety.
- (C) Court systems are voted on.
- (D) People must be treated fairly.
- (E) People can do what they want.
- (F) People are polite to each other.

2 Read the paragraph from the article.

Local governments control communities, such as deciding which areas of the community are set up for businesses.

The word local comes from the Latin root *locus*, meaning "place." What does the word local suggest?

- (A) something that is nationwide
- (B) something that is without any power
- (C) something that is the same everywhere
- (D) something that has to do with a specific area

GO ON →

3 This question has two parts. First, answer part A. Then, answer part B.

Part A: Why does the author explain the effects of food safety laws in the article?

(A) to show that the food you buy is safe to eat

(B) to show that the food sold in stores may be spoiled

(C) to show that food must be priced fairly and cheaply

(D) to show that food must be sold only in grocery stores

Part B: Which sentence from the article **best** supports your answer in part A?

(A) "The government also provides services to people."

(B) "They make sure food safety laws are followed so that no spoiled or unsafe food is sold."

(C) "The national government also makes sure the air is safe to breathe and the water is safe to drink."

(D) "People cannot take anything that is harmful on planes."

4 Read the sentence from the article.

Roads must be kept in good repair so cars and trucks can transport goods and people.

The Latin root of transport means "to carry across." What does this suggest about the goods and people?

(A) They are being moved.

(B) They are being watched.

(C) They are buying something.

(D) They are waiting for something.

GO ON →

5 At the end of the passage, the author explains how people pay for government services. Underline **two** sentences in the paragraphs below that explain this cause-and-effect relationship.

Local governments make sure trash is collected. Without this service, trash would gather in the streets or on sidewalks. Local governments provide police and firefighters to protect the people. They repair local streets and plow them after it snows. Local governments take care of libraries and public parks.

All levels of government collect taxes. People pay national, state, and local taxes. Tax money pays for services. The laws and services provided at each level of government allow citizens to have better lives.

GO ON →

Read the article "Yellowstone" before answering Numbers 6 through 10.

Yellowstone

A national park is a special area set aside by a nation. Once a national park is created, the plants and animals there are protected. The area cannot be developed and remains natural. People who visit a national park can take a journey through nature.

The world's first national park was created in the United States in 1872. That year, President Ulysses S. Grant signed a law creating Yellowstone National Park.

How did this come about? During the 1800s, trappers and hunters returned to the East with tales of the wondrous sights of the West. They told stories of pools of hot water and a hill made of black glass. They also told of towers of water that burst from the ground.

Some people did not believe these strange tales, so, in 1870, a group of men set out to see if the stories were true. They were amazed by the land's beauty and decided to try to protect this special location so everyone could enjoy it. The men wrote newspaper stories. They gave speeches and met with government officials. Yellowstone National Park was created thanks to their hard work.

The park got its name from the yellow rocks found in one river that runs through it. Most of the park is in the northwest corner of Wyoming, but parts of the park are located in Montana and Idaho, as well.

GO ON →

Yellowstone is a very popular park. It is famous for its geysers. These hot-water springs erupt, throwing boiling water and steam into the air. The park's most famous geyser is called Old Faithful. It erupts about every 40 to 70 minutes. Yellowstone also is known as a wildlife reserve. Most of its animals have wandered and roamed the park for many years. There are black bears, grizzly bears, elk, and deer. Moose, bison, bighorn sheep, mountain lions, and wolves live there, too. Many varieties of fish can be found in the park's rivers and streams. In addition, more than 275 kinds of birds can be seen in the park.

If we want to be able to enjoy our national parks for a long time, we have to do what we can to keep them beautiful and wild. We must preserve the balance of nature. Park visitors can help by making sure they do not hurt or disturb animals or plants. Also, people should not leave trash in the parks. If all visitors do their part, people will be able to enjoy Yellowstone and other parks like it for a long time to come.

GO ON →

Name: _____ Date: _____

Now answer Numbers 6 through 10. Base your answers on "Yellowstone."

6 This question has two parts. First, answer part A. Then, answer part B.

Part A: Why did people decide to protect Yellowstone?

(A) Yellowstone was a national park.

(B) It was a good place to hunt and fish.

(C) There was a hill made of black glass.

(D) They wanted everyone to be able to enjoy it.

Part B: Which sentence from the passage **best** supports your answer in part A?

(A) "During the 1800s, trappers and hunters returned to the East with tales of the wondrous sights of the West."

(B) "They told stories of pools of hot water and a hill made of black glass."

(C) "Some people did not believe these strange tales, so, in 1870, a group of men set out to see if the stories were true."

(D) "They were amazed by the land's beauty and decided to try to protect this special location so everyone could enjoy it."

7 What is the author's point of view about Yellowstone? Pick **two** choices.

(A) Visitors to the park should be respectful.

(B) There are not enough places to stop in the park.

(C) There are too many different animals at the park.

(D) Too many people come to visit the park every year.

(E) Yellowstone is the most beautiful park in the country.

(F) The park should be preserved for many years to come.

GO ON →

Name: _____ Date: _____

8 Read the sentence from the article.

These hot-water springs <u>erupt</u>, throwing boiling water and steam into the air.

The Latin root of <u>erupt</u> means "to break out or burst." Which word **most likely** includes the same Latin root found in <u>erupt</u>?

(A) errand

(B) error

(C) intercept

(D) interrupt

9 Draw a line to match each cause on the left with its effect on the right.

Cause

| Yellowstone becomes a national park. |

| Yellow rocks are found in one river in the park. |

| Animals have roamed the park for many years. |

Effect

| The park is named Yellowstone. |

| Yellowstone is known as a wildlife reserve. |

| Plants and animals are protected. |

GO ON →

Name: _____ Date: _____

10 This question has two parts. First, answer part A. Then, answer part B.

Part A: Read the sentence from the article.

Many <u>varieties</u> of fish can be found in the park's rivers and streams.

The Latin root of <u>varieties</u> means "difference." What does it mean if there are many <u>varieties</u> of fish?

Ⓐ There are many kinds of fish.

Ⓑ There are small fish in the park.

Ⓒ There is a lot of one kind of fish.

Ⓓ There are slippery fish in the park.

Part B: Which other word **most likely** includes the root found in <u>varieties</u>?

Ⓐ valid

Ⓑ vanity

Ⓒ various

Ⓓ varsity

Name: _____ Date: _____

Now answer Number 11. Base your answer on "Three Levels of Government" and "Yellowstone."

11 Describe the cause-and-effect relationship of laws in the United States. Support your answer with details from both articles.

_____

_____

_____

_____

_____

_____

_____

_____

_____

_____

_____

_____

_____

_____

Name: _____

Question	Correct Answer	Content Focus	CCSS	Complexity
1	A, B, D	Text Structure: Cause and Effect	RI.4.5	DOK 2
2	D	Latin Roots	L.4.4b	DOK 1
3A	A	Text Structure: Cause and Effect	RI.4.5	DOK 2
3B	B	Text Structure: Cause and Effect/ Text Evidence	RI.4.5/ RI.4.1	DOK 2
4	A	Latin Roots	L.4.4b	DOK 1
5	see below	Text Structure: Cause and Effect	RI.4.5	DOK 2
6A	D	Text Structure: Cause and Effect	RI.4.5	DOK 2
6B	D	Text Structure: Cause and Effect/ Text Evidence	RI.4.5/ RI.4.1	DOK 2
7	A, F	Author's Point of View	RI.4.8	DOK 3
8	D	Latin Roots	L.4.4b	DOK 1
9	see below	Text Structure: Cause and Effect	RI.4.5	DOK 2
10A	A	Latin Roots	L.4.4b	DOK 1
10B	C	Latin Roots	L.4.4b	DOK 1
11	see below	Writing About Text	W.4.9b	DOK 4

Comprehension 1, 3A, 3B, 5, 6A, 6B, 7, 9		/12	%
Vocabulary 2, 4, 8, 10A, 10B		/8	%
Total Weekly Assessment Score		/20	%

5 Students should underline the following two sentences:
• People pay national, state, and local taxes.
• Tax money pays for services.

9 Students should make the following matches of causes to effects:
• Yellowstone becomes a national park.—Plants and animals are protected.
• Animals have roamed the park for many years. —Yellowstone is known as a wildlife reserve.
• Yellow rocks are found in one river in the park. —The park is named Yellowstone.

11 Answers may vary, but to receive full credit for the response, the following information should be included: Because of national laws, people are free and must be treated equally. They cannot be held as slaves. People are checked before boarding airplanes. The effect of the law creating Yellowstone is that plants and animals and the park's natural beauty are protected.

Read the passage "Running for Mayor" before answering Numbers 1 through 5.

Running for Mayor

I stared out the window and watched the falling rain as I thought about issues affecting my city. For one thing, the parks were not kept up. There was broken equipment in almost every park, and I worried that one day someone was going to get seriously hurt. A lot of snow fell in the winter, and the streets were never cleared quickly. There were also a lot of people out of work because companies had moved to new areas. I loved this city, and it made me sad to see these problems. Something needed to change!

I didn't hear my husband, Gary, enter the room until he said, "Alita, you've been sitting here for an hour. Why do you look so down in the dumps?"

"I'm unhappy with what is happening to our city," I said sadly. "I can think of at least three major changes that I would like to see, but I'm just not sure what I can do about it."

GO ON →

Gary smiled at me and patted my hand. "You're a smart woman and a great leader, so maybe you should run for mayor."

I started to laugh, but stopped when I realized Gary's words made sense. I am a member of the Oneida Tribe, which is part of the Iroquois Nation. In our history, women have always held positions of leadership. Women select the male leader, and if the man chosen does not do a good job, they remove him from the job. The current mayor seemed to be putting minimal effort into solving our city's problems, and I thought he was doing a poor job. Maybe he should be replaced, and I should run for mayor!

Gary saw that I needed some time to think. Before he walked out of the room, he said, "If you need to talk, I'm all ears."

I thought about Gary's suggestion for a while longer and began to like his idea. I had been a leader before, when I was in charge of the group that raised money for the local homeless shelter. I also organized volunteers for litter cleanup on the highway. I knew how to take charge and get things done.

I called my mother to find out what she thought about the idea. Should I run for mayor?

"I think that is a wonderful idea," she said. "You come from a long line of women leaders, and your grandmother and great-grandmother would be proud. What do we need to do to get the ball rolling? How do you get your name on the ballot?"

After I said good-bye to my mother, I felt like a million bucks! I had my mother's support and knew that she will help me in the run for mayor. I knew I had Gary's backing, too. Instead of feeling hopeless about the problems in my city, I felt energized. Things would get better, and I wanted to be the one to start the changes.

GO ON →

Now answer Numbers 1 through 5. Base your answers on "Running for Mayor."

1 This question has two parts. First, answer part A. Then, answer part B.

Part A: Who is the narrator of the passage?

Ⓐ Alita

Ⓑ Gary

Ⓒ the mayor

Ⓓ Alita's mother

Part B: Which detail **best** supports your answer in part A?

Ⓐ The narrator calls her mother for advice.

Ⓑ The narrator's husband calls her "Alita."

Ⓒ The narrator considers running for mayor.

Ⓓ The narrator is not happy with the current mayor.

2 Underline **two** sentences from the paragraph that **best** sum up Alita's feelings about her city.

I stared out the window and watched the falling rain as I thought about issues affecting my city. For one thing, the parks were not kept up. There was broken equipment in almost every park, and I worried that one day someone was going to get seriously hurt. A lot of snow fell in the winter, and the streets were never cleared quickly. There were also a lot of people out of work because companies had moved to new areas. I loved this city, and it made me sad to see these problems. Something needed to change!

GO ON →

3 Read the detail from the passage.

". . . 'Alita, you've been sitting here for an hour. Why do you look so down in the dumps?'"

What does the idiom "down in the dumps" mean?

(A) angry

(B) confused

(C) unclean

(D) unhappy

4 What does the first-person point of view help the reader understand? Pick **two** choices.

(A) Alita's job

(B) Alita's family

(C) city problems that worry Alita

(D) the opinions of Alita's mother

(E) Alita's thoughts about running for mayor

(F) traditions in different Native American cultures

GO ON →

Name: _____ Date: _____

5 This question has two parts. First, answer part A. Then, answer part B.

Part A: Read the sentence from the passage.

What do we need to do to <u>get the ball rolling</u>?

What does the idiom "get the ball rolling" mean?

(A) get started

(B) go bowling

(C) solve a problem

(D) play a new game

Part B: Which sentence from the passage **best** suggests the meaning of "get the ball rolling"?

(A) "'I think that is a wonderful idea,' she said."

(B) "'You come from a long line of women leaders, and your grandmother and great-grandmother would be proud.'"

(C) "'How do you get your name on the ballot?'"

(D) "After I said good-bye to my mother, I felt like a million bucks!"

GO ON →

Read the passage "Time to Move On" before answering Numbers 6 through 10.

Time to Move On

It was the end of the workday. Ting reviewed the document on his computer, and made sure to save it before shutting the computer down. Next, he read over some paperwork left by his assistant before finishing his last signature and pushing back from his desk. Ting put his hands behind his head and sighed. He truly loved his job as state senator, for everything he did made a difference in the lives of the people of his state.

Ting looked up when his office door opened. "Do you need anything else tonight?" Ting's assistant, Denise, asked. "I'm getting ready to call it a day."

Ting smiled and answered, "Yes, would you please make sure these get to the right people?" He handed her some papers. "Thanks for your hard work today. I can always count on you to dot all the i's and cross all the t's. I'll see you in the morning."

After Denise left, Ting settled back in his chair. For weeks now, he had been thinking of running for the United States Senate. He had been elected to the state senate three times and had written and passed many laws. "I know the ropes," he thought, and now he felt it was time to work at the national level.

GO ON →

Ting had been interested in politics ever since high school. He remembered winning the election for class president and then organizing service projects to help the community. In college he was elected president of the student body, where he told college officials about concerns the students had and helped to make changes that helped everyone. As a lawyer, Ting represented people who needed his services, and Ting was happy when he represented people in court. As a state senator, he made sure the people in his district were heard and helped pass laws that improved schools and towns.

Now, Ting wanted to be able to help more people, and working in the federal government would give him that opportunity. He called his trusted friend and advisor, Esteban, and asked him to come to his office. When Esteban arrived, Ting asked, "What do you think about me running for the United States Senate?"

Esteban's face went through a quick change of emotions. At first, he looked shocked, but then he slowly started nodding his head. "Ting, I think that should be the next step for you. You have done great things for the people of this state, and now is the time to throw your hat into the ring for the U.S. Senate."

Ting smiled at Esteban and suggested that they talk more tomorrow. He was excited about the future and eager to help more people.

GO ON →

Name: _____ Date: _____

Now answer Numbers 6 through 10. Base your answers on "Time to Move On."

6 This question has two parts. First, answer part A. Then, answer part B.

Part A: Read the sentences from the passage.

He had been elected to the state senate three times and had written and passed many laws. "I know the ropes," he thought, and now he felt it was time to work at the national level.

What does the idiom "know the ropes" mean in the sentences above?

Ⓐ like to sail

Ⓑ write the laws

Ⓒ able to tie knots.

Ⓓ know what to do

Part B: Which phrase from the sentences provides the **best** clue to the meaning of "know the ropes"?

Ⓐ "been elected to the state senate"

Ⓑ "had written and passed many laws"

Ⓒ "it was time to work"

Ⓓ "at the national level"

GO ON →

7 This question has two parts. First, answer part A. Then, answer part B.

Part A: Which sentence **best** describes why Ting wants to run for the United States Senate?

(A) He is tired of being a state senator.

(B) He wants to be able to help more people.

(C) Esteban has nothing to do in his current job.

(D) Esteban told him he would be good at the job.

Part B: Which sentence from the passage **best** supports your answer in part A?

(A) "As a lawyer, Ting represented people who needed his services, and Ting was happy when he represented people in court."

(B) "Now, Ting wanted to be able to help more people, and working in the federal government would give him that opportunity."

(C) "He called his trusted friend and advisor, Esteban, and asked him to come to his office."

(D) "Ting smiled at Esteban and suggested that they talk more tomorrow."

8 Read the sentences from the passage.

"Ting, I think that should be the next step for you. You have done great things for the people of this state, and now is the time to throw your hat into the ring for the U.S. Senate."

What does the idiom "throw your hat into the ring" mean?

(A) keep the same job

(B) throw your hat away

(C) try for a new position

(D) be rewarded for a good job

GO ON →

9 Which sentences summarize the main messages in the passage? Pick **two** choices.

Ⓐ People have different reasons for running for office.

Ⓑ Some people run for office to be able to help others.

Ⓒ All government jobs are difficult in their own ways.

Ⓓ It is important to always improve and set new goals for yourself.

Ⓔ Being a U.S. senator is more important than being a state senator.

Ⓕ It is important to have support from many people when running for office.

10 Write **one** word to show Ting's point of view in the beginning of the passage and **one** word to show his point of view at the end of the passage. Then write the numbers of **two** sentences from the passage that support your choices. Choose from the lists below.

	Ting's Point of View	**Text Evidence**
Beginning		
End		

Ting's Point of View:

anxious   tired

hopeful   unsure

Text Evidence:

1 – "Ting smiled and answered, 'Yes, would you please make sure these get to the right people?'"

2 – "When Esteban arrived, Ting asked, 'What do you think about me running for the United States Senate?'"

3 – "At first, he looked shocked, but then he slowly started nodding his head."

4 – "He was excited about the future and eager to help more people."

Name: _____ Date: _____

Now answer Number 11. Base your answer on "Running for Mayor" and "Time to Move On."

11 How does the point of view presented in each passage affect what the reader learns about the thoughts of the characters? Support your answer with details from both passages.

_____

_____

_____

_____

_____

_____

_____

_____

_____

_____

_____

_____

_____

Answer Key

Name: _____

Question	Correct Answer	Content Focus	CCSS	Complexity
1A	A	Point of View	RL.4.6	DOK 2
1B	B	Point of View/Text Evidence	RL.4.6/ RL.4.1	DOK 2
2	see below	Point of View	RL.4.6	DOK 3
3	D	Figurative Language: Idioms	L.4.5b	DOK 2
4	C, E	Point of View	RL.4.6	DOK 3
5A	A	Figurative Language: Idioms	L.4.5b	DOK 2
5B	C	Figurative Language: Idioms/ Text Evidence	L.4.5b	DOK 2
6A	D	Figurative Language: Idioms	L.4.5b	DOK 2
6B	B	Figurative Language: Idioms/ Text Evidence	L.4.5b	DOK 2
7A	B	Point of View	RL.4.6	DOK 3
7B	B	Point of View/Text Evidence	RL.4.6/ RL.4.1	DOK 3
8	C	Figurative Language: Idioms	L.4.5b	DOK 2
9	B, D	Theme	RL.4.2	DOK 3
10	see below	Point of View	RL.4.6	DOK 3
11	see below	Writing About Text	W.4.9a	DOK 4

Comprehension 1A, 1B, 2, 4, 7A, 7B, 9, 10	/12	%
Vocabulary 3, 5A, 5B, 6A, 6B, 8	/8	%
Total Weekly Assessment Score	/20	%

2 Students should underline the following sentences:
- I loved this city, and it made me sad to see these problems.
- Something needed to change!

10 Students should complete the chart as follows:
- Beginning—Ting's Point of View: unsure; Text Evidence: 2-"When Esteban arrived, Ting asked, 'What do you think about me running for the United States Senate?'"
- End—Ting's Point of View: hopeful; Text Evidence: 4-"He was excited about the future and eager to help more people."

11 To receive full credit for the response, the following information should be included: "Running for Mayor" is told in the first person. The reader learns Alita's frustrations, fear, and excitement directly from her. "Time to Move On" is told in the third person. The reader learns Ting's thoughts from the narrator. Only facts are learned about Ting; no opinions are presented.

Read the passage "Way to Go, Grandma" before answering Numbers 1 through 5.

Way to Go, Grandma

"Jamal, how do you think your sister Kellyn is doing in college?" Grandma asked me. "And how about your brother Michael's new baby, little Jayden, way out there in Oklahoma? I hope he's over his cold by now."

"Grandma," I said, "let me show you how to send emails so you won't have to guess how they're doing. If Kellyn got an email from you, she'd be so amazed that she'd reply to you in seconds, and besides, I think Michael's wife would love to email you every time Jayden coughs!"

Grandma smiled at the thought and then said, "You've been offering to teach me how to use that computer for a long time, Jamal, and I do appreciate it." Sighing, she shook her head in confusion and bewilderment. "Unfortunately, I think technology has passed me by, even though it does take so long for them to answer my letters."

"Why don't I send Kellyn an email now," I suggested, "and you can tell me what to say?"

Grandma's face lit up, her hesitation and doubts gone. She knew she could do this, and she was ready now! She pulled me over to the computer and pushed me down in the chair. "If you insist," she said eagerly.

I opened my email account and typed the first letters of Kellyn's address. The whole address immediately appeared in the "to" box. My grandmother was amazed, and asked, "How did the computer know we were going to write to Kellyn?"

Grinning, I said, "Just lucky, I guess."

Grandma rolled her eyes and started telling me what she wanted to say to Kellyn. As I typed, I purposely made mistakes, and soon Grandma was so frustrated with me that she said, "Oh, get up and let me sit down. I can type better than that!"

GO ON →

"Well, okay," I said, trying to hide my cleverness. My quick thinking even surprised me, as it wasn't often that I outwitted Grandma! I gave her my seat, and with no help or assistance from me, she typed a long email to Kellyn. When she was finished, I pointed out the send button, and she clicked on it.

Smiling from ear to ear, Grandma asked, "Do you think Kellyn will be surprised when she gets my email?"

"I think she will probably faint," I replied honestly.

Then Grandma looked longingly at the computer and asked, "Do you think we can find out how little Jayden is doing today? Sending an email to Jayden's mom would really be the icing on the cake." Without waiting for my answer, Grandma positioned her fingers over the keyboard. "Just tell me the first letters of Michael's email, and the computer will do the rest!"

So I told her, and she started typing. I left to find the book I had been reading, but a few minutes later, Grandma called me back to the computer.

"The computer was dinging," she said with a frown. "Did I do something wrong?"

I glanced at the screen. "You got a reply from Kellyn, so I guess she didn't faint for long!"

Grandma poked me in the ribs with her elbow and demanded, "Show me how to get to her email, young man, and hurry!"

GO ON →

Now answer Numbers 1 through 5. Base your answers on "Way to Go, Grandma."

1 This question has two parts. First, answer part A. Then, answer part B.

Part A: Read the sentences from the passage.

Grandma's face lit up, her <u>hesitation</u> and doubts gone. She knew she could do this, and she was ready now!

Which word means almost the **same** as <u>hesitation</u>?

(A) calm

(B) joy

(C) uncertainty

(D) unhappiness

Part B: Which word from the sentence is a synonym for <u>hesitation</u>?

(A) face

(B) doubts

(C) gone

(D) now

2 Read the sentences from the passage.

She pulled me over to the computer and pushed me down in the chair. "If you insist," she said eagerly.

What conclusion can you make about Grandma based on these sentences?

(A) She is sending an email only to please Jamal.

(B) She is pretending to be eager to send an email.

(C) She is pretending that Jamal is making her send an email.

(D) She does not want Jamal to know she is excited to send an email.

GO ON →

3 Why does Jamal purposely make mistakes as he types? Pick **two** choices.

(A) to help his grandmother solve her problem

(B) to learn how to send an email to a friend

(C) to get his grandmother to type the email

(D) to show how easy it is to send emails

(E) to send an email to his sister Kellyn

(F) to annoy his grandmother

4 Read the sentences from the passage.

"Well, okay," I said, trying to hide my cleverness. My quick thinking even surprised me, as it wasn't often that I outwitted Grandma!

Which word from the sentences gives a clue about the meaning of the word outwitted?

(A) hide

(B) cleverness

(C) surprised

(D) often

GO ON →

Name: _____ Date: _____

5 Draw a line to match each part of the story on the left with Jamal's point of view about his grandmother on the right.

<table>
<tr><th>Part of Story</th><th>Jamal's Point of View</th></tr>
</table>

Part of Story	Jamal's Point of View
Beginning	playful and joking
Middle	serious and helpful
End	proud and happy

GO ON →

Read the passage "The Good Old Days" before answering Numbers 6 through 10.

The Good Old Days

"So, Grandma," Jamal asked with a grin, "how do you like sending emails?"

Smiling proudly, his grandmother told him, "Emailing is a piece of cake!"

Jamal nodded and said, "Would you like to learn some abbreviations to make the words shorter so you can type faster? Or maybe you could get a new phone and use it for your emails."

Shaking her head, Grandma said, "Emailing is already fast enough for me, Jamal. I still don't know how to take a photo with my phone. I realize these new phones do amazing and remarkable things, but it's just a treat for me to be able to call someone from wherever I am."

"You couldn't always do that?" Jamal frowned. "You had to be in a certain place to call people when you were growing up?"

Grandma patted his hand and said, "You have no idea, Jamal. Not only did you have to be next to the phone, but the phone could not be moved, and there was only one phone in our house. It was in the living room. We had our own phone, but we shared the phone line with five other families! It was called a party line, but it wasn't much of a party because Sheila, who lived across the street, hogged the phone every night!"

Jamal was momentarily speechless. How could five families share one phone line? He'd never get to call his friends! "Since the phone was in the living room, what if people were watching TV? Did you have to ask them to turn down the sound all the time?"

Grandma smiled again as she explained, "Well, at first the TV was only on a few hours each day. Everyone wanted to watch it during those hours, so the sound wasn't a problem."

Jamal admitted, "I'm only allowed to watch TV a few hours a day, too."

GO ON →

She shook her head and said, "No, the TV only showed programs for a few hours each day. My parents bought our first TV when I was about six, and we were the first on our street to have one. The neighbors came to our house to watch TV, even though the screen was only about five inches square. The most exciting show on TV was about a cowboy and his horse, and it was black and white with absolutely no special effects. That show would look quaint and unusual now."

Jamal had another question. "I guess you didn't have any computers back then, so how did you do your homework?"

"We did it the hard way, with paper and pencils," Grandma answered. "If you were really lucky, you had a typewriter."

"What's a typewriter?" Jamal wanted to know.

Grandma pointed at the computer. "A typewriter is like this keyboard, but the first ones had no electricity. You pressed a key, and it popped up and printed a letter on the paper, and if you made a mistake, you had to erase it and type the word again. If the paper then looked too messy, you had to start typing all over again on a clean sheet of paper."

Jamal thought about that for a minute before asking, "Grandma, were those 'the good old days'?"

Laughing, she said, "I think any day that you enjoy life is a good old day!"

GO ON →

Now answer Numbers 6 through 10. Base your answers on "The Good Old Days."

6 Circle the word in the paragraph that is a synonym for the word remarkable.

Shaking her head, Grandma said, "Emailing is already fast enough for me, Jamal. I still don't know how to take a photo with my phone. I realize these new phones do amazing and <u>remarkable</u> things, but it's just a treat for me to be able to call someone from wherever I am."

7 This question has two parts. First, answer part A. Then, answer part B.

Part A: What is the **most likely** reason why Jamal is speechless when his grandmother tells him about phone party lines?

(A) He would not want to share his phone time with others.

(B) He did not think his grandmother went to many parties.

(C) He is surprised that a girl named Sheila hogged the phone.

(D) He wonders if other people listened to the phone conversations.

Part B: Which sentence from the passage **best** supports your answer in part A?

(A) "'You had to be in a certain place to call people when you were growing up?'"

(B) "Grandma patted his hand and said, 'You have no idea, Jamal.'"

(C) "How could five families share one phone line?"

(D) "'Did you have to ask them to turn down the sound all the time?'"

GO ON →

8 Read the sentences from the passage.

"The most exciting show on TV was about a cowboy and his horse, and it was black and white with absolutely no special effects. That show would look quaint and unusual now."

Which words mean almost the **same** as quaint? Pick **two** words.

(A) easy

(B) modern

(C) normal

(D) odd

(E) old-fashioned

(F) ugly

9 What is the **most likely** reason why Grandma tells Jamal about the phones and TV from when she was young?

(A) She wants to shock Jamal.

(B) She wants to make Jamal stop complaining.

(C) She wants to show Jamal how things have changed.

(D) She wants to make Jamal wonder what is coming in the future.

GO ON →

10 Which new information would the reader find out if the passage were written from Jamal's point of view? Pick **two** choices.

(A) if Jamal has ever heard of a typewriter before

(B) if Jamal will ever have to share his phone at home

(C) if Jamal wants to learn more about "the good old days"

(D) if Jamal would like to watch a black-and-white TV show

(E) If Jamal thinks Grandma should learn email abbreviations

(F) if Jamal is surprised that his grandmother used to have a party line

Name: _____ Date: _____

Now answer Number 11. Base your answer on "Way to Go, Grandma"
and "The Good Old Days."

11 "Way to Go, Grandma" is told in the first person, while "The Good Old Days" is told in the third person. How does point of view affect the way a reader sees characters in a passage? Support your answer with details from both passages.

_____

_____

_____

_____

_____

_____

_____

_____

_____

_____

_____

_____

_____

Answer Key

Name: _____

Question	Correct Answer	Content Focus	CCSS	Complexity
1A	C	Context Clues: Synonyms	L.4.5c	DOK 2
1B	B	Context Clues: Synonyms/ Text Evidence	L.4.5c/ RL.4.1	DOK 2
2	C	Point of View	RL.4.6	DOK 3
3	A, C	Character, Setting, Plot: Problem and Solution	RL.4.3	DOK 2
4	B	Context Clues: Synonyms	L.4.5c	DOK 1
5	see below	Point of View	RL.4.6	DOK 3
6	see below	Context Clues: Synonyms	L.4.5c	DOK 2
7A	A	Point of View	RL.4.6	DOK 3
7B	C	Point of View/Text Evidence	RL.4.6/ RL.4.1	DOK 3
8	D, E	Context Clues: Synonyms	L.4.5c	DOK 2
9	C	Point of View	RL.4.6	DOK 3
10	C, D	Point of View	RL.4.6	DOK 3
11	see below	Writing About Text	W.4.9a	DOK 4

Comprehension 2, 3, 5, 7A, 7B, 9, 10	/12	%
Vocabulary 1A, 1B, 4, 6, 8	/8	%
Total Weekly Assessment Score	/20	%

5 Students should match the parts of the story with Jamal's point of view as follows:
- Beginning—serious and helpful
- Middle—playful and joking
- End—proud and happy

6 Students should circle the word "amazing" in the paragraph.

11 To receive full credit for the response, the following information should be included: In the first-person point of view, you see exactly how a character feels through his or her thoughts, words, and actions. Jamal tells what he thinks and feels in "Way to Go, Grandma." In the third-person point of view, thoughts and feelings are interpreted through what the characters say and do and how they interact. In "The Good Old Days," Jamal says he is surprised. You don't know more than what he says because you don't know his thoughts.

Read the article "Stories in the Sky" before answering Numbers 1 through 5.

Stories in the Sky

For thousands of years, people have been guided by the stars. Farmers used the stars to decide when to plant or harvest crops, and sailors and other travelers used stars to guide their journeys. Stars guided people long before maps or computers.

Long ago, people noticed that stars form patterns in the sky. They told stories about these groups of stars, called constellations. These stories used people, animals, or objects to describe the stars, and each story reflected the storyteller's culture. Most stories come from the ancient Greeks, and the names of the constellations come from Latin words. Today, astronomers recognize eighty-eight constellations. These scientists study stars and use history to describe each constellation.

Many people can find the Big Dipper, which looks like a cup with a long handle. This group of stars is actually part of a larger constellation called Ursa Major. The Greek myth about Ursa Major describes the constellation as a large bear. In this story, Zeus, the king of the gods, changes a woman named Callisto into a bear. Then he places the bear in the sky. Native American stories about this constellation also use a bear, and other cultures use a wagon, a plow, a chariot, or a reindeer. Escaped enslaved workers looked for this constellation because the two stars at the front of the cup always point North. This led to freedom on the Underground Railroad.

GO ON →

The Little Dipper looks like a smaller version of the Big Dipper. It is part of a larger constellation called Ursa Minor. The stories of the two dippers are related. In the Greek myth, the bear Callisto wanders in the woods. Callisto's son is hunting when he sees the bear and he does not recognize the bear as his mother. The son is about to kill her when Zeus stops him by turning him into a bear as well. Zeus flings both bears by their tails into the night sky. This unusual detail explains why the bears have long tails.

Bright stars make Orion another easy constellation to find. This constellation can be identified by the three bright stars in Orion's belt. The Greek myth about Orion tells of a great hunter with a big ego. Orion thinks that he is the best hunter in the world. He brags that he can kill any animal. The goddess of Earth is worried that Orion might harm animals, so she sends a scorpion to sting and kill him. Because of this fight, the constellation Scorpius is on the other side of the sky from Orion. This distance keeps Orion and the scorpion from fighting. Many cultures have tales of Orion. In China, Orion is part of a larger constellation called the White Tiger.

Learning about the constellations and their stories is interesting. On the next starry night, grab a star chart and go outside. There are many stories waiting to be told.

GO ON →

Now answer Numbers 1 through 5. Base your answers on "Stories in the Sky."

1 This question has two parts. First, answer part A. Then, answer part B.

Part A: Why does the author explain how travelers used the stars at the beginning of the article?

(A) to show that stars are pretty to look at in the night sky

(B) to show that stars can show people in which direction to go

(C) to show that stars are the subject of stories told by travelers

(D) to show that stars can be seen only at certain times of the year

Part B: Which sentence from the article **best** supports your answer in part A?

(A) "Stars guided people long before maps or computers."

(B) "Long ago, people noticed that stars form patterns in the sky."

(C) "They told stories about these groups of stars, called constellations."

(D) "Today, astronomers recognize eighty-eight constellations."

2 Read the sentences from the article.

These stories used people, animals, or objects to describe the stars, and each story reflected the storyteller's culture. Most stories come from the ancient Greeks, and the names of the constellations come from Latin words.

What does the word culture mean in the sentences above?

(A) songs and tales

(B) inventions and creations

(C) traditions and ways of life

(D) pets and household items

GO ON →

3 This question has two parts. First, answer part A. Then, answer part B.

Part A: Which sentence explains the effect of Zeus flinging the bears into the sky?

(A) The son does not recognize his mother as a bear.

(B) The North Star lands in the sky inside the cup.

(C) The bears in the constellations have long tails.

(D) Zeus turns Callisto and her son into bears.

Part B: Which sentence from the article **best** explains the effect of Zeus flinging the bears into the sky?

(A) "The Little Dipper looks like a smaller version of the Big Dipper."

(B) "The stories of the two dippers are related."

(C) "The son is about to kill her when Zeus stops him by turning him into a bear as well."

(D) "This unusual detail explains why the bears have long tails."

4 According to the article, why **most likely** did enslaved workers look for the North Star? Pick **two** choices.

(A) It was part of a bear constellation.

(B) It was the brightest star in the sky.

(C) It guided them in the right direction.

(D) It moved across the sky as they traveled.

(E) It showed them which way to travel at night.

(F) It was found among constellations in the sky.

GO ON →

5 Read the paragraph from the article. Underline **two** sentences in the paragraph that help to explain what the word <u>ego</u> means.

Bright stars make Orion another easy constellation to find. This constellation can be identified by the three bright stars in Orion's belt. The Greek myth about Orion tells of a great hunter with a big <u>ego</u>. Orion thinks that he is the best hunter in the world. He brags that he can kill any animal. The goddess of Earth is worried that Orion might harm animals, so she sends a scorpion to sting and kill him. Because of this fight, the constellation Scorpius is on the other side of the sky from Orion. This distance keeps Orion and the scorpion from fighting. Many cultures have tales of Orion. In China, Orion is part of a larger constellation called the White Tiger.

GO ON →

Read the article "A Giant Star" before answering Numbers 6 through 10.

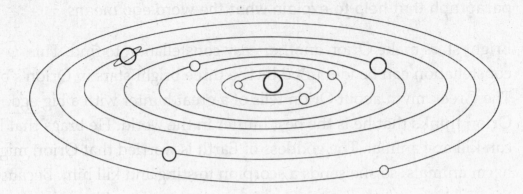

A Giant Star

Do you know that the sun is really a giant star at the center of our solar system? The sun is a large ball made of many kinds of gases. It gives light and heat to the planets that move around it and make up our solar system.

The sun rises in the eastern sky each morning, swallowing up the eerie darkness from the night before. Some people find the darkness creepy. The sun chases away the moon and stars that lurk in the night sky where they have been waiting, barely able to be seen. The shimmer and sparkle of sunlight mark the beginning of a new day. At the end of the day, the sun sets in the western sky, and when night returns, the stars can be seen in the dark sky overhead.

Without the sun, there would be no life on Earth as we know it. There would be no spiders spinning their silken webs and no elephants lumbering their enormous bodies across vast stretches of land. The large land area on Earth would be empty.

All living plants and animals need the sun to survive. Without it they would die. Plants use sunlight to make food. While doing this, they give off oxygen. Animals and people eat plants and breathe in oxygen. They breathe out carbon dioxide. Plants use carbon dioxide, energy from sunlight, and water to make more food.

GO ON →

Not only do people, animals, and plants depend on the sun, but Earth's climate and temperature do, too. The temperature of a place on Earth depends on the position of the sun. It is cooler in the morning when the sun is lower in the sky. As the sun rises, it becomes hotter, and then it cools down as the sun sets. Places near the equator are hot because the sun shines almost directly overhead at noon. The equator is an imaginary line that circles the middle of Earth. Places near the North Pole and South Pole are cold because the sun does not rise high in the sky in those places.

Every 365 days, Earth makes a trip around the sun. For six months, the northern half of Earth leans toward the sun, causing spring and summer in that part of the world. The southern half of Earth has fall and winter during this time. During the other six months, the northern half of Earth leans away from the sun, causing fall and winter in that part of the world. This is also when the southern half has spring and summer.

As you can see, the sun controls many things on Earth. It controls the food that we eat and the air that we breathe. Without the sun, nothing would survive.

GO ON →

Now answer Numbers 6 through 10. Base your answers on "A Giant Star."

6 This question has two parts. First, answer part A. Then, answer part B.

Part A: Read the sentences from the article.

The sun rises in the eastern sky each morning, swallowing up the <u>eerie</u> darkness from the night before. Some people find the darkness creepy.

What does the word <u>eerie</u> mean?

(A) comforting

(B) exciting

(C) quiet

(D) spooky

Part B: Which word from the sentences **best** helps the reader understand what <u>eerie</u> means?

(A) sun

(B) eastern

(C) swallowing

(D) creepy

GO ON →

7 This question has two parts. First, answer part A. Then, answer part B.

Part A: Which sentence summarizes a point the author makes about the sun?

Ⓐ The sun is a mystery to us.

Ⓑ The sun is always changing.

Ⓒ The sun is necessary for life.

Ⓓ The sun is bigger than we think.

Part B: Which detail from the article **best** supports your answer in part A?

Ⓐ The sun is a giant star.

Ⓑ Plants and animals need the sun to live.

Ⓒ The sun rises in the eastern sky each morning.

Ⓓ Every 365 days, Earth makes a trip around the sun.

8 Read the sentences from the article.

All living plants and animals need the sun to survive. Without it they would die. Plants use sunlight to make food.

What does the word survive mean?

Ⓐ fade

Ⓑ live

Ⓒ fall apart

Ⓓ start again

GO ON →

9 Complete the chart below to show causes and effects. Choose the correct causes and effects from the list below and write them in the chart. Not all causes and effects will be used.

Cause	Effect/Cause	Effect
	→	→

Causes and Effects:
Plants use carbon dioxide to help make food.
Animals and people eat plants.
Plants continue to live and grow.
Animals and people breathe out carbon dioxide.

10 What happens as a result of Earth traveling around the sun? Pick **two** choices.

Ⓐ Places on Earth have different seasons.

Ⓑ Places near Earth's Poles always have winter.

Ⓒ Places near Earth's equator have a mild climate.

Ⓓ Parts of Earth lean toward or away from the sun.

Ⓔ Places near Earth's equator are very cold at night.

Ⓕ Parts of Earth are sunny and other parts are rainy.

Name: _____ Date: _____

Now answer Number 11. Base your answer on "Stories in the Sky" and "A Giant Star."

11 How did stars affect life on Earth in the past? How do they affect life on Earth today? Support your answer with details from both articles.

_____

_____

_____

_____

_____

_____

_____

_____

_____

_____

_____

_____

_____

Answer Key

Name: _____

Question	Correct Answer	Content Focus	CCSS	Complexity
1A	B	Text Structure: Cause and Effect	RI.4.5	DOK 2
1B	A	Text Structure: Cause and Effect/ Text Evidence	RI.4.5/ RI.4.1	DOK 2
2	C	Context Clues: Paragraph Clues	L.4.4a	DOK 2
3A	C	Text Structure: Cause and Effect	RI.4.5	DOK 2
3B	D	Text Structure: Cause and Effect/ Text Evidence	RI.4.5/ RI.4.1	DOK 2
4	C, E	Text Structure: Cause and Effect	RI.4.5	DOK 2
5	see below	Context Clues: Paragraph Clues	L.4.4a	DOK 2
6A	D	Context Clues: Paragraph Clues	L.4.4a	DOK 2
6B	D	Context Clues: Paragraph Clues/ Text Evidence	L.4.4a/ RI.4.1	DOK 2
7A	C	Author's Point of View	RI.4.8	DOK 3
7B	B	Author's Point of View/ Text Evidence	RI.4.8/ RI.4.1	DOK 3
8	B	Context Clues: Paragraph Clues	L.4.4a	DOK 2
9	see below	Text Structure: Cause and Effect	RI.4.5	DOK 2
10	A, D	Text Structure: Cause and Effect	RI.4.5	DOK 2
11	see below	Writing About Text	W.4.9b	DOK 4

Comprehension 1A, 1B, 3A, 3B, 4, 7A, 7B, 9, 10	/12	%
Vocabulary 2, 5, 6A, 6B, 8	/8	%
Total Weekly Assessment Score	/20	%

5 Students should underline the following sentences:
- Orion thinks that he is the best hunter in the world.
- He brags that he can kill any animal.

9 Students should complete the chart with the following details:
- Cause—Animals and people breathe out carbon dioxide.
- Effect/Cause—Plants use carbon dioxide to help make food.
- Effect—Plants continue to live and grow.

11 To receive full credit for the response, the following information should be included: People in the past used the stars to determine direction or to know when to plant crops. The sun determines the temperature and climate on Earth. The sun controls the air we breathe and the food we eat. Without the sun, there would be no life on Earth.

Read the passage "A Friendly Contest" before answering Numbers 1 through 5.

A Friendly Contest

A poetry contest sounded interesting, so Jason read the rest of the article in the local newspaper. The contest was for ages 8–15, and the deadline was two weeks away.

Jason was too bashful to try out for the fourth-grade talent show, but he was pretty sure he had a talent for writing poetry. No one besides his parents had ever read his poems. His mom and dad said he was a remarkable poet, but he guessed they were a little biased. In fact, his parents showed favoritism toward everything he did. This contest might be a good way to see if anyone else liked his poems, and maybe he could enter a poem under a fake name.

Jason thought he had a good start on a poem that might win this contest:

> Are you a friend in word?
> Or are you a friend in deed?
> Sometimes the line is blurred.
> Sometimes our acts mislead.

Jason worked on his poem for the next week trying to explain a real friend. He told his parents about the contest, but decided not to mention it to anyone else. He still couldn't decide whether to put his real name on his poem. What if no one liked it? What an embarrassment that would be!

Finally, Jason finished the last part of his poem.

> In sadness or laughter,
> A friend knows what to say,
> In hard times or awfter,
> Friends help you find your way.

GO ON →

Before Jason emailed his poem to the newspaper, he changed the name to his own and then crossed his fingers.

At last, it was Thursday, delivery day for the weekly newspaper, and after school, Jason did not even wait to walk home with Kyle. He ran all the way to his house and burst through the front door. His mom was waiting for him, smiling and holding the newspaper with his poem printed on the front page! He had won the contest!

Crushing him in a hug, she said, "We are so proud of you, Jason!"

The phone rang, so Jason grabbed it. "I thought I was your best friend!" Kyle grumbled. "Why didn't you tell me you entered that contest? Do you have other poems? I want to read them!"

Suddenly Jason was regretful, telling himself that he should have trusted Kyle to read his poems.

Jason told Kyle, "I'll bring my poems over right now because I do want to know what you think, and maybe you could even give me some ideas for more poems!"

The next day at school, everyone congratulated Jason on winning the contest. When a girl named Ashley told him she had memorized the last part, he blushed. That was the first time she had ever talked to him!

A week later, a literary magazine called and asked to print Jason's poem. He was pleased, for sure. Still, he was even happier when kids at school asked if they could read more of his poems. That was true success!

GO ON →

Now answer Numbers 1 through 5. Base your answers on "A Friendly Contest."

1 This question has two parts. First, answer part A. Then, answer part B.

Part A: Which sentence **best** states the theme of the passage?

Ⓐ Learn from your mistakes.

Ⓑ Not everyone can be trusted.

Ⓒ If you don't try, you won't succeed.

Ⓓ Friends come in all shapes and sizes.

Part B: Which detail from the passage **best** supports the theme?

Ⓐ "The contest was for ages 8–15, and the deadline was two weeks away."

Ⓑ "This contest might be a good way to see if anyone else liked his poems, . . ."

Ⓒ "Before Jason emailed his poem to the newspaper, he changed the name to his own . . ."

Ⓓ "When a girl named Ashley told him she had memorized the last part, he blushed."

2 Read the sentences from the passage.

What if no one liked it? What an embarrassment that would be!

What does the use of the word embarrassment suggest about Jason?

Ⓐ He is trying to not upset his parents.

Ⓑ He is sure no one will like his poem.

Ⓒ He will feel ashamed if no one likes his poem.

Ⓓ He thinks that his poem might upset someone.

GO ON →

3 Based on the passage, what does Jason consider to be true success? Pick **two** choices.

Ⓐ winning a poetry contest

Ⓑ having a poem published

Ⓒ sharing your poems with others

Ⓓ having your friends congratulate you

Ⓔ having your friends enjoy your poems

Ⓕ making new friends because of your poems

4 This question has two parts. First, answer part A. Then, answer part B.

Part A: Read the sentence from the passage.

Suddenly Jason was <u>regretful</u>, telling himself that he should have trusted Kyle to read his poems.

What does the word <u>regretful</u> mean?

Ⓐ feeling sorry

Ⓑ thinking hard

Ⓒ not understanding

Ⓓ changing his mind

Part B: Which word has a similar connotation to that of <u>regretful</u>?

Ⓐ proud

Ⓑ puzzled

Ⓒ shocked

Ⓓ upset

GO ON →

5 Circle **three** sentences below that support the theme of the passage.

Sentences that Support the Theme of "A Friendly Contest"
"A poetry contest sounded interesting, so Jason read the rest of the article in the local newspaper."
"In fact, his parents showed favoritism toward everything he did."
"He still couldn't decide whether to put his real name on his poem."
"Jason told Kyle, 'I'll bring my poems over right now because I do want to know what you think, and maybe you could even give me some ideas for more poems!'"
"That was the first time she had ever talked to him!"
"Still, he was even happier when kids at school asked if they could read more of his poems."

GO ON →

Read the passage "The Rockin' Rhymer" before answering Numbers 6 through 10.

The Rockin' Rhymer

I am in my usual disguise as an ordinary fourth-grade girl, and my friends have no idea that I am actually the Rockin' Rhymer. I am like the superhero of poetry, but without a cape. For example, when I grabbed my backpack out of my locker yesterday, this poem sprang to my mind.

> My backpack is full of books.
> It's heavier than it looks.

My poems usually don't have much use, until today. This morning as I walk to school with my friend, Celia, she is moving slowly and calling, "Daisy, Daisy! Come here, kitty!"

"Daisy's probably just investigating the neighborhood," I tell Celia. "No telling what she'll find!" As I speak, the Rockin' Rhymer is wondering what rhymes with *neighborhood.*
Understood? That is an intriguing pair of words!

As we near the school, more friends join us, all calling for Daisy, and Celia is fighting back tears. "Maybe Daisy's lost forever," she whispers, and scanning the busy street, she adds fearfully, "Look at all those cars and trucks."

I give her a hug and we head inside to our lockers, but later, as I sit in class, I think about how miserable Celia is and I write down a poem that has been floating around in my head.

GO ON →

Your kitten named Daisy
Is not really crazy.
She'll come home when school's out.
Of that there's no doubt!

On the way to history class, I tell Celia I forgot something in my locker. I rush back and stick the poem in Celia's locker before sprinting to get to history on time.

At lunchtime, Celia meets me in the cafeteria, looking more puzzled than worried. "Someone left me a poem about Daisy," she tells me. "Who would do that?"

Smiling, I say, "It was probably one of the kids who helped us look for her this morning."

"Hmmm....," she mumbles, frowning. It's not easy to deceive Celia, who can spot a lie a mile away, and she gives me another doubtful look before going up to the lunch counter to buy some milk. Another poem comes to my mind, and I hurriedly scribble it on a slip of paper.

Don't decide that all is lost!
That's a line we haven't crossed!

Celia gets back before I can conceal my latest poem in her lunch bag, so I quickly drop it on the floor. "What's this?" she asks, picking up the scrap of paper.

I shrug innocently and tell her, "Keisha just walked by, so maybe she dropped it."

Shaking her head, Celia reads my poem. Then she smiles and says, "I don't know who is writing these poems, but I like them." Celia glances up at the clock. "School will be out soon, and I think Daisy will be waiting for me. She'll probably be hungry and cold."

We run home from school, and there is Daisy, pacing impatiently back and forth in front of Celia's door. "Oh, Daisy!" Celia cries joyfully as she reaches for her cat. I pet Daisy too, glad that my poems finally have a good use!

GO ON →

Name: _____ Date: _____

Now answer Numbers 6 through 10. Base your answers on "The Rockin' Rhymer."

6 What does the narrator's point of view help to explain in the passage? Pick **two** choices.

Ⓐ where Daisy went for the day

Ⓑ who Celia thinks is writing the poems

Ⓒ how important the poems are to Celia

Ⓓ why the narrator and Celia are friends

Ⓔ why the narrator writes poems for Celia

Ⓕ how much the narrator enjoys writing poems

7 This question has two parts. First, answer part A. Then, answer part B.

Part A: Which sentence **best** states the theme of the passage?

Ⓐ Helping others makes you feel good.

Ⓑ People love to read good poems.

Ⓒ Everyone has a hidden talent.

Ⓓ Don't let your pets run loose.

Part B: Which evidence from the passage **best** supports the theme?

Ⓐ "I am in my usual disguise as an ordinary fourth-grade girl, and my friends have no idea that I am actually the Rockin' Rhymer."

Ⓑ "I rush back and stick the poem in Celia's locker before sprinting to get to history on time."

Ⓒ "At lunchtime, Celia meets me in the cafeteria, looking more puzzled than worried."

Ⓓ "I pet Daisy too, glad that my poems finally have a good use!"

GO ON →

8 Read the sentence from the passage.

It's not easy to deceive Celia, who can spot a lie a mile away, and she gives me another doubtful look before going up to the lunch counter to buy some milk.

Which word has a connotation similar to that of doubtful in the sentence?

(A) accusing

(B) angry

(C) uncertain

(D) worried

9 Read the sentence from the passage.

Celia gets back before I can conceal my latest poem in her lunch bag, so I quickly drop it on the floor.

What does the use of the word conceal suggest about the narrator?

(A) She drops the poem accidentally.

(B) She does not think the poem is good.

(C) She does not want Celia to know she wrote the poem.

(D) She wants someone other than Celia to find the poem.

GO ON →

Name: _____ Date: _____

10 Write **two** words from the box to complete the sentence about the
theme of the passage.

Sentence: You can tell the narrator thinks _____ is using

your poetry to _____ others.

```
Words:

help

lunch

success

teach

tease

work
```

Name: _____ Date: _____

Now answer Number 11. Base your answer on "A Friendly Contest" and "The Rockin' Rhymer."

11 How are Jason's feelings toward poetry in "A Friendly Contest" similar to the narrator's feelings toward poetry in "The Rockin' Rhymer"? Support your answer with details from both passages.

_____

_____

_____

_____

_____

_____

_____

_____

_____

_____

_____

_____

_____

Answer Key

Name: _____

Question	Correct Answer	Content Focus	CCSS	Complexity
1A	C	Theme	RL.4.2	DOK 3
1B	B	Theme/Text Evidence	RL.4.2/ RL.4.1	DOK 3
2	C	Connotation and Denotation	L.5.5c	DOK 2
3	C, E	Theme	RL.4.2	DOK 3
4A	A	Connotation and Denotation	L.5.5c	DOK 2
4B	D	Connotation and Denotation	L.5.5c	DOK 2
5	see below	Theme	RL.4.2	DOK 3
6	E, F	Point of View	RL.4.6	DOK 3
7A	A	Theme	RL.4.2	DOK 3
7B	D	Theme/Text Evidence	RL.4.2/ RL.4.1	DOK 3
8	C	Connotation and Denotation	L.5.5c	DOK 2
9	C	Connotation and Denotation	L.5.5c	DOK 2
10	see below	Theme	RL.4.2	DOK 3
11	see below	Writing About Text	W.4.9a	DOK 4

Comprehension 1A, 1B, 3, 5, 6, 7A, 7B, 10	/12	%
Vocabulary 2, 4A, 4B, 8, 9	/8	%
Total Weekly Assessment Score	/20	%

5 Students should circle the following sentences:
- "He still couldn't decide whether to put his real name on his poem."
- "Jason told Kyle, 'I'll bring my poems over right now because I do want to know what you think, and maybe you could even give me some ideas for more poems!'"
- "Still, he was even happier when kids at school asked if they could read more of his poems."

10 Students should complete the sentence as follows:
- You can tell the narrator thinks success is using your poetry to help others.

11 To receive full credit for the response, the following information should be included: Both Jason and the narrator of "The Rockin' Rhymer" enjoy writing poetry. They feel they are successful when others read their poems and like them or are helped by them.

Read the passage "A Hug in a Box" before answering Numbers 1 through 5.

A Hug in a Box

The Herrera family was having a discussion. Cousin Flora was a soldier serving overseas, and the family wanted to let her know they were thinking of her. They already send a weekly email that updated Flora on family news, but they wanted to do more.

Dorinda asked if Flora could receive regular mail. "I love to get cards and packages in the mail, and I bet Flora would love to get mail, too!" Dorinda said excitedly.

Mrs. Herrera answered that they could mail things to Flora. "In fact, we could put together a box of things that would remind Flora of home. Boxes like that are called care packages," Mrs. Herrera added.

"What kinds of things could we put in the box?" asked Matias. "We should put in things that she can't get over there. We want to fill the box with great things so she knows that we care."

Mr. Herrera suggested they look online for ideas, and they found a Web site that listed items often included in care packages for soldiers.

"When Flora gets this package, she will be as happy as a lark!" Dorinda exclaimed. "I can't wait to buy things to send."

Matias was quiet for a minute, and then he said, "I think that other soldiers would enjoy care packages, too. Could we send packages to lots of soldiers?"

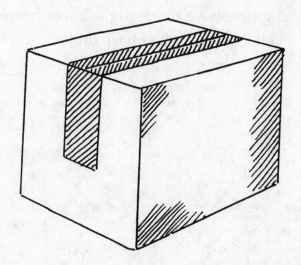

GO ON →

Mrs. Herrera told Matias that she liked the idea, but sending many care packages would be expensive. Matias wilted in defeat, but after a few minutes he became excited again. He suggested they tell other families in the neighborhood about their idea. Maybe other families would be able to send a care package to a soldier, and then lots of soldiers would know people care about them.

Mr. Herrera hugged his son and praised his idea. Just then Dorinda had a concern that struck like a bolt of lightning. How would they get the names and addresses of other soldiers? They decided to ask Flora for the names of some other soldiers serving with her.

The family spent the rest of the afternoon working on the plan. Mr. Herrera and Dorinda made fliers explaining their project. They printed the fliers and handed them to their neighbors. Mrs. Herrera and Matias made a list of the items they wanted to put in Flora's care package, and then they emailed her to ask for the names of the soldiers serving with her. The next day, the family went shopping for items, and when they got home, they put Flora's package together and mailed it.

A few weeks went by. One afternoon, Mr. Herrera opened an email from Flora that said she had received the care package. "Thanks so much for the hug in a box," wrote Flora. "I cannot thank you enough for your affection. These reminders of home really brightened my day, and some of my fellow soldiers have received packages from your kind neighbors, as well. Thank you for all that you have done!"

GO ON →

Now answer Numbers 1 through 5. Base your answers on "A Hug in a Box."

1 This question has two parts. First, answer part A. Then, answer part B.

Part A: Which sentence describes a **main** lesson in the passage?

(A) The Herrera family wants to do more for cousin Flora.

(B) The Herrera family needs to send an email once a week.

(C) The Herrera family needs to find information on the Internet.

(D) The Herrera family wants to update cousin Flora on family news.

Part B: Which detail from the passage **best** supports your answer in part A?

(A) "The Herrera family was having a discussion."

(B) ". . . the family wanted to let her know they were thinking of her."

(C) "They already send a weekly email that updated Flora on family news, . . ."

(D) "Dorinda asked if Flora could receive regular mail."

GO ON →

2 This question has two parts. First, answer part A. Then, answer part B.

Part A: Read the sentence from the passage.

Matias <u>wilted in defeat</u>, but after a few minutes he became excited again.

What does the use of the phrase "wilted in defeat" suggest about Matias?

(A) He feels happy.

(B) He is disappointed.

(C) He looks like a flower.

(D) He wants to be a soldier.

Part B: Which detail helps to show the meaning of "wilted in defeat"?

(A) Matias has an idea to send care packages to other soldiers.

(B) Mrs. Herrera tells Matias she likes his idea.

(C) Mrs. Herrera explains that it is expensive to send care packages.

(D) Matias thinks they should tell other families about his idea.

3 Read the sentence from the passage.

Just then Dorinda had a concern that struck <u>like a bolt of lightning</u>.

What does the simile "like a bolt of lightning" suggest about Dorinda's concern?

(A) It is sudden.

(B) It is dangerous.

(C) It causes confusion.

(D) It takes a long time to form.

GO ON →

4 Draw a line to match each problem from the passage on the left with its solution on the right.

Problem

Mr. Herrera wonders what items go in a care package.	
It is too expensive to send care packages to a lot of soldiers.	
The family wants to do more to show Flora they are thinking of her.	
Flora is overseas and does not know what is happening at home.	

Solution

The family asks neighbors to send care packages.
The family sends their cousin a care package.
The family sends Flora an email every week.
The family looks up information on a Web site.

5 How does the Herrera family **most likely** feel at the end of the passage? Pick **two** choices.

(A) excited

(B) grateful

(C) nervous

(D) proud

(E) tired

(F) unsure

GO ON →

Read the passage "A Neighbor's Helping Hand" before answering Numbers 6 through 10.

A Neighbor's Helping Hand

A strong wind blew as I trudged down the sidewalk to Mrs. Goodman's house. She had just had knee surgery, and Mom told her that I would do her yard work until she was able to again. I had been going to her house every Saturday for a month, but I didn't mind because Mrs. Goodman was very kind.

The wind blew as cold as ice across my face as I rang Mrs. Goodman's doorbell, and after what seemed like forever, the door finally opened. "Hi, Rodney," Mrs. Goodman said. "Sorry it took me so long to answer the door, but I am a snail with this knee brace! Today, I need you to clean out my flowerbeds and rake the yard. Do you have any questions?"

I paused before answering because I was unsure of how to do either task. I didn't know how to clean out a flowerbed, and the last time I raked leaves my dad helped me. Mrs. Goodman was kind and patient, and I knew I could ask my questions.

"Mrs. Goodman, could you tell me how to clean out a flowerbed? I know how to rake leaves, but I'm not sure how to do it by myself." I blushed and said, "I'm sorry I have so many questions!"

Mrs. Goodman smiled warmly as she said, "Rodney, you never have to apologize for asking questions." She explained how to complete each task, and soon I was ready to get started.

GO ON →

First I cleaned out the flowerbeds, and then I started raking the leaves as the wind blew and the leaves twirled around the yard. While I worked, I thought about a problem I was having at school. I did not understand my math homework and we were having a test soon. I remembered my mom saying that Mrs. Goodman was a retired teacher, so I wondered if she might help me with my math. Even though she was kind when answering my yard work questions, I was nervous to ask her for math help.

A little while later, Mrs. Goodman opened the door and called, "Would you like to come inside and warm up?"

Inside, she handed me a mug of steamy hot chocolate. She sighed and said, "You have done a great job these past few weeks, Rodney. It was hard for me to admit that I needed help with my yard work. Have you ever had a hard time asking for help?"

Now I knew that I didn't have to keep my math troubles bottled up inside. "I sure have, Mrs. Goodman," I answered, "and I wanted to ask you a question. Is it true that you used to be a teacher?"

"Yes, Rodney," Mrs. Goodman replied. "I taught high school math for many years."

I could not believe my ears! She was the perfect person to help me with my math homework! I explained my problem and asked if she would help me. She replied, "You have done so much to help me, so of course I would be happy to help you!" I knew that I would help Mrs. Goodman again whenever she needed me.

GO ON →

Now answer Numbers 6 through 10. Base your answers on "A Neighbor's Helping Hand."

6 This question has two parts. First, answer part A. Then, answer part B.

Part A: Which sentence **best** describes why Mrs. Goodman needs help with her yard work?

(A) She is not home to rake her yard.

(B) She does not like to do yard work.

(C) She does not know how to rake her yard.

(D) She is not able to do yard work right now.

Part B: Which sentence from the passage **best** supports your answer in part A?

(A) "She had just had knee surgery, and Mom told her that I would do her yard work until she was able to again."

(B) "I had been going to her house every Saturday for a month, but I didn't mind because Mrs. Goodman was very kind."

(C) "She explained how to complete each task, and soon I was ready to get started."

(D) "I knew that I would help Mrs. Goodman again whenever she needed me."

7 Read the sentence from the passage.

The wind blew as cold as ice across my face as I rang Mrs. Goodman's doorbell, and after what seemed like forever, the door finally opened.

What does the simile "as cold as ice" mean?

(A) cool

(B) dry

(C) freezing

(D) moist

GO ON →

Weekly Assessment • Unit 5, Week 1

8 This question has two parts. First, answer part A. Then, answer part B.

Part A: Read the sentence from the passage.

"Sorry it took me so long to answer the door, but I am a snail with this knee brace!"

What does the metaphor "I am a snail" suggest about Mrs. Goodman?

(A) She feels very weak.

(B) She is often stubborn.

(C) She moves very slowly.

(D) She wiggles around a lot.

Part B: Which detail from the passage **best** supports your answer in part A?

(A) Mrs. Goodman is happy to see Rodney.

(B) Mrs. Goodman used to be a math teacher.

(C) Mrs. Goodman has tasks for Rodney to do.

(D) Mrs. Goodman apologizes for taking so long.

GO ON →

9 Read the paragraphs from the passage. Underline **two** sentences that state the problem Rodney has after Mrs. Goodman tells him what to do.

". . . Today, I need you to clean out my flowerbeds and rake the yard. Do you have any questions?"

I paused before answering because I was unsure of how to do either task. I didn't know how to clean out a flowerbed, and the last time I raked leaves my dad helped me. Mrs. Goodman was kind and patient, and I knew I could ask my questions.

10 Which sentences **best** explain why Rodney is happy that Mrs. Goodman used to be a math teacher? Pick **two** choices.

(A) Math is Rodney's favorite subject.

(B) Mrs. Goodman will know how to help Rodney.

(C) Rodney does not understand his math homework.

(D) Rodney's school is looking for a new math teacher.

(E) Mrs. Goodman will not be interested in the yard work.

(F) Rodney thinks that Mrs. Goodman will be his math teacher.

Name: _____ Date: _____

Now answer Number 11. Base your answer on "A Hug in a Box" and "A Neighbor's Helping Hand."

11 What problems do the Herrera family, Mrs. Goodman, and Rodney face in the passages? Support your answer with details from both passages.

_____

_____

_____

_____

_____

_____

_____

_____

_____

_____

_____

_____

_____

Answer Key

Question	Correct Answer	Content Focus	CCSS	Complexity
1A	A	Character, Setting, Plot: Problem and Solution	RL.4.3	DOK 2
1B	B	Character, Setting, Plot: Problem and Solution/Text Evidence	RL.4.3/ RL.4.1	DOK 2
2A	B	Figurative Language: Metaphors	L.4.5a	DOK 2
2B	C	Figurative Language: Metaphors/ Text Evidence	L.4.5a/ RL.4.1	DOK 2
3	A	Figurative Language: Similes	L.4.5a	DOK 2
4	see below	Character, Setting, Plot: Problem and Solution	RL.4.3	DOK 1
5	A, D	Point of View	RL.4.6	DOK 2
6A	D	Character, Setting, Plot: Problem and Solution	RL.4.3	DOK 1
6B	A	Character, Setting, Plot: Problem and Solution/Text Evidence	RL.4.3/ RL.4.1	DOK 1
7	C	Figurative Language: Similes	L.4.5a	DOK 2
8A	C	Figurative Language: Metaphors	L.4.5a	DOK 2
8B	D	Figurative Language: Metaphors/ Text Evidence	L.4.5a/ RL.4.1	DOK 2
9	see below	Character, Setting, Plot: Problem and Solution	RL.4.3	DOK 1
10	B, C	Character, Setting, Plot: Problem and Solution	RL.4.3	DOK 1
11	see below	Writing About Text	W.4.9a	DOK 4

Comprehension 1A, 1B, 4, 5, 6A, 6B, 9, 10	/12	%
Vocabulary 2A, 2B, 3, 7, 8A, 8B	/8	%
Total Weekly Assessment Score	/20	%

4 Students should match the following problems and solutions:
- Mr. Herrera wonders what items go in a care package.—The family looks up information on a Web site.
- It is too expensive to send care packages to a lot soldiers.—The family asks neighbors to send care packages.
- The family wants to do more to show Flora they are thinking of her.—The family sends their cousin a care package.
- Flora is overseas and does not know what is happening at home.—The family sends Flora an email every week.

9 Students should underline the following sentences in the paragraphs:
- I paused before answering because I was unsure of how to do either task.
- I didn't know how to clean out a flowerbed, and the last time I raked leaves my dad helped me.

11 To receive full credit for the response, the following information should be included:
The Herrera family wants to find a way to send care packages to soldiers overseas.
Mrs. Goodman needs help with her yard work after having surgery, and Rodney needs help with math homework that he does not understand.

Read the passage "Land of Their Own" before answering Numbers 1 through 5.

Land of Their Own

The Carpenter family lived in a small house near a large farm in Tennessee. The Carpenters worked for the family who owned the farm. Mr. Carpenter worked in the fields and Mrs. Carpenter worked in the house, cooking and cleaning for the family. Althea watched over her two younger brothers while their parents worked. She knew her parents were working hard to save enough money to move to Kansas. The people of Kansas fought to keep slavery out of its borders, and Althea's parents wanted to live in a place that had never known slavery. They wanted better lives for their children.

Mr. and Mrs. Carpenter were born into slavery. All enslaved workers were freed during the Civil War. After the war, the Carpenters married and moved into their own little house. They had been enslaved workers, but now they dreamed of having their own farm. They knew that it would take lots of hard work to make this dream come true, and they saved every penny they could.

Late at night, Althea sat as quiet as a mouse while her parents talked about moving. She had heard of the open land west of the Mississippi River. The government was giving this land to anyone who was twenty-one years old and who had never fought against the United States government. In order to keep this land, the person had to live on the land for five years and improve it. This meant that houses and barns had to be built and the land had to be farmed. After five years, the person could apply for the land deed. This paper gave the land to the person who improved it.

GO ON →

One night, Mr. and Mrs. Carpenter brought their children together. The parents had huge smiles on their faces. They told the children that they had finally saved enough money to move to Kansas. The family hugged, cheered, and cried as they began planning the trip west.

A few weeks later, Althea said goodbye to her friends. She had to refrain from crying, for she knew she might never see her friends again. She hugged each one and told them that she would write letters. Althea's friend, Dorothy, gave her a doll made from scraps of fabric. Dorothy was worried Althea would forget their friendship. Althea held the doll tightly as she and her family set off in the jerky wagon.

The trip to Kansas was long and difficult. The family did their best to forge on and travel as far as they could each day in order to reach Kansas before winter. Sometimes, they had to stop for a few days because of bad weather.

After months of traveling, the family finally reached their new home, Kansas. A big job lay ahead of them. Many trees had to be cut down so a house could be built before winter, and Althea and her brothers spent many days helping their father hack down the trees and cut them into boards. Finally a small house was built and at last, the Carpenter family had land of their own.

GO ON →

Now answer Numbers 1 through 5. Base your answers on "Land of Their Own."

1 This question has two parts. First, answer part A. Then, answer part B.

Part A: Which sentence **best** explains why the Carpenters want to live in Kansas?

Ⓐ They do not want to be enslaved workers again.

Ⓑ They want to live where there was never slavery.

Ⓒ They hear the land is better in Kansas than in Tennessee.

Ⓓ They do not want to meet any of the enslaved workers they once knew.

Part B: Which sentence from the passage **best** supports your answer in part A?

Ⓐ "The Carpenter family lived in a small house near a large farm in Tennessee."

Ⓑ "The Carpenters worked for the family who owned the farm."

Ⓒ "She knew her parents were working hard to save enough money to move to Kansas."

Ⓓ "The people of Kansas fought to keep slavery out of its borders, and Althea's parents wanted to live in a place that had never known slavery."

2 Read the sentence from the passage.

She had to <u>refrain</u> from crying, for she knew she might never see her friends again.

What does the word <u>refrain</u> mean in the sentence?

Ⓐ repeat

Ⓑ a saying

Ⓒ hold back

Ⓓ a song part

GO ON →

3 What causes the Carpenters to get a farm?

(A) They want something of their own.

(B) They want to see what Kansas looks like.

(C) They want to help others who are enslaved.

(D) They save enough money to move to Kansas.

(E) They want to make a lot of money as farmers.

(F) They become bored with working the same land.

4 Complete the chart below to show causes and effects. Choose the correct sentences from the list below and write them in the chart. Not all sentences will be used.

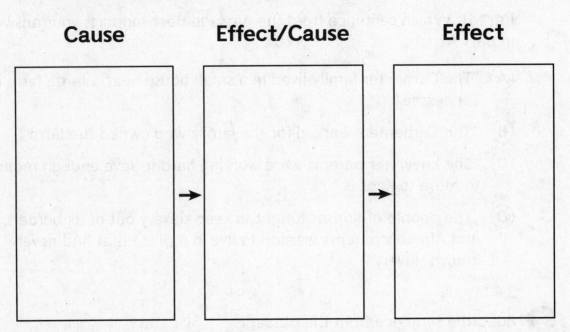

Cause	Effect/Cause	Effect
	→	→

Causes and Effects:
Dorothy gives Althea a doll.
Althea's family reaches their new home.
Althea's family decides to move to Kansas.
Dorothy worries Althea will forget her.

GO ON →

5 This question has two parts. First, answer part A. Then, answer part B.

Part A: Read the sentence from the passage.

Many trees had to be cut down so a house could be built before winter, and Althea and her brothers spent many days helping their father hack down the trees and cut them into boards.

What does the word hack mean in the sentence?

Ⓐ manage

Ⓑ cough dryly

Ⓒ chop roughly

Ⓓ carry for money

Part A: Which word from the sentence **best** shows what hack means?

Ⓐ cut

Ⓑ house

Ⓒ winter

Ⓓ helping

GO ON →

Read the passage "A Golden Moment" before answering Numbers 6 through 10.

A Golden Moment

Big Bob Benton was well known among the prospectors who had all moved west to look for gold. They said that where Big Bob went, gold followed. When he heard that, Bob got annoyed. Any real prospector knew gold did not follow anyone. You had to hunt for it, and it took a lot of hard work to find it, as well as a lot of luck.

Sure, he had struck it rich three times, but he did not give up at the first disappointment like a lot of other prospectors. Bob worked tirelessly on all of his gold claims. Other prospectors would start out with big plans to strike it rich, and then quit when they did not find gold after a few days. Bob was always prepared to work hard when he started a claim.

GO ON →

Now he was going out a fourth time, and there were murmurings among the prospectors about wanting to follow him. People wanted to set up diggings next to Bob's new claim. Bob was bound for the mountain slope, but he decided to take an exhausting route to get to his destination. His plan was to lose and frustrate those who were following him. Bob alternated his direction of travel this way and that way for hours.

As he started to cross a stream a twig snapped behind some elder trees. Just then, Jokin' Joe, the one prospector Bob admired and respected, appeared from behind the trees. "Howdy," Joe greeted Bob with an outstretched hand. "Find gold yet?"

"Nope," Bob answered, wondering what Joe was doing there.

"Too bad. Hoped you'd lead me right to it," bluffed Joe.

"I thought you were a better man than that," Bob replied.

"Just joking," Joe assured Bob. "That was a reference to the talk going around town. You know what people are saying about following you, but I *am* a better man than that. I'm content to try my luck on the other side of the mountain, so I'll leave this side to you. Happy hunting!"

Big Bob remained still until Jokin' Joe had vanished around a curve up the mountain. When he was sure he was alone again, he got back on his horse and was about to continue when something caught his eye. Next to the stream, something as bright as the morning sunrise sparkled on the bank. He got off his horse, scooped up what appeared to be a pebble, and found himself holding a shiny gold nugget.

GO ON →

Now answer Numbers 6 through 10. Base your answers on "A Golden Moment."

6 This question has two parts. First, answer part A. Then, answer part B.

Part A: Which sentence **best** describes the message about human nature that is told in the passage?

(A) Most people are not completely truthful.

(A) Most people naturally like to be left alone.

(C) No one likes it when others make fun of them.

(D) No one wants others to take advantage of them.

Part B: Which sentence from the passage **best** supports your answer in part A?

(A) "Big Bob Benton was well known among the prospectors who had all moved west to look for gold."

(B) "His plan was to lose and frustrate those who were following him."

(C) "As he started to cross a stream a twig snapped behind some elder trees."

(D) "Big Bob remained still until Jokin' Joe had vanished around a curve up the mountain."

7 Which details from the passage support the idea that Big Bob is annoyed when the other prospectors say that gold follows him? Pick **two** choices.

(A) He has found gold three times already.

(B) He finds gold shortly after Joe leaves him.

(C) He does not like it when Joe jokes with him.

(D) He goes out to look for gold for the fourth time.

(E) He tries to lose the people who are following him.

(F) He respects Joe and thinks of him as a good person.

8 This question has two parts. First, answer part A. Then, answer part B.

Part A: Read the sentence from the passage.

Bob was <u>bound</u> for the mountain slope, but he decided to take an exhausting route to get to his destination.

What does the word <u>bound</u> mean in the sentence?

Ⓐ required

Ⓑ tied up to

Ⓒ held tightly

Ⓓ determined to go

Part B: Which word from the sentence **best** shows what <u>bound</u> means?

Ⓐ slope

Ⓑ decided

Ⓒ exhausting

Ⓓ destination

9 Read the sentence from the passage.

I'm <u>content</u> to try my luck on the other side of the mountain, so I'll leave this side to you.

What does the word <u>content</u> mean in the sentence?

Ⓐ relaxed

Ⓑ satisfied

Ⓒ information

Ⓓ overall meaning

GO ON →

10 Write **one** effect for each cause listed in the chart. Then write the number for **one** example of evidence from the passage that supports each effect. Choose from the lists in the box below.

Cause	Effect	Text Evidence
Bob sees something shiny.		
Bob gets upset with Jokin' Joe.		

Effect:

Bob discovers a gold nugget.

Joe meets Bob while on the trail.

Joe tells Bob that he is just joking.

Bob waits for Joe to go around the bend.

Text Evidence:

1 – "People wanted to set up diggings next to Bob's new claim."

2 – "Jokin' Joe, the one prospector Bob admired and respected, appeared from behind the trees."

3 – "You know what people are saying about following you, but I *am* a better man than that."

4 – "He got off his horse, scooped up what appeared to be a pebble, and found himself holding a shiny gold nugget."

Name: _____ Date: _____

Now answer Number 11. Base your answer on "Land of Their Own" and "A Golden Moment."

11 Both passages show examples of the effects of hard work and determination. How does hard work cause the Carpenters and Big Bob to reach their goals? Support your answer with details from both passages.

_____

_____

_____

_____

_____

_____

_____

_____

_____

_____

_____

_____

_____

_____

_____

Answer Key

Name: _____

Question	Correct Answer	Content Focus	CCSS	Complexity
1A	B	Character, Setting, Plot: Cause and Effect	RL.4.3	DOK 1
1B	D	Character, Setting, Plot: Cause and Effect/ Text Evidence	RL.4.3/ RL.4.1	DOK 1
2	C	Homographs	L.4.4a	DOK 2
3	A, D	Character, Setting, Plot: Cause and Effect	RL.4.3	DOK 2
4	see below	Character, Setting, Plot: Cause and Effect	RL.4.3	DOK 2
5A	C	Homographs	L.4.4a	DOK 2
5B	A	Homographs/Text Evidence	L.4.4a/ RL.4.1	DOK 2
6A	D	Theme	RL.4.2	DOK 3
6B	B	Theme/Text Evidence	RL.4.2/ RL.4.1	DOK 3
7	C, E	Character, Setting, Plot: Cause and Effect	RL.4.3	DOK 2
8A	D	Homographs	L.4.4a	DOK 2
8B	D	Homographs/Text Evidence	L.4.4a/ RL.4.1	DOK 2
9	B	Homographs	L.4.4a	DOK 2
10	see below	Character, Setting, Plot: Cause and Effect	RL.4.3	DOK 2
11	see below	Writing About Text	W.4.9a	DOK 4

Comprehension 1A, 1B, 3, 4, 6A, 6B, 7, 10		/12	%
Vocabulary 2, 5A, 5B, 8A, 8B, 9		/8	%
Total Weekly Assessment Score		/20	%

4 Students should choose the following causes and effects:
- Cause—Althea's family decides to move to Kansas.
- Effect/Cause —Dorothy worries Althea will forget her.
- Effect—Dorothy gives Althea a doll.

10 Students should complete the chart as follows:
- Cause—Bob sees something shiny; Effect—Bob discovers a gold nugget.; Text Evidence—4
- Cause—Bob gets upset with Jokin' Joe; Effect—Joe tells Bob that he is just joking.; Text Evidence—3

11 To receive full credit for the response, the following information should be included: The Carpenters work hard to save money to move to Kansas and to build a house for themselves. This allows them to get their own land. Big Bob works hard and tirelessly to find gold. This allows him to be successful in striking it rich.

Read the article "Staying Fresh" before answering Numbers 1 through 5.

Staying Fresh

For thousands of years, growing and preparing food took up a lot of time. People grew or hunted their own food, and then they struggled to find ways to keep it fresh. All food spoils or grows mold eventually, and the challenge is to slow or stop food from spoiling. This challenge led to inventions that are now used every day. Today, most people do not think much about food safety. Inventions such as refrigerators and freezers allow us to eat all types of food in any season.

One early food storage problem was keeping meat safe to eat. People hunted animals for meat, which needed to last a long time. The meat was preserved by drying it. It was cut into thin strips and hung to dry in sunlight or by a fire. Today, modern machines are used to dehydrate meat. Without water, the tiny organisms that cause food to spoil cannot survive and dried meat stays good for a long time.

A balanced diet includes fruits and vegetables along with meat. Another challenge is keeping fruits and vegetables safe to eat all year round. Fruits and vegetables grow in warm weather and spoil within a few days or weeks after they ripen. Canning keeps food safe for a long time. When canning, food is placed in a glass or metal container and the air is removed from the container. The container is sealed, heated, then cooled. If unopened, the canned food stays good for months, and sometimes years.

GO ON →

Some foods need to be kept cold to stay fresh. Dairy products spoil within a few hours if they are not kept cold. Cold storage has been used for many years. This is easy to do in winter, but the challenge is keeping food cold in warm weather. The first invention to solve this problem was the icebox. Blocks of ice were placed in box-like containers that held food. The ice kept the food cold, but people who lived in warm climates had a hard time getting ice. Inventors looked for other ways to cool air.

Eventually, the modern refrigerator was invented. Compressors cool the air in a refrigerator, and a thermostat keeps the inside of the refrigerator at a constant temperature. Refrigeration helped metropolitan areas grow. People no longer needed to live close to farms in order to get fresh food since food was moved to cities using refrigerated trucks and trains.

Canned food keeps for a long time, but nutrients can be lost and the flavor can change in the canning process. Another method for long term storage was needed. The solution to this problem was the freezer. Freezing has the least effect on the flavor and nutrients found in foods. Many foods can stay frozen for months at a time and still be safe to eat.

Food storage helps avoid food shortages. Floods, droughts, or other natural disasters can kill crops. Being able to store food keeps us from running out of food. The next time you get a bite to eat, think of the ways that your food was stored and kept safe before you dig in.

GO ON →

Name: _____ Date: _____

Now answer Numbers 1 through 5. Base your answers on "Staying Fresh."

1 This question has two parts. First, answer part A. Then, answer part B.

Part A: Read the paragraph from the article.

One early food storage problem was keeping meat safe to eat. People hunted animals for meat, which needed to last a long time. The meat was preserved by drying it. It was cut into thin strips and hung to dry in sunlight or by a fire. Today, modern machines are used to dehydrate meat. Without water, the tiny organisms that cause food to spoil cannot survive and dried meat stays good for a long time.

Which statement **best** explains how the author organized this paragraph?

(A) by describing a few solutions to food storage problems

(B) by explaining what caused people to hunt for animals

(C) by sequencing the steps for preserving meat

(D) by contrasting different places to store food

Part B: Which detail from the paragraph **best** supports your answer in part A?

(A) "One early food storage problem . . ."

(B) "People hunted animals for meat, . . ."

(C) ". . . which needed to last a long time."

(D) ". . . dried meat stays good for a long time."

GO ON →

2 Underline **two** sentences that **best** help the reader understand why canning is a good food storage solution.

A balanced diet includes fruits and vegetables along with meat. Another challenge is keeping fruits and vegetables safe to eat all year round. Fruits and vegetables grow in warm weather and spoil within a few days or weeks after they ripen. Canning keeps food safe for a long time. When canning, food is placed in a glass or metal container and the air is removed from the container. The container is sealed, heated, then cooled. If unopened, the canned food stays good for months, and sometimes years.

3 Read the sentence from the passage.

Compressors cool the air in a refrigerator, and a <u>thermostat</u> keeps the inside of the refrigerator at a constant temperature.

The word thermostat includes the Greek root *therme*. What is the **most likely** meaning of this root?

(A) heat

(B) speed

(C) time

(D) weight

4 Read the sentence from the passage.

Refrigeration helped <u>metropolitan</u> areas grow.

The word <u>metropolitan</u> includes a Greek root meaning "city." What does this suggest about a <u>metropolitan</u> area?

(A) It has dirt roads.

(B) It has open land.

(C) It has many farms.

(D) It has tall buildings.

5 Why does the author share problems and solutions to organize the article? Pick **two** choices.

(A) to explain the cause of food storage problems

(B) to explain that there is more than one way to store food

(C) to describe the best way to store food so that it is preserved

(D) to describe how food storage problems can be solved step-by-step

(E) to show that people have been trying to solve this problem for years

(F) to show that food storage is not needed as often as most people would think

GO ON →

Read the article "What's Next?" before answering Numbers 6 through 10.

What's Next?

People have been inventing things for thousands of years. Many of these inventions have become part of our daily lives. Some of them are extremely useful while others might be considered hilarious. The silly inventions that we laugh at often do not get much attention, but the really useful ones can make an enormous difference in the way we live. Some inventions, such as the telegraph, were very important at a certain time in history, but now their use is rare.

Thinking about all these inventions can make a person feel dizzy, yet it can also make us aware of just how much inventions have changed our world. Can you imagine what your life would be like without electric lights, television, computers, or automobiles? Nowadays, we do not even think about the things that make our lives easier and give us so much independence. There was a time, though, when they did not exist.

Before the wheel was invented, people had to carry loads on their backs and drag heavy things behind them. Can you sympathize with those people? With the wheel, people were able to build carts and wagons that helped them move heavy things much more easily. It also helped them move larger loads.

Before the seed drill, farmers planted seeds by simply throwing them on the ground. This wasted a lot of seeds. Then the seed drill was invented. This machine was a huge advancement in technology for agriculture. Farmers could make straight rows of holes in the ground and then drop their seeds into these holes. Farmers used fewer seeds and had more control over where they planted crops. This helped them grow more crops, which meant more food for people.

GO ON →

The first cars had to be started using a hand crank. This crank was hard to turn and was not convenient in rainy or cold weather. Charles Kettering was convinced that there had to be a better way. He invented the electric starter, which made it possible for people to start a car's engine by pushing a button.

While flying a kite during a storm, Ben Franklin discovered something important about the physical properties of lightning. He discovered that lightning conducts electricity. This little bit of creative mischief led him to invent the lightning rod. Before his invention, people had problems protecting their houses from lightning damage. The lightning rod protects buildings and ships from lightning strikes. It has saved a lot of property from being destroyed. It has saved many lives, too.

We welcome inventions that make our lives safer, better, and easier. Even silly inventions have their place. Think about how far all our inventions have brought us. Can you imagine the exciting things that might be next?

GO ON →

Name: _____ Date: _____

Now answer Numbers 6 through 10. Base your answers on "What's Next?"

6 Circle **one** main idea of the article. Then circle **two** sentences from the article that support the main idea.

Main Idea of "What's Next?"	Text Evidence
Many inventions create problems for people.	"People have been inventing things for thousands of years."
Inventions are usually created to make people laugh.	"Can you imagine what your life would be like without electric lights, television, computers, or automobiles?"
Many inventions change our lives and change the world.	"With the wheel, people were able to build carts and wagons that helped them move heavy things much more easily."
Inventions often have the effect of bringing people together.	"Even silly inventions have their place."

7 How does the author help the reader understand how inventions help people? Pick **two** choices.

(A) by comparing and contrasting inventions

(B) by discussing problems that people needed to solve

(C) by asking and answering questions about inventions

(D) by describing how some inventions solved problems

(E) by listing inventions in the order of their importance to people

(F) by telling how important events in history caused people to invent things

GO ON →

8 Read the sentences from the article.

Before the wheel was invented, people had to carry loads on their backs and drag heavy things behind them. Can you <u>sympathize</u> with those people?

The Greek root of <u>sympathize</u> means "feeling." What does the word <u>sympathize</u> **most likely** mean?

(A) explain

(B) join

(C) remember

(D) understand

9 This question has two parts. First, answer part A. Then, answer part B.

Part A: Read the sentences from the article.

Then the seed drill was invented. This machine was a huge advancement in <u>technology</u> for agriculture.

The word <u>technology</u> includes the Greek root *logy*. What does this root **most likely** mean?

(A) shaped like

(B) hidden from

(C) relating to the center

(D) the study or science of

Part B: Which other word has the same root as the one in <u>technology</u>?

(A) biology

(B) clog

(C) kilogram

(D) logger

GO ON →

10 This question has two parts. First, answer part A. Then, answer part B.

Part A: Which statement **best** explains why the author tells about Ben Franklin flying a kite during a storm?

(A) to show how a problem was solved by an invention

(B) to explain the effect of lightning strikes on houses

(C) to explain how Franklin invented many things

(D) to show that Franklin liked to do silly things

Part B: Which sentence from the article **best** supports your answer in part A?

(A) "While flying a kite during a storm, Ben Franklin discovered something important about the physical properties of lightning."

(B) "He discovered that lightning conducts electricity."

(C) "The lightning rod protects buildings and ships from lightning strikes."

(D) "Can you imagine the exciting things that might be next?"

STOP

Name: _____ Date: _____

Now answer Number 11. Base your answer on "Staying Fresh" and "What's Next?"

11 How is the text structure of "Staying Fresh" similar to the text structure of "What's Next?" Support your answer with details from both articles.

_____

_____

_____

_____

_____

_____

_____

_____

_____

_____

_____

_____

Answer Key

Name: _____

Question	Correct Answer	Content Focus	CCSS	Complexity
1A	A	Text Structure: Problem and Solution	RI.4.5	DOK 2
1B	D	Text Structure: Problem and Solution/ Text Evidence	RI.4.5/ RI.4.1	DOK 2
2	see below	Text Structure: Problem and Solution	RI.4.5	DOK 2
3	A	Greek Roots	L.4.4b	DOK 2
4	D	Greek Roots	L.4.4b	DOK 1
5	B, E	Text Structure: Problem and Solution	RI.4.5	DOK 2
6	see below	Main Idea and Key Details	RI.4.2	DOK 2
7	B, D	Text Structure: Problem and Solution	RI.4.5	DOK 2
8	D	Greek Roots	L.4.4b	DOK 2
9A	D	Greek Roots	L.4.4b	DOK 2
9B	A	Greek Roots	L.4.4b	DOK 2
10A	A	Text Structure: Problem and Solution	RI.4.5	DOK 2
10B	C	Text Structure: Problem and Solution/ Text Evidence	RI.4.5/ RI.4.1	DOK 2
11	see below	Writing About Text	W.4.9b	DOK 4

Comprehension 1A, 1B, 2, 5, 6, 7, 10A, 10B	/12	%
Vocabulary 3, 4, 8, 9A, 9B	/8	%
Total Weekly Assessment Score	/20	%

2 Students should underline the following sentences in the paragraph:
- Canning keeps food safe for a long time.
- If unopened, the canned food stays good for months, and sometimes years.

6 Students should circle the following sentences:
- Main Idea of "What's Next?"—Many inventions change our lives and change the world.
- Text Evidence—"Can you imagine what your life would be like without electric lights, television, computers, or automobiles?"; "With the wheel, people were able to build carts and wagons that helped them move heavy things much more easily."

11 To receive full credit for the response, the following information should be included: Both articles follow a problem-and-solution text structure. The paragraphs in each article begin with a problem. The solution to that problem is given in the same paragraph. Many problem/solution relationships are explained in each article.

Read the article "Stargazing" before answering Numbers 1 through 5.

Stargazing

Many people enjoy looking at the sky on a clear night. Some people might want a closer look at the stars and planets. A telescope lets you view objects more closely than you can with just your eye. It takes preparation for a night of looking at the stars, but the results will make your viewing successful. Here are some tips for enjoying the stars.

Before using your telescope, you should do some planning. You need to wait for a night that is clear, without many clouds, and you need to choose a night when the moon is not very full. You might think that a full moon will help you see more stars, but the moon's brilliance can make it difficult to see some stars. Wait for a night when there is more darkness.

Decide where to set up your telescope. A good location would be very dark and far from buildings. It is important to check this spot during the day, too, to make sure the area you choose is safe. The tripod holding the telescope should stand on solid, level ground. A telescope is fragile and not very sturdy, and it can break easily if it falls.

GO ON →

After finding a good spot and choosing a clear night, you are ready to set up your telescope. The first basic step is to open the tripod's legs and to make sure they are planted firmly on the ground. This will keep the image in the telescope steady so it does not waver. Next, attach the long tube to the tripod mount. Then attach the low-power eyepiece, which is marked with the highest number. This eyepiece makes the telescopic images sharper. Then attach the finderscope, which is the little spotting scope on the top of the telescope that helps center a star's image. Now, look through the eyepiece. Move the lens until the image is focused and not blurry. Remember that all telescopes can be a bit different so first read the instructions that come with your scope!

Star maps will help you identify the objects you locate in the night sky. Monthly star maps tell which stars and planets can be seen from your area of Earth. A star map shows the entire night sky. The center of the map is the part of the sky that is directly overhead. Hold the star map so that the direction you are facing is the direction written at the bottom of the map. Then look up and see if you can find a star or group of stars that match the stars on the map. Star maps list stars that can be seen with or without a telescope.

If you take care of your telescope, it can last for many years. With practice, you can look for more challenging objects, such as galaxies. You can share your hobby with your friends and relatives. Looking at the stars can be fun for people of all ages.

GO ON →

Name: _____ Date: _____

Now answer Numbers 1 through 5. Base your answers on "Stargazing."

1 This question has two parts. First, answer part A. Then, answer part B.

Part A: Read the sentences from the article.

You might think that a full moon will help you see more stars, but the moon's <u>brilliance</u> can make it difficult to see some stars. Wait for a night when there is more darkness.

What does the word <u>brilliance</u> mean in the sentences?

Ⓐ distance

Ⓑ light

Ⓒ shape

Ⓓ size

Part B: Which word from the sentences means the **opposite** of <u>brilliance</u>?

Ⓐ full

Ⓑ stars

Ⓒ difficult

Ⓓ darkness

2 Pick **two** things that must be done **before** setting up your telescope.

Ⓐ Set up the finderscope.

Ⓑ Choose a well-lit area.

Ⓒ Wait for a clear night.

Ⓓ Look for a full moon.

Ⓔ Find a safe spot.

Ⓕ Use a star map.

GO ON →

3 Read the sentences from the article.

The tripod holding the telescope should stand on solid, level ground. A telescope is <u>fragile</u> and not very sturdy, and it can break easily if it falls.

Which word from the sentence has the **opposite** meaning of <u>fragile</u>?

Ⓐ level

Ⓑ sturdy

Ⓒ easily

Ⓓ falls

4 A telescope is put together in a certain sequence. Write the steps in the correct order in the chart below.

Step 1	
Step 2	
Step 3	
Step 4	
Step 5	

Events:
Attach the finderscope.
Attach the low-power eyepiece.
Move the lens to focus the image.
Attach the long tube to the tripod mount.
Open the tripod's legs and plant them on the ground.

GO ON →

5 This question has two parts. First, answer part A. Then, answer part B.

Part A: When using a star map, what must be done **before** looking at the sky?

(A) You must find planets and stars.

(B) You must hold the map correctly.

(C) You must look for faraway galaxies.

(D) You must loosen the telescope's eyepiece.

Part B: Which text from the article **best** supports your answer in part A?

(A) "Star maps will help you identify the objects you locate in the night sky."

(B) "A star map shows the entire night sky. The center of the map is the part of the sky that is directly overhead."

(C) "Hold the star map so that the direction you are facing is the direction written at the bottom of the map. Then look up and see if you can find a star or group of stars that match the stars on the map."

(D) "Star maps list stars that can be seen with or without a telescope."

GO ON →

Read the article "Prehistoric Art" before answering Numbers 6 through 10.

Prehistoric Art

Many people today think that ancient people spent all their time trying to survive, yet prehistoric cave art proves that some of these people took time to draw, just like modern artists of today. Carvings from this time show that ancient people were not unskilled, but rather they were talented at creating many kinds of art.

Archeologists say this art might have been used in rituals, or maybe it was used to pass on messages. Maybe these early people just enjoyed creating art. Scientists have many theories about why early humans created art.

One discovery that left many people wondering was the discovery of a group of numerous statues found in the Czech Republic. The statues are about twenty-six thousand years old. Most carvings done around this time were made of bone, soft stone, or ivory. These were materials that were easily found. Some heads made of ivory were found there, too. But what surprised everyone were the terra-cotta figures. These were made by people who knew how to make pottery by heating soft clay.

GO ON →

Scientists did not think that early humans knew how to use fire to make pottery. They thought that pottery was invented much later, but these statues proved them wrong.

When scientists excavated buried objects at this site, they dug up more than seven thousand pieces of fired clay. They even found two kilns, or special ovens used for firing clay. They also dug up more than two thousand balls of burnt clay. Many of the other pieces they found are only small bits, but some pieces looked like people or animals.

One expert who studied the pieces said the clay had lime added to it. The people had to mix the lime into the clay first. Then they could fire the clay at low temperatures. That way they could harden it in a small open fire, such as a campfire. The heat made the clay hard and turned it into terra-cotta, a shiny brown pottery. The fire also made the clay turn black in some places.

These early humans may have discovered how to make pottery by accident, but the statues they made took real talent. The statues were detailed likenesses, not just general shapes. One of the statues is a woman. She is only four and a half inches tall. There are also animals, such as a bear, lion, fox, and rhino. The artists who made them must have known what all these animals looked like. They also knew how to fire the clay to make it hard. Firing the clay saved the sculptures. It is amazing to think that they have lasted all these years!

GO ON →

Now answer Numbers 6 through 10. Base your answers on "Prehistoric Art."

6 Read the sentence from the article.

Carvings from this time show that ancient people were not unskilled, but rather they were <u>talented</u> at creating many kinds of art.

Which word from the sentence means the **opposite** of <u>talented</u>?

Ⓐ carvings

Ⓑ ancient

Ⓒ unskilled

Ⓓ art

7 This question has two parts. First, answer part A. Then, answer part B.

Part A: Which sentence **best** states a main idea about prehistoric art that is presented in the article?

Ⓐ Prehistoric art is a lot like modern art.

Ⓑ The purpose of prehistoric art is unknown.

Ⓒ Prehistoric art is more important than other types of art.

Ⓓ There is a lot of prehistoric art that has not been found yet.

Part B: Which detail from the article **best** supports your answer in part A?

Ⓐ ". . . some of these people took time to draw, just like modern artists of today."

Ⓑ "Scientists have many theories about why early humans created art."

Ⓒ "The statues are about twenty-six thousand years old."

Ⓓ "These early humans may have discovered how to make pottery by accident, . . ."

GO ON →

8 Which details tell what happened **after** scientists dug up buried objects at the site in the Czech Republic? Pick **two** choices.

(A) Burnt clay was rolled into balls.

(B) Scientists found lime in the clay.

(C) Terra-cotta animal figures were made.

(D) Experts studied pieces of the fired clay.

(E) Scientists thought that pottery was invented much later.

(F) People began to create different types of prehistoric art.

9 This question has two parts. First, answer part A. Then, answer part B.

Part A: Read the sentences from the article.

The statues were detailed likenesses, not just general shapes. One of the statues is a woman. She is only four and a half inches tall.

What does the word detailed mean in the sentences?

(A) pretty

(B) large

(C) specific

(D) unusual

Part B: Which word from the sentences means the **opposite** of detailed?

(A) statues

(B) likenesses

(C) general

(D) tall

GO ON →

10 Put the steps for making terra-cotta pottery in the correct sequence. Number the steps from 1 to 4. Write the correct number in front of each step.

_____ | Fire the clay at low temperatures.

_____ | Wait until the clay hardens and turns brown.

_____ | Mix the lime into the clay.

_____ | Heat the clay over a small fire.

Name: _____ Date: _____

Now answer Number 11. Base your answer on "Stargazing" and "Prehistoric Art."

11 Both articles discuss the steps in a process. How is each article structured to help the reader understand the processes? Support your answer with details from both articles.

_____

_____

_____

_____

_____

_____

_____

_____

_____

_____

_____

_____

_____

_____

Answer Key

Name: _____

Question	Correct Answer	Content Focus	CCSS	Complexity
1A	B	Context Clues: Antonyms	L.4.5c	DOK 2
1B	D	Context Clues: Antonyms/ Text Evidence	L.4.5c	DOK 2
2	C, E	Text Structure: Sequence	RI.4.3	DOK 2
3	B	Context Clues: Antonyms	L.4.5c	DOK 2
4	see below	Text Structure: Sequence	RI.4.3	DOK 2
5A	B	Text Structure: Sequence	RI.4.3	DOK 2
5B	C	Text Structure: Sequence/ Text Evidence	RI.4.3/ RI.4.1	DOK 2
6	C	Context Clues: Antonyms	L.4.5c	DOK 2
7A	B	Main Idea and Key Details	RI.4.2	DOK 2
7B	B	Main Idea and Key Details/ Text Evidence	RI.4.2/ RI.4.1	DOK 2
8	B, D	Text Structure: Sequence	RI.4.3	DOK 2
9A	C	Context Clues: Antonyms	L.4.5c	DOK 2
9B	C	Context Clues: Antonyms/ Text Evidence	L.4.5c	DOK 2
10	see below	Text Structure: Sequence	RI.4.3	DOK 2
11	see below	Writing About Text	W.4.9b	DOK 4

Comprehension 2, 4, 5A, 5B, 7A, 7B, 8, 10	/12	%
Vocabulary 1A, 1B, 3, 6, 9A, 9B	/8	%
Total Weekly Assessment Score	/20	%

4 Students should put the steps in the following order:
- Step 1—Open the tripod's legs and plant them on the ground.
- Step 2—Attach the long tube to the tripod mount.
- Step 3—Attach the low-power eyepiece.
- Step 4—Attach the finderscope.
- Step 5—Move the lens to focus the image.

10 Students should put the steps in the following order:
- 2 – Fire the clay at low temperatures.
- 4 – Wait until the clay hardens and turns brown.
- 1 – Mix the lime into the clay.
- 3 – Heat the clay over a small fire.

11 To receive full credit for the response, the following information should be included: The author of each article describes the process in order. The authors use other text structure techniques such as cause/effect and compare/contrast to help the reader understand what happens in each process. "Stargazing" describes how to assemble a telescope and how to use it. "Prehistoric Art" describes the discoveries that changed archaeologists' opinions of prehistoric art and how terra-cotta was made by early peoples.

    Weekly Assessment · Unit 5, Week 4

Read the article "Mary Anning: First Fossil Hunter" before answering Numbers 1 through 5.

Mary Anning: First Fossil Hunter

Smack! Smash! Splash! In 1799, Mary Anning was born to the sound of ocean waves crashing against the cliffs of Lyme Regis, England. When Mary was just a few years old, she and her older brother, Joseph, would go to the town's seashore with her father. Here Mary's father taught his children how to hunt for fossils in the rocks and cliffs. At this time, scientists were just beginning to understand fossils, or the remains of plants and animals that lived long, long ago. Wealthy visitors would come to Lyme Regis to vacation. The Anning family had little money, so they would sell the small fossils they found to these tourists.

Mary was a quiet girl. Some might say that in Mary's case still waters run deep because she was also bright, curious, and a hard worker who spent long days on the beach looking for fossils. She needed to help her family survive. Life was hard and when it rains, it pours. Soon, Mary's father died. Although she was only ten, Mary was forced to quit school, and now she needed to work even harder to find fossils to sell. Because of unstable cliffs, battering waves, and sudden storms, Mary had to be bold and daring. It was dangerous work.

But one day, something happened to show that every cloud has a silver lining. When Mary was about twelve, Joseph made a fantastic find. He found a large fossil skull that had a long nose and many teeth.

First, Mary planned how to uncover the rest of the creature. Then, over several months, she unearthed each part of the fossil. Since haste makes waste, Mary did not want to hurry and damage the fossil. She chiseled and chipped slowly, tapping and brushing carefully. Finally, Mary uncovered an almost complete skeleton of a prehistoric creature. A wealthy neighbor bought the fossils and later, scientists named the creature, ichthyosaur, or fish-lizard.

GO ON →

The discovery of the ichthyosaur called attention to Mary as a fossil hunter, but her family was still poor. Mary continued to uncover fossils to sell. Even though she had little formal schooling, Mary knew how to read and write. During her teenage years, Mary taught herself about rocks, animals, fish, and the earth. She wrote letters to well-known scientists. Some scientists came to visit her in Lyme Regis.

About eleven years after finding ichthyosaur, Mary made another astonishing discovery. She dug out another reptile that had lived in the sea, the first complete plesiosaur. The plesiosaur was nine feet long with a lizard's head and crocodile teeth. Scientists called the long-necked plesiosaur the sea dragon. This was followed by her discovery of the rare fossil of the flying dragon, pterodactyl.

With each discovery, Mary's fame grew. Visitors followed her on fossil hunts, and scientists combed the beach with her. Throughout her life, Mary looked for fossils. She was one of the first persons to make a living as a fossil hunter. Mary helped solve the puzzle of what life was like long ago.

After her death in 1847, Mary was honored with a stained-glass window in the church of Lyme Regis. Many of the fossils Mary Anning uncovered are still studied and displayed in museums.

GO ON →

Now answer Numbers 1 through 5. Base your answers on "Mary Anning: First Fossil Hunter."

1 This question has two parts. First, answer part A. Then, answer part B.

Part A: Which statement **best** explains how the passage is organized?

(A) The author tells the sequence of events in Mary's life.

(B) The author lists the reasons why Mary became a fossil hunter.

(C) The author compares the different dinosaur skeletons that were discovered.

(D) The author describes the problems that led to the discovery of the ichthyosaur.

Part B: Which sentences from the passage **best** support your answer in part A? Pick **two** choices.

(A) "Wealthy visitors would come to Lyme Regis to vacation."

(B) "Although she was only ten, Mary was forced to quit school, and now she needed to work even harder to find fossils to sell."

(C) "Because of unstable cliffs, battering waves, and sudden storms, Mary had to be bold and daring."

(D) "Even though she had little formal schooling, Mary knew how to read and write."

(E) "During her teenage years, Mary taught herself about rocks, animals, fish, and the earth."

(F) "Scientists called the long-necked plesiosaur the sea dragon."

GO ON →

2 Read the sentences from the article.

Mary was a quiet girl. Some might say that in Mary's case <u>still waters run deep</u> because she was also bright, curious, and a hard worker who spent long days on the beach looking for fossils.

What does the adage "still waters run deep" suggest about Mary?

(A) She is quiet but likes to swim in the ocean.

(B) She is calm on the outside but nervous on the inside.

(C) She does not talk a lot but when she does she is funny.

(D) She does not have a lot to say but she is smart and thoughtful.

3 This question has two parts. First, answer part A. Then, answer part B.

Part A: Read the sentence from the passage.

But one day, something happened to show that <u>every cloud has a silver lining</u>. When Mary was about twelve, Joseph made a fantastic find.

What mood does the author create with the use of the adage "every cloud has a silver lining"?

(A) anger

(B) fear

(C) hope

(D) sadness

Part B: Which phrase from the sentences helps to explain the meaning of the adage?

(A) "but one day"

(B) "something happened"

(C) "about twelve"

(D) "a fantastic find"

GO ON →

4 Explain the events in the article that are related to the ichthyosaur. Write the events in the correct order in the chart below.

1	
2	
3	
4	
5	
6	

Events:
Mary uncovers almost a complete skeleton.
Scientists name the creature an ichthyosaur.
Joseph discovers the skull of an ichthyosaur.
Mary makes a plan to dig up the ichthyosaur.
A neighbor buys the fossils that Mary digs up.
Mary slowly chisels away the rest of the fossils.

5 Why does the author state the date of Mary's birth at the beginning of the passage and the date of her death at the end of the passage?

Ⓐ to show the time order of events in Mary's life

Ⓑ to show what caused Mary to be interested in fossils

Ⓒ to show how Mary's life was different from Joseph's life

Ⓓ to show the effects of the hard life that Mary's family lived

GO ON →

Read the article "Science in Your Bones" before answering Numbers 6 through 10.

Science in Your Bones

What was Earth like a long time ago? What kinds of plants lived on Earth? What kinds of animals were here? There are professionals whose job is to answer questions like these. They are called *paleontologists*.

Paleo is a Greek word that means "old." *Logy* also comes from Greek, meaning "study." So *paleontology* means "the study of old things."

The "old things" that these scientists study are fossils, the remains of plants or animals left behind in rocks. Some fossils are shells, leaves, or bones, and some are tracks that were left by animals as they passed by. It is said that there's nothing new in things as old as the hills, but you can learn from an old fossil!

How did the fossils get into the rocks? The rocks were formed millions of years ago. At that time, the animals and plants were alive, but then the animals and plants died and were buried in the rocks. Over time, the rocks piled up and the shape of the plant or the animal's bones became part of the rock. By studying fossils, paleontologists can determine what the animal or plant looked like.

GO ON →

The oldest fossils found so far are the remains of bacteria. Scientists think these bacteria lived more than 3 billion years ago. These microscopic fossils are not large enough to be seen without the aid of a microscope.

Fossils have been found all over the United States, but scientists believe these fossils represent just a small fraction of the animals and plants that have lived on Earth. After all, looking for a particular fossil is like looking for a needle in a haystack! Scientists also believe that many living things vanished from the planet without leaving a single fossil behind.

Paleontologists learn many things from fossils. It takes a lot of painstaking work to gain a small amount of knowledge, but good things come to those who wait! One thing they learn is what kinds of animals roamed the planet long before there were people. They also learn whether rocks were formed on land or in the sea. Most rocks that have fossils of sea creatures were formed in water. Most rocks that have fossils of land creatures were formed on land. Knowing where rocks were formed tells us what Earth may have looked like millions of years ago.

Like other kinds of science, paleontology can be very exciting. Think about the first paleontologists who stumbled upon a dinosaur fossil. Imagine what they felt like when they inspected the fossil and realized what they had found. As some paleontologists might say, "Leave no stone unturned!"

GO ON →

Now answer Numbers 6 through 10. Base your answers on "Science in Your Bones."

6 This question has two parts. First, answer part A. Then, answer part B.

Part A: How does the author help the reader understand what paleontologists learn from fossils?

(A) by explaining the sequence of how fossils are formed

(B) by contrasting sea creatures with land animals

(C) by explaining why sea creatures formed fossils

(D) by listing the kinds of rocks that make fossils

Part B: Which sentence from the passage **best** supports your answer in part A?

(A) "There are professionals whose job is to answer questions like these."

(B) "Over time, the rocks piled up and the shape of the plant or the animal's bones became part of the rock."

(C) "Scientists think these bacteria lived more than 3 billion years ago."

(D) "Scientists also believe that many living things vanished from the planet without leaving a single fossil behind."

7 How does the author organize the last paragraph on page 294? Pick **two** choices.

(A) by explaining the effects of finding fossils

(B) by describing a specific sequence of events

(C) by contrasting animal fossils and plant fossils

(D) by contrasting the different ways rocks pile up

(E) by describing how rocks formed millions of year ago

(F) by explaining how living things become part of rocks

GO ON →

8 This question has two parts. First, answer part A. Then, answer part B.

Part A: Read the sentences from the article.

Paleontologists learn many things from fossils. It takes a lot of painstaking work to gain a small amount of knowledge, but good things come to those who wait!

What is the meaning of the adage "good things come to those who wait"?

(A) You may wait a long time and get nothing.

(B) It is better to wait and let others do the work.

(C) If you are patient, you will get what you want.

(D) If you wait too long you will miss your chance.

Part B: Which word from the sentences **best** supports the meaning of the adage?

(A) paleontologists

(B) fossils

(C) amount

(D) knowledge

GO ON →

9 The author suggests that paleontology can be very exciting. Write the numbers of **two** sentences from the article that support this point of view. Choose the sentences from the box and write the sentence numbers in the chart.

Point of View:	
Paleontology can be very exciting.	
Sentence:	Sentence:

Sentences:

1 – "Some fossils are shells, leaves, or bones, and some are tracks that were left by animals as they passed by."

2 – "These microscopic fossils are not large enough to be seen without the aid of a microscope."

3 – "Most rocks that have fossils of sea creatures were formed in water."

4 – "Think about the first paleontologists who stumbled upon a dinosaur fossil."

5 – "Imagine what they felt like when they inspected the fossil and realized what they had found."

10 Read the sentence from the article.

As some paleontologists might say, "Leave no stone unturned!"

What does the adage "leave no stone unturned" suggest about paleontologists?

(A) They are suspicious.

(B) They look at every detail.

(C) They worry about their work.

(D) They like to joke around a lot.

Weekly Assessment · Unit 5, Week 5

Now answer Number 11. Base your answer on "Mary Anning: First Fossil Hunter" and "Science in Your Bones."

11 How does the use of sequencing help to present the information in "Mary Anning: First Fossil Hunter" and "Science in Your Bones"? Support your answer with details from both articles.

_____

_____

_____

_____

_____

_____

_____

_____

_____

_____

_____

_____

_____

_____

_____

Answer Key

Name: _____

Question	Correct Answer	Content Focus	CCSS	Complexity
1A	A	Text Structure: Sequence	RI.4.5	DOK 2
1B	B, E	Text Structure: Sequence/Text Evidence	RI.4.5/ RI.4.1	DOK 2
2	D	Figurative Language: Proverbs and Adages	L.4.5b	DOK 2
3A	C	Figurative Language: Proverbs and Adages	L.4.5b	DOK 2
3B	D	Figurative Language: Proverbs and Adages/ Text Evidence	L.4.5b/ RI.4.1	DOK 2
4	see below	Text Structure: Sequence	RI.4.5	DOK 2
5	A	Text Structure: Sequence	RI.4.5	DOK 2
6A	A	Text Structure: Sequence	RI.4.5	DOK 2
6B	B	Text Structure: Sequence/Text Evidence	RI.4.5/ RI.4.1	DOK 2
7	B, F	Text Structure: Sequence	RI.4.5	DOK 2
8A	C	Figurative Language: Proverbs and Adages	L.4.5b	DOK 2
8B	D	Figurative Language: Proverbs and Adages/ Text Evidence	L.4.5b/ RI.4.1	DOK 2
9	see below	Author's Point of View	RL.4.8	DOK 3
10	B	Figurative Language: Proverbs and Adages	L.4.5b	DOK 2
11	see below	Writing About Text	W.4.9b	DOK 4

Comprehension 1A, 1B, 4, 5, 6A, 6B, 7, 9	/12	%
Vocabulary 2, 3A, 3B, 8A, 8B, 10	/8	%
Total Weekly Assessment Score	/20	%

4 Students should put the events in the following order:
- 1 — Joseph discovers the skull of an ichthyosaur.
- 2 — Mary makes a plan to dig up the ichthyosaur.
- 3 — Mary slowly chisels away the rest of the fossils.
- 4 — Mary uncovers almost a complete skeleton.
- 5 — A neighbor buys the fossils that Mary digs up.
- 6 — Scientists name the creature an ichthyosaur.

9 Students should write the following sentence numbers in the chart:
- 4 ("Think about the first paleontologists who stumbled upon a dinosaur fossil.")
- 5 ("Imagine what they felt like when they inspected the fossil and realized what they had found.")

11 To receive full credit for the response, the following information should be included: Telling events in the order in which they happened can help readers visualize and better understand a process. It also shows how something developed over time. "Mary Anning: First Fossil Hunter" provides the series of events in Mary's life that led to her finding many fossils and becoming a famous fossil hunter. "Science in Your Bones" explains how fossils are formed and what information scientists can learn by studying fossils.

Read the passage "The Babushka" before answering Numbers 1 through 5.

The Babushka

The winters were always harsh, but the one Mary Kowalski remembered was especially fierce. For weeks, snow, ice, and strong winds had battered her village in Poland. Mary dreaded the long, frigid walk to school each day. Very soon, her mother found a way to solve the problem. Before she went out, Mary's mother would tie her own babushka, or kerchief, under Mary's chin. The babushka was large and colorful. In spite of the freezing weather, Mary could feel the warmth of the soft babushka, and she imagined the touch of her mother's hands. The babushka made Mary feel cozy and safe.

When Mary came to the United States, the babushka was one of the few things she brought with her. She landed a job as a cook in a restaurant that served Polish food. Mary would stand in the kitchen all day and make handmade *golabki*, or cabbage leaves stuffed with meat and rice. The city where Mary lived had severe winters, so Mary wore her mother's babushka to work every day. The weather reminded her of winters in Poland, and the babushka reminded Mary of her mother.

The years passed, and before long Mary was a mother. When her daughter Jenny left for college, Mary gave her the babushka. Jenny had no intentions of wearing it since it was not stylish, yet she didn't want to hurt her mother's feelings. Jenny knew why the babushka was special to her mother. She had heard the story, so Jenny pointed out, "Since the babushka's color is starting to fade, I'll try not to wear it too much."

After Jenny unpacked at college, she lovingly placed the babushka on her bed. I'll find a drawer for it tonight, Jenny thought before she hurried out to her first class.

GO ON →

That day, Jenny was surprised by all the work that was required in college. There were books to read, reports to write, and research to do. Jenny was overwhelmed and scared, and she plopped down on her bed and laid her head on the babushka.

It was not long before Jenny started to feel better. The babushka made her think of her mom and gave her encouragement. "Mom worked hard at the restaurant, and I'll work hard at school. I'll do whatever it takes," Jenny promised herself. From then on, Jenny would lay her head on the babushka at the end of the day. If she was upset or worried, the feel of her mom's faded babushka would calm her. It was as if she was hearing her mom's voice soothing her.

By the time Jenny was ready to pass the babushka on to her own daughter, the material was very thin. The colors were even lighter. "Why would I want this shabby, faded piece of cloth?" asked Marie.

"I think it's lovely, but then beauty is in the eye of the beholder," Jenny answered. Then she realized that Marie did not know the story of the babushka. "Sit down, Marie. I want to tell you a story that begins years ago in a village in Poland. One harsh, fierce winter . . ."

Now answer Numbers 1 through 5. Base your answers on "The Babushka."

1 This question has two parts. First, answer part A. Then, answer part B.

Part A: Which sentence **best** describes the theme in the passage?

Ⓐ You can learn from your mistakes.

Ⓑ Life is filled with many adventures.

Ⓒ Families love and support each other.

Ⓓ To have a friend, you must be a friend.

Part B: Which detail from the passage **best** supports your answer in part A?

Ⓐ "The city where Mary lived had severe winters, so Mary wore her mother's babushka to work every day."

Ⓑ "She had heard the story, so Jenny pointed out, 'Since the babushka's color is starting to fade, I'll try not to wear it too much.'"

Ⓒ "That day, Jenny was surprised by all the work that was required in college."

Ⓓ "The babushka made her think of her mom and gave her encouragement."

2 Underline **two** sentences in the paragraph that support the theme of the passage.

The winters were always harsh, but the one Mary Kowalski remembered was especially fierce. For weeks, snow, ice, and strong winds had battered her village in Poland. Mary dreaded the long, frigid walk to school each day. Very soon, her mother found a way to solve the problem. Before she went out, Mary's mother would tie her own babushka, or kerchief, under Mary's chin. The babushka was large and colorful. In spite of the freezing weather, Mary could feel the warmth of the soft babushka, and she imagined the touch of her mother's hands. The babushka made Mary feel cozy and safe.

3 This question has two parts. First, answer part A. Then, answer part B.

Part A: Read the sentence from the passage.

After Jenny unpacked at college, she lovingly placed the babushka on her bed.

What does the use of the word lovingly suggest?

Ⓐ The babushka reminds Jenny to dress warmly.

Ⓑ The babushka is very important to Jenny.

Ⓒ Jenny does not want to upset her mother.

Ⓓ Jenny thinks the babushka is very old.

Part B: Which word has a connotation **most** similar to the word lovingly?

Ⓐ finally

Ⓑ gently

Ⓒ slowly

Ⓓ suddenly

GO ON →

4 Which actions **best** describe the lesson of the passage? Pick **two** choices.

(A) Mary makes Polish food for others.

(B) Jenny lays her head on the babushka.

(C) The babushka becomes old and faded.

(D) The babushka reminds Mary of her mother.

(E) Marie is not sure what to do with the babushka.

(F) Mary walks to school through snow and fierce winds.

5 Read the paragraph from the passage.

By the time Jenny was ready to pass the babushka on to her own daughter, the material was very thin. The colors were even lighter. "Why would I want this shabby, faded piece of cloth?" asked Marie.

Which word from the paragraph has a negative connotation?

(A) ready

(B) pass

(C) shabby

(D) piece

Read the passage "The Night Before" before answering Numbers 6 through 10.

The Night Before

Running Deer sat on the hill under the countless stars that lit the night sky of the Great Plains. He was a Native American. He was also the leader of the Lakota, and his people were a powerful nation. But the settlers were coming, and with them would come their greed for land. It was a need that could never be satisfied for no matter how much land these people had, they still wanted more.

The settlers viewed the land as a wilderness that needed *them* to settle it. They thought of themselves as the civilized people.

The settlers had started in the east, taking land as they spread west. It was Native American land, but the settlers had loosened the Native Americans' hold on the land and had taken what they wanted. To the east, Native American land was just like a patchwork quilt now—a little land here, a little land there.

GO ON →

At first, Running Deer listened to the stories about the settlers with amazement. In the midst of so much land, how could these people always want more? Then his amazement turned to anger, but now he was filled with great sadness because the settlers had reached the eastern edge of the Great Plains. What would happen now?

As leader of the Lakota, it was Running Deer's responsibility to make the right decisions for his people. Running Deer had heard of a group of Native Americans to the east called the Algonquin that had traditions similar to those of the Lakota. At first, they had welcomed the settlers and the settlers had promised that the Algonquin could keep their land, but their actions spoke louder than words. The settlers took the land and forced the Algonquin to leave. Now the settlers were building a town with big wooden houses on the land that had belonged to the Algonquin. They were putting up fences and they had rules about who could use the land and what they could do with it. The Native Americans who had lived there had been pushed west.

Running Deer was willing to fight for Lakota land. He would stay on his horse for days if that would help, but would it help? There were so many settlers, and the settlers had better weapons. Was it better to give up their land so his people might live in peace, or was it better to fight for what was theirs? And what if, by fighting, they lost everything? The Lakota were part of a group of related Sioux tribes. Tomorrow was the great council, when all the Sioux chiefs would talk this over. Sitting here alone tonight, Running Deer did not know what the council would decide, but he did know that, for his people, life would never be the same after the settlers came.

GO ON →

Name: _____ Date: _____ →

Now answer Numbers 6 through 10. Base your answers on "The Night Before."

6 Read the paragraph from the passage.

Running Deer sat on the hill under the countless stars that lit the night sky of the Great Plains. He was a Native American. He was also the leader of the Lakota, and his people were a powerful nation. But the settlers were coming, and with them would come their greed for land. It was a need that could never be satisfied for no matter how much land these people had, they still wanted more.

Which word from the paragraph has a negative connotation?

(A) countless

(B) greed

(C) powerful

(D) satisfied

7 Circle the **one** main problem of the passage. Then circle **one** sentence from the passage that supports your choice.

Main Problem	Text Evidence
The settlers broke their promise to the Algonquin.	"They thought of themselves as the civilized people."
The settlers are about to take over the Lakota's land.	"The settlers had started in the east, taking land as they spread west."
The settlers took over the Algonquin land and pushed them west.	"As leader of the Lakota, it was Running Deer's responsibility to make the right decisions for his people."
Running Deer does not have anyone to help him with his difficult decisions.	"The settlers took the land and forced the Algonquin to leave."

GO ON →

8 This question has two parts. First, answer part A. Then, answer part B.

Part A: Read the sentence from the passage.

At first, Running Deer listened to the stories about the settlers with <u>amazement</u>.

What does the use of the word <u>amazement</u> suggest about Running Deer?

(A) He has a difficult time believing the stories he hears.

(B) He wishes his people told stories like the settlers.

(C) He thinks the settlers are very smart.

(D) He is confused about the situation.

Part B: Which other word has the same connotation as the word <u>amazement</u>?

(A) disbelief

(B) doubt

(C) question

(D) wonder

9 This question has two parts. First, answer part A. Then, answer part B.

Part A: Which sentence **best** summarizes the theme of the passage?

(A) Promises are never broken.

(B) A new neighbor is a new friend.

(C) It is difficult to know how to deal with change.

(D) The future is always bright if you have the right plan.

Part B: Which detail from the passage **best** supports your answer in part A?

(A) "The settlers viewed the land as a wilderness that needed *them* to settle it."

(B) "... the settlers had reached the eastern edge of the Great Plains."

(C) "He would stay on his horse for days if that would help, but would it help?"

(D) "... for his people, life would never be the same after the settlers came."

10 Read the sentences from the passage.

Was it better to give up their land so his people might live in peace, or was it better to fight for what was theirs? And what if, by fighting, they lost everything?

How do these sentences support the passage's theme? Pick **two** choices.

(A) They show how the Lakota were a peaceful people.

(B) They show how the Lakota faced a difficult decision.

(C) They show how the Lakota wanted to fight the settlers.

(D) They show how the Lakota felt they deserved more land.

(E) They show how life for the Lakota was changed by the settlers' arrival.

(F) They show how life for the Lakota was made up of one battle after another.

Weekly Assessment • Unit 6, Week 1

Name: _____ Date: _____

Now answer Number 11. Base your answer on "The Babushka" and "The Night Before."

11 How are the themes of "The Babushka" and "The Night Before" alike? Support your answer with details from both passages.

_____

_____

_____

_____

_____

_____

_____

_____

_____

_____

_____

_____

Answer Key

Name: _____

Question	Correct Answer	Content Focus	CCSS	Complexity
1A	C	Theme	RL.4.2	DOK 3
1B	D	Theme/Text Evidence	RL.4.2/ RL.4.1	DOK 3
2	see below	Theme	RL.4.2	DOK 2
3A	B	Connotation and Denotation	L.5.5c	DOK 2
3B	B	Connotation and Denotation/ Text Evidence	L.5.5c/ RL.4.1	DOK 2
4	B, D	Theme	RL.4.2	DOK 2
5	C	Connotation and Denotation	L.5.5c	DOK 1
6	B	Connotation and Denotation	L.5.5c	DOK 1
7	see below	Character, Setting, Plot: Problem and Solution	RL.4.3	DOK 2
8A	A	Connotation and Denotation	L.5.5c	DOK 2
8B	D	Connotation and Denotation/ Text Evidence	L.5.5c/ RL.4.1	DOK 2
9A	C	Theme	RL.4.2	DOK 3
9B	D	Theme/Text Evidence	RL.4.2/ RL.4.1	DOK 3
10	B, E	Theme	RL.4.2	DOK 2
11	see below	Writing About Text	W.4.9a	DOK 4

Comprehension 1A, 1B, 2, 4, 7, 9A, 9B, 10	/12	%
Vocabulary 3A, 3B, 5, 6, 8A, 8B	/8	%
Total Weekly Assessment Score	/20	%

2 Students should underline the following sentences in the paragraph:
- In spite of the freezing weather, Mary could feel the warmth of the soft babushka, and she imagined the touch of her mother's hands.
- The babushka made Mary feel cozy and safe.

7 Students should circle the following sentences in the chart:
- Main Problem—The settlers are about to take over the Lakota's land.
- Text Evidence—"The settlers had started in the east, taking land as they spread west."

11 To receive full credit for the response, the following information should be included: Both passages have themes about surviving. In "The Babushka," the theme is about families surviving and remembering each other through the years. In "The Night Before," the theme is about the Lakota surviving, or trying to live on as the people of a nation. Both have an element of the importance of tradition and carrying on a culture.

Read the passage "The Cranberry Connection" before answering Numbers 1 through 5.

The Cranberry Connection

"What is this book?" Anna mumbled to herself as she helped her mom look through cardboard boxes that had been stored in their basement for years. Most of the boxes belonged to her grandparents who died when Anna was a baby, so she did not remember anything about them.

Anna pulled the book out of the box, releasing a cloud of dust that made her sneeze three times in a row. The cover, which was once blue, was now a dusty gray, and as Anna opened the book, she had to catch some loose pages before they fell onto the floor.

"I think I found Grandma's diary," she told her mother.

Her mother quickly came closer and said, "What a find! I can't wait to read it. I miss her." Then seeing Anna's frown, Mom added, "But you found Grandma's diary, so you can read it first."

Nodding happily, Anna read the date on the first entry, August 13, 1953. "How old was your mom in 1953?" she asked.

Her mom wrinkled her brows and thought for a minute. "She was born in 1944, so she must have been about nine, the same age as you are right now."

GO ON →

Wow, Anna thought, for she had seen photos of her mom's parents, but they looked so old that it was hard to imagine that her grandma was ever nine.

Anna read the first entry:

> *The county fair is only two weeks away and today I'm going to practice making Mother's cranberry bread. Last time, the dough was a big problem, for it was so thick that I couldn't even knead it! I get mad at myself when my baking turns out wrong, but Mother keeps telling me to have more patience. I'll use less flour today and hope for the best.*

Then Anna realized that her mother made cranberry bread, too, and the recipe for that bread must have been passed down through the generations. Anna suddenly wanted to learn how to make it, and quickly asked, "Mom, could you help me make cranberry bread today?"

She could tell by the long pause that her mom was a little surprised by her request. "I guess we could make some after we're done here," she replied, "but you'll have to do the kneading because my shoulder is sore from all this work in the basement."

"I want to do all of it," Anna told her. "Your only contribution will be to make sure I'm doing it exactly the way you do it."

Her mom smiled and pointed out, "Anna, you don't have a lot of . . ."

"Patience!" Anna interrupted. "I'm just like Grandma! But I want to learn how to make that bread just like you do it—and like your mother did it, and her mother did it, and . . ."

Laughing, her mom held up her hand. "I get it, but I'm wondering why you're suddenly so interested in that bread. Maybe I'd better read the diary before we start!"

Anna smiled and handed the dusty diary to her mom. "I don't want to break the cranberry connection," she said. "I have to be ready to teach my own kids how to make that bread!"

GO ON →

Now answer Numbers 1 through 5. Base your answers on "The Cranberry Connection."

1 This question has two parts. First, answer part A. Then, answer part B.

Part A: Which sentence **best** summarizes the message of the passage?

(A) The only way to know the future is to study the past.

(B) Some traditions are good enough to continue.

(C) Old boxes can be full of surprises.

(D) People need to be more patient.

Part B: Which sentences from the passage **best** support your answer in part A? Pick **two** choices.

(A) "'I think I found Grandma's diary,' she told her mother."

(B) "Then seeing Anna's frown, Mom added, 'But you found Grandma's diary, so you can read it first.'"

(C) "Then Anna realized that her mother made cranberry bread, too, and the recipe for that bread must have been passed down through the generations."

(D) "She could tell by the long pause that her mom was a little surprised by her request."

(E) "'But I want to learn how to make that bread just like you do it—and like your mother did it, and her mother did it, and . . .'"

(F) "'I get it, but I'm wondering why you're suddenly so interested in that bread.'"

GO ON →

2 Read the sentences from the passage.

Her mother quickly came closer and said, "What a find! I can't wait to read it. I miss her."

Why **most likely** is Anna's mom excited to read the diary?

Ⓐ She misses her mom.

Ⓑ She needs to learn old family recipes.

Ⓒ She wants to learn all the family's secrets.

Ⓓ She wants to see if her mom was like Anna.

3 Draw a line to match the underlined word in each sentence on the left with the definition for a homophone for the underlined word.

Last time, the dough was a big problem, for it was so thick that I couldn't even <u>knead</u> it!	people who see a doctor
I get mad at myself when my baking turns out wrong, but Mother keeps telling me to have more <u>patience</u>.	to fly without flapping wings
I guess we could make some after we're done here," she replied, "but you'll have to do the kneading because my shoulder is sore from all this work <u>in</u> the basement.	to require something

GO ON →

4 This question has two parts. First, answer part A. Then, answer part B.

Part A: Read the sentence from the passage.

I'll use less <u>flour</u> today and hope for the best.

Which definition fits the word <u>flour</u> in the sentence?

(A) a plant

(B) to open

(C) a baking ingredient

(D) to show one's talents

Part B: Which word is a homophone for the word <u>flour</u>?

(A) flier

(B) floor

(C) flower

(D) four

5 Read the sentences from the passage.

"I don't want to break the cranberry connection," she said. "I have to be ready to teach my own kids how to make that bread!"

How do the sentences support the theme of the passage?

(A) by showing how much Anna enjoys baking

(B) by showing how much Anna likes cranberry bread

(C) by showing how Anna needs to learn patience just like her grandmother

(D) by showing how Anna understands that baking cranberry bread is a tradition

GO ON →

Read the passage "Mysterious Neighbors" before answering Numbers 6 through 10.

Mysterious Neighbors

"How can something that old be right here in Illinois?" Rob asked himself. He had been using the Internet to research lost civilizations for a history project. Rob had found some interesting places around the world, and then he found a place called Cahokia.

After a quick search, Rob was amazed to find that Cahokia was a lost civilization about two hours from his home! Between 20,000 to 40,000 people once lived there and built 120 mounds, yet researchers disagree about exactly how many people lived there and the purpose of the mounds. Why don't they know? The Cahokia people disappeared and left behind no written records.

Rob read that long ago Cahokia covered 4,000 acres and was the largest city north of Mexico. Living there were farmers, hunters, craftsmen, traders, and priests. He already knew that researchers vary in their conclusions about Cahokia, but most of them think that the city was settled before the year 1000. What really surprised Rob was that everyone abandoned the city about 300 years later, about 100 years before Columbus or any other Europeans arrived in North America.

"Why would people build a big city and then abandon it?" Rob wondered. He was excited to tell his parents about what he had learned. They had heard about Cahokia but hadn't been there, and before Rob could even ask, his mom suggested that they go there the following weekend.

On Saturday morning, they stopped at the Visitor Center. A model of the ancient city showed the mounds and hundreds of homes, some with their own gardens. Next, Rob wanted to explore the huge Monks Mound, which was ten stories high. He had read that this mound was bigger at its base than the largest pyramid in Egypt. Rob wondered how many trips it took to haul enough dirt to make a mound that big.

The family climbed 156 steps to the top of the mound, which seemed to soar into the sky. From there, they looked out over an enormous flat, grassy area and the other mounds. The view was astounding. It was more amazing than Rob had expected.

"I can see parts of a wooden wall around the city," Rob said. "Maybe the people who lived here were attacked and killed by their enemies."

"Maybe," his mom agreed as she checked the booklet from the Visitor Center. "The ruler of Cahokia probably lived right here on this mound."

"But no one knows for sure that this ruler existed," Rob said, "and no one knows what role he had. Why didn't the Cahokia people leave behind any records?"

"They didn't forget to write down their history, Rob," his dad explained. "Long ago, many groups didn't have a written language, so they couldn't record their history. Instead, parents told stories to their children, and the children told the same stories to their own kids. That's how they tried to preserve their history, yet those stories are lost now."

"That's too bad," Rob said, "because I'd really like to know more about the people who lived here. After all, they were our neighbors!"

GO ON →

Now answer Numbers 6 through 10. Base your answers on "Mysterious Neighbors."

6 This question has two parts. First, answer part A. Then, answer part B.

Part A: Which sentence **best** describes the message in this passage?

Ⓐ History is very exciting.

Ⓑ Some things cannot be explained.

Ⓒ You can find amazing facts on the Web.

Ⓓ Some stories from history may be lost to us.

Part B: Which detail from the passage **best** supports your answer in part A?

Ⓐ Rob and his family go to visit Cahokia.

Ⓑ Rob wishes he knew more about Cahokia.

Ⓒ Rob researches lost civilizations on the Internet.

Ⓓ Rob gets to see what an ancient city might have looked like.

7 Read the sentence from the passage.

Rob read that long ago Cahokia covered 4,000 acres and was the largest city north of Mexico.

Which word from the sentence is a homophone for a word that means "a type of color"?

Ⓐ read

Ⓑ long

Ⓒ acres

Ⓓ city

8 Which sentences explain why Rob **most likely** wants to visit Cahokia? Pick **two** choices.

(A) He wants to tell his friends about it.

(B) He is interested in the city's history.

(C) He wants to see where the ruler lived.

(D) He wants to see what the city looked like.

(E) He is interested in spending time with family.

(F) He is interested in having a class trip to see it.

9 This question has two parts. First, answer part A. Then, answer part B.

Part A: Read the sentence from the passage.

Rob wondered how many trips it took to haul enough dirt to make a mound that big.

Which definition fits the word haul in the sentence?

(A) a passage from one place to another

(B) a large room for events

(C) to carry something

(D) to find something

Part B: Which word is a homophone for the word haul?

(A) hail

(B) hall

(C) heal

(D) howl

GO ON →

10 Read the sentence.

Information that is not recorded may be lost forever.

Circle the paragraph that **best** supports the theme of the passage stated in the sentence above.

The family climbed 156 steps to the top of the mound, which seemed to soar into the sky. From there, they looked out over an enormous flat, grassy area and the other mounds. The view was astounding. It was more amazing than Rob had expected.

"I can see parts of a wooden wall around the city," Rob said. "Maybe the people who lived here were attacked and killed by their enemies."

"Maybe," his mom agreed as she checked the booklet from the Visitor Center. "The ruler of Cahokia probably lived right here on this mound."

"But no one knows for sure that this ruler existed," Rob said, "and no one knows what role he had. Why didn't the Cahokia people leave behind any records?"

Name: _____ Date: _____

Now answer Number 11. Base your answer on "The Cranberry Connection" and "Mysterious Neighbors."

11 Compare the themes of "The Cranberry Connection" and "Mysterious Neighbors." Support your answer with details from both passages.

_____

_____

_____

_____

_____

_____

_____

_____

_____

_____

_____

_____

_____

_____

_____

Answer Key

Question	Correct Answer	Content Focus	CCSS	Complexity
1A	B	Theme	RL.4.2	DOK 3
1B	C, E	Theme/Text Evidence	RL.4.2/ RL.4.1	DOK 3
2	A	Theme	RL.4.2	DOK 2
3	see below	Homophones	L.4.4c	DOK 2
4A	C	Homophones	L.4.4c	DOK 1
4B	C	Homophones	L.4.4c	DOK 1
5	D	Theme	RL.4.2	DOK 2
6A	D	Theme	RL.4.2	DOK 3
6B	B	Theme/Text Evidence	RL.4.2/ RL.4.1	DOK 3
7	A	Homophones	L.4.4c	DOK 1
8	B, D	Character, Setting, Plot: Cause and Effect	RL.4.3	DOK 2
9A	C	Homophones	L.4.4c	DOK 1
9B	B	Homophones	L.4.4c	DOK 1
10	see below	Theme	RL.4.2	DOK 2
11	see below	Writing About Text	W.4.9a	DOK 4

Comprehension 1A, 1B, 2, 5, 6A, 6B, 8, 10	/12	%
Vocabulary 3, 4A, 4B, 7, 9A, 9B	/8	%
Total Weekly Assessment Score	/20	%

3 Students should draw lines to match the following sentences and homophone definitions:
- Last time, the dough was a big problem, for it was so thick that I couldn't even knead it!—to require something
- I get mad at myself when my baking turns out wrong, but Mother keeps telling me to have more patience.—people who see a doctor
- I guess we could make some after we're done here," she replied, "but you'll have to do the kneading because my shoulder is sore from all this work in the basement.—to fly without flapping wings

10 Students should circle the following paragraph:
- "But no one knows for sure that this ruler existed," Rob said, "and no one knows what role he had. Why didn't the Cahokia people leave behind any records?"

11 To receive full credit for the response, the following information should be included:
Both passages show that keeping records of the past is important. In "The Cranberry Connection," Anna learns she shares a trait with her grandmother and that the cranberry bread her mom makes is a family tradition. In "Mysterious Neighbors," because an ancient culture did not keep written records, we know little about it.

Read the article "Nonrenewable Resources" before answering Numbers 1 through 5.

Nonrenewable Resources

Fuels used to produce energy come from many different sources, some of which are nonrenewable. These resources have a limited supply and cannot be replaced, so once they are used, they are gone forever.

Some examples of nonrenewable resources are coal, oil, and natural gas. They are usually found in deposits deep underground. Scientists look for these resources in areas that were covered by water before the time of the dinosaurs. Dead plants and animals were buried under layers of rock and soil, and then heat and pressure were applied to the remains. After millions of years, these fuels were created.

Throughout time, our use of these resources has changed. Oil has been used as a fuel for many years. Before the 1890s, the main product made from oil was kerosene, which heated homes and lit lamps. The invention of the automobile created a need for gasoline, which replaced kerosene as the main product made from oil. The amount of gasoline needed increased as the number of cars on the road got larger, and oil became the most used energy source.

Like oil, natural gas has been used for a long time. One early use of natural gas was lighting street lamps in the predawn hours. In the past, natural gas had problems as a fuel source. The wooden pipes used to carry natural gas leaked. It was hard to move gas safely. The invention of strong pipes that did not leak changed the gas industry by allowing natural gas to be carried far from where it was found. Today, people use natural gas to heat their homes and water. Natural gas may be used to preheat your oven when you want to bake something, and it powers clothes dryers, fireplaces, and gas grills.

GO ON →

Coal burns like oil and natural gas. Coal is a black or brownish-black rock that is removed from the ground using giant machines. There are four types of coal. Microscopes are used to help determine the type of coal. Each type of coal burns differently and is used for different things.

Coal has had many uses. In the past, it was used to make items for the military, such as shot and shells. It was burned to produce steam for train engines and steamboats, and it was also used as fuel to heat homes. Today, coal is used to create almost half of all the electricity generated in the United States. It is used by the cement, steel, and paper industries. By-products of coal are used to make plastics, tar, and medicine. Coal is also used to make steel, which is used to make building materials and automobiles.

Nonrenewable resources provide electricity that powers many things. They are used to create products we use every day. Oil, coal, and natural gas have been used as fuel for many years. Our use of these fuels has changed over time, and it will most likely continue to change.

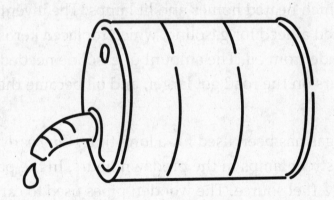

Now answer Numbers 1 through 5. Base your answers on "Nonrenewable Resources."

1 This question has two parts. First, answer part A. Then, answer part B.

Part A: Which sentence **best** describes what the article is about?

(A) Natural gas has been used as a fuel for many years.

(B) Coal was used to power train engines and steamboats.

(C) Before the 1890s, the main product made from oil was kerosene.

(D) The uses for nonrenewable resources have changed through time.

Part B: Which detail from the article **best** supports your answer in part A?

(A) Nonrenewable resources help to provide electricity.

(B) There are different types of coal buried in the ground.

(C) Gasoline replaced kerosene as the main product made from oil.

(D) Fuels were created from dead plants and animals over millions of years.

2 Read the sentence from the article.

Fuels used to produce energy come from many different sources, some of which are <u>nonrenewable</u>.

The prefix *non-* means "not." What does it mean if something is <u>nonrenewable</u>?

(A) It will always be available.

(B) It can be made in factories.

(C) It is at risk of being used up.

(D) It is always increasing in amount.

GO ON →

3 Which of the following are examples of nonrenewable resources? Pick **three** choices.

(A) animals

(B) coal

(C) gas

(D) oil

(E) paper

(F) plants

4 Underline the sentence in the paragraph that shows how a problem was solved in the gas industry.

Like oil, natural gas has been used for a long time. One early use of natural gas was lighting street lamps in the predawn hours. In the past, natural gas had problems as a fuel source. The wooden pipes used to carry natural gas leaked. It was hard to move gas safely. The invention of strong pipes that did not leak changed the gas industry by allowing natural gas to be carried far from where it was found. Today, people use natural gas to heat their homes and water. Natural gas may be used to preheat your oven when you want to bake something, and it powers clothes dryers, fireplaces, and gas grills.

GO ON →

5 This question has two parts. First, answer part A. Then, answer part B.

Part A: Read the sentence from the article.

Microscopes are used to help determine the type of coal.

The prefix *micro-* means "tiny." What do a microscopes do?

(A) They allow you to look at very small things.

(B) They make large things look smaller than they are.

(C) They allow you to look at things that were once very small.

(D) They make small things larger so you can see them without a machine.

Part B: Which other words have the same prefix as the word microscopes? Pick **two** choices.

(A) macaroni

(B) machetes

(C) microphones

(D) microwave

(E) periscope

(F) telescopes

GO ON →

Read the article "Renewable Resources" before answering Numbers 6 through 10.

Renewable Resources

Renewable resources are used to produce energy. Renewable resources are nondepletable, which means that they can never be used up. On the other hand, nonrenewable resources can be depleted, or used up. In the past, it was more expensive to use renewable resources than nonrenewable resources to produce energy. But today, the price of nonrenewable resources, such as oil and natural gas, has increased. Scientists are searching for new ways to use renewable resources.

One renewable resource is biomass, which is a material that comes from plants and animals and contains microorganisms. You cannot see these tiny organisms without a microscope. This resource is renewable because there will always be plants and animals. Wood is a type of biomass that once created most of the energy used. People burned wood to produce heat, but this changed when people began to use other fuels. Today, some people still use wood to heat their homes and to cook. Most wood fuel is used by the paper and wood industries, which burn their wood scraps to produce electricity.

Another renewable resource is geothermal energy, which comes from heat within Earth. This heat is always in the ground and is recovered as steam or hot water. Geothermal energy can be seen at a hot spring. This natural pool is filled with water heated underground. Long ago, people used hot springs for bathing, cooking, and heating, and today, some people still bathe in hot springs. Geothermal energy can be used to heat buildings, and it is also used for drying food and gold mining.

Water is another renewable resource. Hydropower is created when water falls or flows. Water is one of the oldest energy sources. For instance, it was used to turn a paddle wheel to grind grain thousands of years ago. Today, about one-third of the power that comes from renewable resources comes from hydropower.

GO ON →

The sun is a renewable resource because it does not stop shining. You can feel solar energy when you feel the warmth of the sun's rays. During World War II, there was a limited supply of electricity, so to increase the electric supply in our country, buildings were designed so that the windows, walls, and floors collected and stored solar energy. Today, some homes and businesses use solar panels to collect solar energy.

The wind is a powerful renewable resource. Wind power has been used since ancient times as an energy source. Windmills have pumped water, have ground wheat and corn, and have generated electricity. Today, windmills are a nonstandard way of generating power. However, their popularity is growing. Some areas of the country have seen an increase in the number of windmills that are used to generate electricity. Using windmills requires some preplanning. You need another energy source for days when the wind does not blow.

Renewable resources have been used for thousands of years. Some people are looking at renewable resources in new ways. They are finding ways to replace some nonrenewable resources.

GO ON →

Name: _____ Date: _____

Now answer Numbers 6 through 10. Base your answers on "Renewable Resources."

6 Complete the chart to show the main idea of the article and **two** details that support the main idea. Write the sentences from the list. Not all of the sentences will be used.

Main Idea

Supporting Details

Sentences:

Windmills generate electricity using wind power.

Hydropower is one of the earliest forms of power.

The price of nonrenewable resources has increased.

Renewable resources come from sources that cannot be depleted.

GO ON →

7 Which of the following are types of biomass? Pick **three** choices.

(A) animals

(B) oil

(C) plants

(D) steam

(E) water

(F) wood

8 This question has two parts. First, answer part A. Then, answer part B.

Part A: Which statement explains why geothermal energy is a renewable resource?

(A) Earth will always produce heat.

(B) Hot springs will always have hot water.

(C) There will always be heat coming from the sun.

(D) The flow of water will always produce electricity.

Part B: Which sentence from the article **best** supports your answer in part A?

(A) "Most wood fuel is used by the paper and wood industries, which burn their wood scraps to produce electricity."

(B) "This heat is always in the ground and is recovered as steam or hot water."

(C) "Geothermal energy can be used to heat buildings, and it is also used for drying food and gold mining."

(D) "Today, about one-third of the power that comes from renewable resources comes from hydropower."

GO ON →

9 Read the sentence from the article.

Today, windmills are a <u>nonstandard</u> way of generating power.

If the prefix *non-* means "not," what is a <u>nonstandard</u> way of doing something?

- Ⓐ an old way of doing it
- Ⓑ the best way of doing it
- Ⓒ not the usual way of doing it
- Ⓓ not the correct way of doing it

10 This question has two parts. First, answer part A. Then, answer part B.

Part A: Read the sentence from the article.

Using windmills requires some <u>preplanning</u>.

The prefix *pre-* means "before" What does the word <u>preplanning</u> mean?

- Ⓐ forgetting to plan
- Ⓑ planning ahead
- Ⓒ waiting to plan
- Ⓓ planning again

Part B: Which word has the same prefix as <u>preplanning</u>?

- Ⓐ prefer
- Ⓑ preview
- Ⓒ president
- Ⓓ pressure

Name: _____ Date: _____

Now answer Number 11. Base your answer on "Nonrenewable Resources" and "Renewable Resources."

11 How has the way we use nonrenewable and renewable resources changed throughout the years? What has led to these changes? Support your answer with details from both passages.

_____

_____

_____

_____

_____

_____

_____

_____

_____

_____

_____

_____

_____

_____

_____

_____

Answer Key

Name: _____

Question	Correct Answer	Content Focus	CCSS	Complexity
1A	D	Main Idea and Key Details	RI.4.2	DOK 2
1B	C	Main Idea and Key Details/ Text Evidence	RI.4.2/ RI.4.1	DOK 2
2	C	Latin and Greek Prefixes	L.4.4b	DOK 2
3	B, C, D	Main Idea and Key Details	RI.4.2	DOK 1
4	see below	Text Structure: Problem and Solution	RI.4.5	DOK 2
5A	A	Latin and Greek Prefixes	L.4.4b	DOK 2
5B	C, D	Latin and Greek Prefixes	L.4.4b	DOK 2
6	see below	Main Idea and Key Details	RI.4.2	DOK 2
7	A, C, F	Main Idea and Key Details	RI.4.2	DOK 1
8A	A	Main Idea and Key Details	RI.4.2	DOK 2
8B	B	Main Idea and Key Details/ Text Evidence	RI.4.2/ RI.4.1	DOK 2
9	C	Latin and Greek Prefixes	L.4.4b	DOK 2
10A	B	Latin and Greek Prefixes	L.4.4b	DOK 2
10B	B	Latin and Greek Prefixes	L.4.4b	DOK 2
11	see below	Writing About Text	W.4.9b	DOK 4

Comprehension 1A, 1B, 3, 4, 6, 7, 8A, 8B	/12	%
Vocabulary 2, 5A, 5B, 9, 10A, 10B	/8	%
Total Weekly Assessment Score	/20	%

4 Students should underline the following sentence in the paragraph:
- The invention of strong pipes that did not leak changed the gas industry by allowing natural gas to be carried far from where it was found.

6 Students should complete the chart with the following sentences:
- Main Idea— Renewable resources come from sources that cannot be depleted.
- Supporting Details—Windmills generate electricity using wind power.; Hydropower is one of the earliest forms of power.

11 To receive full credit for the response, the following information should be included: In the past, more nonrenewable resources were used. Then people began to use more renewable resources. Now, people are looking for ways to use more renewable resources because they will never run out.

Weekly Assessment · Unit 6, Week 3

Read the article "A Shirt for Two Chickens" before answering Numbers 1 through 5.

A Shirt for Two Chickens

Long ago, if you needed a shirt, you might trade with your neighbor. You would give your neighbor two chickens and in exchange, your neighbor would make you a shirt. What if your neighbor had her own flock of chickens? What if she didn't need tomatoes from your garden or corn from your fields? How would you get a shirt?

Thousands of years ago, people bartered, or traded, for what they could not make or grow. At first, they traded animals for what they needed. Then they traded their extra crops for eggs, clothing, and other necessities, and they also traded their services. But sometimes no one wanted what people had to trade.

Because necessity is the mother of invention, people began to use money, which made sure people had something others wanted. Money was a lot easier to carry around than crops and animals, and it also made trading less messy. Trading money for a pair of socks was much neater than giving someone half of a chicken! However, it took a very long time to develop the money system we use today.

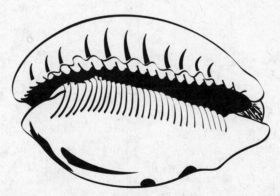

For thousands of years, cowrie shells like this one were used as money.

GO ON →

The cowrie snail lives near the Pacific and Indian Oceans. Its egg-shaped shell is shiny and smooth with a flat underside. Cowrie shells are the oldest and most widely used form of money. More than three thousand years ago, people in China and Africa began using cowrie shells as money.

Then several hundred years later, the Chinese began forming metal into the shape of cowrie shells, and they used these metal shells as money. In time, the metal shapes became round coins that had holes in the middle and could be strung together, like a necklace.

About 2,500 years ago, people began to make coins out of silver, bronze, and gold, and they were often stamped with a picture of the current ruler or king. The metal used in the coins made them valuable.

By the 700s, the Chinese tired of carrying around heavy coins, so they began printing and using paper money. But they printed so much paper money that it lost its value. After all, if you could print money nonstop, everyone would have plenty of it. In time, no one accepted the worthless money in exchange for goods.

For many years, much of the paper money in our own nation was worthless. Now the printing of money in the United States is tightly controlled to keep our money valuable. Did anyone ever tell you, "Money doesn't grow on trees"? They wanted you to know that money is hard to get. However, if money did grow on trees, no one would bother picking it. It, too, would be worthless.

GO ON →

Now answer Numbers 1 through 5. Base your answers on "A Shirt for Two Chickens."

1 This question has two parts. First, answer part A. Then, answer part B.

Part A: Which sentence **best** describes the main idea of the article?

Ⓐ Not everyone wants to trade for chickens.

Ⓑ Cowrie shells are the oldest form of money.

Ⓒ Paper money has been used for many years.

Ⓓ Money was invented to make trading easier.

Part B: Which sentence from the article **best** supports your answer in part A?

Ⓐ "Long ago, if you needed a shirt, you might trade with your neighbor."

Ⓑ "Trading money for a pair of socks was much neater than giving someone half of a chicken!"

Ⓒ "The cowrie snail lives near the Pacific and Indian Oceans."

Ⓓ "For many years, much of the paper money in our own nation was worthless."

2 Read the sentence from the article.

Because necessity is the mother of invention, people began to use money, which made sure people had something others wanted.

What is the meaning of the saying "necessity is the mother of invention"?

Ⓐ Mothers need more inventions.

Ⓑ Invention needs to have a mother.

Ⓒ Mothers invent things to make work easier.

Ⓓ Inventions are created when something is needed.

GO ON →

3 Write the effect for each cause in the chart. Choose from the effects in the list. Not all of the effects will be used.

Cause	Effect
Metals were used to make coins.	
Coins became too heavy to carry.	
Too much money was printed.	

Effects:
Money became worthless.
Coins were considered valuable.
People used cowrie shells as money.
People bartered for what they needed.
The Chinese began to print paper money.

GO ON →

4 Which conclusions can be drawn about why forms of money kept changing? Pick **two** choices.

(A) Some forms of money were hard to use.

(B) Money wore out and had to be replaced.

(C) Not everyone agreed on the best form of money.

(D) People grew tired of always using the same money.

(E) People found too many cowrie shells on the beaches.

(F) Everyone had enough chickens and did not need to trade.

5 This question has two parts. First, answer part A. Then, answer part B.

Part A: Read the sentences from the article.

Did anyone ever tell you, "Money doesn't grow on trees"? They wanted you to know that money is hard to get. However, if money did grow on trees, no one would bother picking it.

What does the saying "money doesn't grow on trees" mean?

(A) Money must be printed by the government.

(B) You have to be an adult to get money.

(C) Money grows only on certain bushes.

(D) You have to work to get money.

Part B: Which phrase from the sentences **best** explains what the saying means?

(A) "anyone ever tell you"

(B) "wanted you to know"

(C) "is hard to get"

(D) "no one would bother"

GO ON →

Read the article "What Good Is Money?" before answering Numbers 6 through 10.

What Good Is Money?

Before the United States became a country, the colonists used a mixture of Spanish, French, and English money, and banks were even allowed to print their own money. By 1860, about 8,000 banks were offering paper money that they had printed themselves. However, much of this money was worthless. Have you heard people say, "It's not worth the paper it's printed on"? They could have been describing paper money during this time of our history. It's not surprising that people began to distrust paper money and they relied more on coins and old-fashioned trading.

It was not until the Civil War that our government started to control the printing of money. In 1861, Congress issued paper money in the amounts of $5, $10, and $20. Most importantly, you could take this paper money to the bank and exchange it for coins. Special paper with special ink was used to print the money. People could not easily print their own money, so for the first time, Americans could trust their paper money. In fact, the money printed back in 1861 can still be used, but most of it is in museums.

GO ON →

Since then, the size of paper money and the words printed on it have changed slightly. Money is now printed in $50 and $100 bills, too, but the money we use is much the same as it was back in 1861. In fact, now most nations use paper money and coins that are printed by their governments.

What has changed is how we use money. We buy many things with credit and debit cards now, and often, no real money changes hands. Still, no one is ready to predict that paper money and coins are likely to disappear anytime soon!

What role does money play in our lives? Prices are set in terms of money. For example, a farmer does not have to figure out how many chickens to trade for a computer. A teacher does not have to guess how many hours of teaching to trade for a car. An item has a price tag that tells what it costs in dollars, and instead of trading something for a computer or a car, we simply use money.

Money is also used to pay people for the work they do. Have you heard the saying, "Time is money"? If you are getting paid by the hour, that's true. The longer you work, the more money you earn. Everyone is willing to accept money for working. Imagine being paid in tomatoes or chickens when what you really need is money to buy gas for your car.

We can save money, too. While chickens get old and tomatoes rot, money keeps nicely, so in this way, money helps us plan for our future.

Anything, even shells, can be used as money, but everyone must be willing to accept that form of money. When people stop accepting a form of money, it loses its value. Are you thinking about inventing a new kind of money, using something you have lots of? Chances are you won't succeed. Inventing a new money system is easier said than done!

GO ON →

Now answer Numbers 6 through 10. Base your answers on "What Good Is Money?"

6 This question has two parts. First, answer part A. Then, answer part B.

Part A: Which sentence **best** explains the main idea of the first two paragraphs of the article?

(A) Americans struggled many years before setting up a trusted money system.

(B) The main thing that has changed about our money is the way we use it.

(C) The Civil War was a turning point for our money system.

(D) Printing too much paper money leads to problems.

Part B: Which detail from the article **best** supports your answer in part A?

(A) ". . . the colonists used a mixture of Spanish, French, and English money, . . ."

(B) ". . . they relied more on coins and old-fashioned trading."

(C) ". . . Congress issued paper money in the amounts of $5, $10, and $20."

(D) ". . . so for the first time, Americans could trust their paper money."

7 Read the sentences from the article.

Have you heard the saying, "Time is money"? If you are getting paid by the hour, that's true.

What is the meaning of the saying "time is money"?

(A) Time is valuable.

(B) Money is valuable.

(C) The more money you have, the more time you have.

(D) The more time you have, the more money you have.

GO ON →

8 Read the sentence.

For better or worse, the worth of products and services is measured in dollars.

Circle the paragraph that is **best** supported by the detail above.

What has changed is how we use money. We buy many things with credit and debit cards now, and often, no real money changes hands. Still, no one is ready to predict that paper money and coins are likely to disappear anytime soon!

What role does money play in our lives? Prices are set in terms of money. For example, a farmer does not have to figure out how many chickens to trade for a computer. A teacher does not have to guess how many hours of teaching to trade for a car. An item has a price tag that tells what it costs in dollars, and instead of trading something for a computer or a car, we simply use money.

Money is also used to pay people for the work they do. Have you heard the saying, "Time is money"? If you are getting paid by the hour, that's true. The longer you work, the more money you earn. Everyone is willing to accept money for working. Imagine being paid in tomatoes or chickens when what you really need is money to buy gas for your car.

We can save money, too. While chickens get old and tomatoes rot, money keeps nicely, so in this way, money helps us plan for our future.

GO ON →

9 Why do most people want money instead of goods as a payment for working? Pick **two** choices.

(A) It is easy to save money.

(B) Everyone accepts money as payment.

(C) People will not agree to work for free.

(D) Money is worth more now than it used to be.

(E) People can use money to buy things that they need.

(F) Prices of products and services are set in dollar amounts.

10 This question has two parts. First, answer part A. Then, answer part B.

Part A: Read the sentences from the article.

Are you thinking about inventing a new kind of money, using something you have lots of? Chances are you won't succeed. Inventing a new money system is <u>easier said than done</u>!

What does the saying "easier said than done" mean?

(A) Talk means nothing and actions mean everything.

(B) Some people talk a lot but never do anything.

(C) Do not brag about what you are going to do.

(D) The task is easier to talk about than to do.

Part B: Which phrase from the sentences **best** explains what the saying means?

(A) "thinking about inventing"

(B) "using something you have"

(C) "you won't succeed"

(D) "a new money system"

Name: _____ Date: _____

Now answer Number 11. Base your answer on "A Shirt for Two Chickens" and "What Good Is Money?"

11 Has the role or purpose of money changed throughout time? Support your answer with details from both passages.

_____

_____

_____

_____

_____

_____

_____

_____

_____

_____

_____

_____

_____

_____

Question	Correct Answer	Content Focus	CCSS	Complexity
1A	D	Main Idea and Key Details	RI.4.2	DOK 2
1B	B	Main Idea and Key Details/ Text Evidence	RI.4.2/ RI.4.1	DOK 2
2	D	Proverbs and Adages	L.4.5b	DOK 2
3	see below	Text Structure: Cause and Effect	RI.4.5	DOK 2
4	A, C	Main Idea and Key Details	RI.4.2	DOK 2
5A	D	Proverbs and Adages	L.4.5b	DOK 2
5B	C	Proverbs and Adages/Text Evidence	L.4.5b/ RI.4.1	DOK 2
6A	A	Main Idea and Key Details	RI.4.2	DOK 2
6B	D	Main Idea and Key Details/ Text Evidence	RI.4.2/ RI.4.1	DOK 2
7	A	Proverbs and Adages	L.4.5b	DOK 2
8	see below	Main Idea and Key Details	RI.4.2	DOK 2
9	B, E	Main Idea and Key Details	RI.4.2	DOK 2
10A	D	Proverbs and Adages	L.4.5b	DOK 2
10B	C	Proverbs and Adages/Text Evidence	L.4.5b/ RI.4.1	DOK 2
11	see below	Writing About Text	W.4.9b	DOK 4

Comprehension 1A, 1B, 3, 4, 6A, 6B, 8, 9	/12	%
Vocabulary 2, 5A, 5B, 7, 10A, 10B	/8	%
Total Weekly Assessment Score	/20	%

3 Students should complete the chart with the following sentences:
- Cause—Metals were used to make coins.; Effect—Coins were considered valuable.
- Cause—Coins became too heavy to carry.; Effect—The Chinese began to print paper money.
- Cause—Too much money was printed.; Effect—Money became worthless.

8 Students should circle the following paragraph:
- What role does money play in our lives? Prices are set in terms of money. For example, a farmer does not have to figure out how many chickens to trade for a computer. A teacher does not have to guess how many hours of teaching to trade for a car. An item has a price tag that tells what it costs in dollars, and instead of trading something for a computer or a car, we simply use money.

11 To receive full credit for the response, the following information should be included: The role of money is essentially unchanged. It provides something everyone wants so we can trade for the things we need and pay people for working. It also allows us to save for the future. Those functions have always been the role of money.

Read the passage "Thinking Big" before answering Numbers 1 through 5.

Thinking Big

"Good evening, and welcome to our first ever poetry slam!" announced Mrs. Harmon. "We're happy to see that so many of our families and friends turned out for this event in support of our local food bank."

Olivia sat in the back of the classroom in a row with the other poets and listened as Mrs. Harmon thanked everyone for bringing cans and boxes of food as their entrance ticket to the slam. Olivia glanced at the shelves and tables. She always thought big, and to her, the boxes were grocery warehouses stocked with good things to eat and the cans were colorful barn silos filled with food.

Olivia thought back to the day when the class had the idea to support hungry people in their community. They noticed a photo in the local newspaper that showed families receiving bags of groceries from the food bank. There was no article or caption, but a picture is worth a thousand words. The students could see there was a need, and they were determined to help fill it.

It took a while to come up with the perfect way to help. Students thought of raising money by holding a car wash or a walk-a-thon, and a baked goods sale and a garage sale were ideas they considered. Olivia suggested soccer games between students and teachers and between other schools in the district. All their ideas were snowflakes, melting one by one until finally, one stuck. They decided to hold a poetry slam.

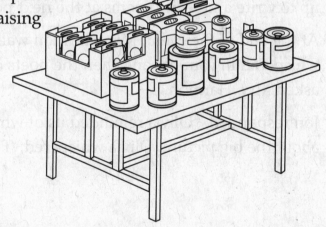

Olivia was brought back to the present by Mrs. Harmon's voice. "In a poetry slam, poets focus on what they are saying and how they are saying it," she explained. "The best part is that the audience is free to show the poets how much they like the poems."

GO ON →

The poetry slam seemed like a good idea, until now. Olivia was nervous, and she could tell her classmates were jittery too. How would the audience react to their poetry? Then Olivia thought big. She whispered in Jon's ear and said, "Pass it on." When it was time to perform, the poets were ready, and Jon confidently stepped up first.

> *Sharing food and a smiling face,*
> *Our food bank is a caring place!*

Afterward, the audience was a pod of seals, clapping and clapping for Jon. Then it was Kenji's turn to perform.

> *No one should go hungry, this much we all know.*
> *We can fill our food bank, let's give it a go!*

Kenji's spunky reading gave the audience a good reason to stomp their feet and snap their fingers. Olivia was last, and she recited from the heart.

> *A slam each year is not enough,*
> *One each month won't be so tough.*
> *Poems are fun. Who will write?*
> *Will you join the hunger fight?*

"Bravo! Right on! Yes!" shouted the crowd, and soon, twenty people signed up to write and recite poems at the next poetry slam.

At the end of the event, Mrs. Harmon walked up to Jon. "I noticed Olivia whispered in your ear and then the poets calmed down. What did she say?" asked Mrs. Harmon.

Jon responded, "Olivia reminded us of why we were here. She thought about the big picture. Olivia whispered, 'Feed the hungry!'"

GO ON →

Now answer Numbers 1 through 5. Base your answers on "Thinking Big."

1 This question has two parts. First, answer part A. Then, answer part B.

Part A: Which statement **best** describes the theme of the passage?

(A) People need to work together to get anything done.

(B) Eat good foods to stay strong and healthy.

(C) You can find a way to help those in need.

(D) Stick with a task until you are finished.

Part B: Which detail from the passage **best** supports your answer in part A?

(A) Mrs. Harmon welcomes everyone to the poetry slam.

(B) The students want to raise money for a local food bank.

(C) At first, the students do not know the best way to raise money.

(D) The students feel nervous when they get up in front of the audience.

GO ON →

2 Read the sentence from the passage.

All their ideas were snowflakes, melting one by one until finally, one stuck.

Which feeling does the author create by using the metaphor "their ideas were snowflakes, melting one by one"?

- Ⓐ anger
- Ⓑ disappointment
- Ⓒ fear
- Ⓓ happiness

3 Underline the sentence in the paragraph that **best** supports the overall message of the passage.

Olivia thought back to the day when the class had the idea to support hungry people in their community. They noticed a photo in the local newspaper that showed families receiving bags of groceries from the food bank. There was no article or caption, but a picture is worth a thousand words. The students could see there was a need, and they were determined to help fill it.

GO ON →

4 Read the sentence from the passage.

Afterward, the audience was a pod of seals, clapping and clapping for Jon.

Which feelings does the author create with this sentence? Pick **two** choices.

(A) failure

(B) hope

(C) fear

(D) sadness

(E) success

(F) support

5 Read the lines from a poem in the passage.

Poems are fun. Who will write?
Will you join the hunger fight?

Which sentence **best** explains how these lines support the theme of the passage?

(A) They tell what happens when you join a fun group.

(B) They tell why many people like to write poems.

(C) They tell how people can help others in need.

(D) They tell how to avoid ever being hungry.

GO ON →

Read the passage "The Next President" before answering Numbers 6 through 10.

The Next President

Boom, boom, boom—my heart is a drum beating loud and fast as I walk up on stage to speak. I am thrilled because today I will become the best president of the student government—ever.

Last night, my parents talked to me about the school election because they thought I was overly confident. "You waged a hard campaign, Connor, but so did Vanessa," noted Dad, "and either one of you could be elected."

"You may be too sure of winning," warned Mom, "and I don't want you to count your chickens before they hatch."

But how can I miss? I am a ticking clock, and my time is now. It is my final chance to get their votes, and I will deliver a speech that the students will never forget.

"I'll find a way to get handheld electronic games for every classroom and a vending machine for the lunchroom. Homework will be optional, and short recesses will be extinct dinosaurs. From now on, morning and afternoon recesses will last for an hour, maybe longer. Bring your cell phones to school, as there will be rules about using them in class, but only a few. Vote for me—Connor Storms—as your next president!"

To conclude, I start a cheer that I wrote myself:

Connor, Connor, he's the one
To get the job done, done, done!

GO ON →

Most students join in, and I feel great about my chances. While Vanessa is speaking, I take the opportunity to pass around flyers I made because I know this poem will help students decide I am right for the job.

When put to any kind of test,
Connor is by far the best!
It's the start of a brand new day,
Vote for Connor. Hip! Hip! Hooray!

As students vote, I try not to show how happy I am. I notice that Vanessa is a wooden toy soldier, standing tall and stiff, and I can see why, for it is no fun to lose.

At the end of the day, the votes are counted, and our principal is ready to announce the results. "Connor Storms," I can hear him say, but instead, he says, "The next president of our student government is . . . Vanessa Gainous!"

I cannot believe what I am hearing! How can this be? I thought I would be the next president. I see Vanessa coming toward me, but I turn and walk out of the building.

Tonight, Mom and Dad could have said, "We told you so," but they know how stunned I am. I did not see the defeat coming, and we talk a long time about what it means to be a good sport. I realize there were times when I did not respect my opponent and I was not polite, and I definitely was not a gracious loser, but I will change. The first thing I do is call and congratulate Vanessa, and I offer to help her in any way I can. Then I get busy making flyers to hand out in school tomorrow.

Keeping all her promises and working for our school,
Vanessa, our new president, is smart and very cool!

GO ON →

Now answer Numbers 6 through 10. Base your answers on "The Next President."

6 This question has two parts. First, answer part A. Then, answer part B.

Part A: Which statement **best** summarizes the theme of the passage?

(A) Winners never lose.

(B) Always be a good sport.

(C) Do not be afraid to take advice.

(D) Get involved in student government.

Part B: Which sentence from the passage **best** supports your answer in part A?

(A) "Most students join in, and I feel great about my chances."

(B) "As students vote, I try not to show how happy I am."

(C) "I see Vanessa coming toward me, but I turn and walk out of the building."

(D) "The first thing I do is call and congratulate Vanessa, and I offer to help her in any way I can."

7 Read the paragraph from the passage.

But how can I miss? I am a ticking clock, and my time is now. It is my final chance to get their votes, and I will deliver a speech that the students will never forget.

Why does the author compare Connor to a ticking clock in the paragraph?

(A) Connor has a heart that keeps on ticking.

(B) Connor always likes to know what time it is.

(C) Connor will promise to give the students watches.

(D) Connor does not have much time left before the election.

GO ON →

8 This question has two parts. First, answer part A. Then, answer part B.

Part A: Read the sentence from the passage.

I notice that Vanessa is a <u>wooden toy soldier, standing tall and stiff</u>, and I can see why, for it is no fun to lose.

Which feeling does the author create with the metaphor "a wooden toy soldier, standing tall and stiff"?

(A) confusion

(B) joy

(C) playfulness

(D) tenseness

Part B: Which phrase from the sentence **best** explains what the saying means?

(A) "notice that Vanessa"

(B) "I can see why"

(C) "for it is"

(D) "no fun to lose"

GO ON →

9 Read the sentence from the passage.

While Vanessa is speaking, I take the opportunity to pass around flyers
I made because I know this poem will help students decide I am right
for the job.

How does this sentence support the theme of the passage? Pick
two choices.

(A) It tells why speakers often cannot be heard.

(B) It explains how to treat your opponent fairly.

(C) It explains the importance of respecting others.

(D) It tells why Connor wants to be the next president.

(E) It tells how someone acts who is not a good sport.

(F) It explains the best time to pass papers to a group.

10 The passage is told from a first-person point of view. Circle the
conclusions that can be drawn about how this point of view helps the
reader understand the passage.

First-Person Point of View
The point of view reveals how Connor feels when he loses.
The point of view compares Connors feelings with Vanessa's feelings.
The point of view show how sure Connor is about winning the election.
The point of view suggests who the students think will be the best president.
The point of view explains what Mom and Dad say while Connor is at school.
The point of view describes why Vanessa does not complain about her opponent.

Name: _____ Date: _____

Now answer Number 11. Base your answer on "Thinking Big" and "The Next President."

11 How do the themes of "Thinking Big" and "The Next President" present a positive message about how to treat others? Support your answer with details from both passages.

_____

_____

_____

_____

_____

_____

_____

_____

_____

_____

_____

_____

_____

_____

Answer Key

Name: _____

Question	Correct Answer	Content Focus	CCSS	Complexity
1A	C	Theme	RL.4.2	DOK 3
1B	B	Theme/Text Evidence	RL.4.2/ RL.4.1	DOK 3
2	B	Figurative Language: Metaphor	L.4.5a	DOK 2
3	see below	Theme	RL.4.2	DOK 2
4	E, F	Figurative Language: Metaphor	L.4.5a	DOK 2
5	C	Theme	RL.4.2	DOK 2
6A	B	Theme	RL.4.2	DOK 3
6B	D	Theme/Text Evidence	RL.4.2/ RL.4.1	DOK 3
7	D	Figurative Language: Metaphor	L.4.5a	DOK 2
8A	D	Figurative Language: Metaphor	L.4.5a	DOK 2
8B	D	Figurative Language: Metaphor/Text Evidence	L.4.5a/ RL.4.1	DOK 2
9	C, E	Theme	RL.4.2	DOK 2
10	see below	Point of View	RL.4.6	DOK 2
11	see below	Writing About Text	W.4.9a	DOK 4

Comprehension 1A, 1B, 3, 5, 6A, 6B, 9, 10		/12	%
Vocabulary 2, 4, 7, 8A, 8B		/8	%
Total Weekly Assessment Score		/20	%

3 Students should underline the following sentence in the paragraph:
- The students could see there was a need, and they were determined to help fill it.

10 Students should circle the following sentences:
- The point of view reveals how Connor feels when he loses.
- The point of view show how sure Connor is about winning the election.

11 To receive full credit for the response, the following information should be included:
"Thinking Big" helps readers understand they should help others in need, sometimes by organizing fundraisers and functions to achieve a goal. "The Next President" helps readers understand that they should respect others, be gracious losers, and not be overconfident.